GROUNDS FOR HOPE
A Cup of Blessing for Each Day of the Year

By
Jan Unfried

Grounds for Hope Copyright © 2024 by Jan Unfried. All Rights Reserved.

All rights reserved. No part of this book may be reproduced in any form or by any electronic or mechanical means including information storage and retrieval systems, without permission in writing from the author. The only exception is by a reviewer, who may quote short excerpts in a review.

Follow all of Jan's blogs on Facebook at Jan Unfried's Grounds for Hope page

For all other information and how to get Jan to speak at your events
Visit her website at www.janunfried.com

Printed in the United States of America

First Printing: November 2024
J & J Unfried Publishing

ISBN 979-8-3458-5391-7

Books and Resources by Jan Unfried

Coffee Shop Chronicles Series:

1) *Common Ground, Coffee Shop Chronicles to Warm Your Heart and Soul*

2) *Solid Ground, Coffee Shop Chronicles to Anchor Your Heart and Soul*

   ***Solid Ground Bible Study*

3) *Higher Ground, Coffee Shop Chronicles to Lift Your Heart and Soul*

   ***Higher Ground Bible Study*

**Companion Bible studies that can be done with or without the accompanying book

Acknowledgements

There are a couple of people who read my Grounds for Hope Facebook blogs almost every morning--My loyal mom and my amazing friend Patti. They respond to most of those posts. That is really my favorite part of putting a devotional thought out there each day—getting the responses from my followers! It makes me feel connected to them, and being connected is one of my goals for you and for me.

"Stay Grounded. Keep Connected. One Cup, One Story at a Time."

I think that's why I have hesitated to write this daily devotional book. There will be no way for me to know how you are responding to the thoughts and truths from Scripture. But Patti has been relentless. She has bugged me for years to translate the daily posts into a devotional book.

Thanks, Patti King, for continuing to pursue this idea and spur me to finally write it! Thanks to my husband for putting up with my lack of presence for hours on end, loving me through my writing processes, and encouraging me in the Lord.

Thank you, most, to my Heavenly Father and Lord Jesus Christ for choosing to use words, True and Inspired Words, to communicate with us. And thanks to the Holy Spirit who led and guided me along the way. The Trinity's wisdom and help throughout this project were sought and found.

TABLE OF CONTENTS

Introduction..1

January..2

February...33

March... 62

April...93

May...125

June..157

July..187

August..218

September..249

October..279

November..310

December..340

Introduction

Welcome to *Grounds for Hope, A Cup of Blessing for Each Day of the Year*. I have prayed over each of these daily devotionals. When you read them, I pray that the Holy Spirit will do His work in your heart and mind. When you put forth the effort to gather your daily manna, God's provision for you, He will be faithful to fill your cup to overflowing.

These devotionals are purposefully short and to the point. You can read it while you are waiting for your cup of coffee to brew. You can use it to be a part of your quiet time as you sit with the Lord each day. You can read it first thing in the morning, right before bed, or any time in between.

The primary source of Truth is God's Word. I have written out a key verse for each day, but I encourage you to have your Bible open and your journal nearby. Read the verse in the context of the rest of the chapter. Think about who is saying it, what the setting is, and why it is being said. Try using the C.U.P strategy described on February 2.

Most of all, I pray that the Lord will give you wisdom and discernment as you apply His Words to your life. My words are secondary, a way to bring some present-day context to the Scriptures.

I will leave you with this prayer, one that I pray before I ever write or speak:

"May the words of my mouth and the meditation of my heart be pleasing in your sight, O Lord, my Rock and my Redeemer." Psalm 19:14 (NIV)

January 1

"O give thanks to the Lord, for he is good; for his steadfast love endures forever!" 1 Chronicles 16:34 (ESV)

Happy New Year! As we begin the new year, it would be good to do a little reflecting.

What were the best and worst moments? My husband and I have a weekly phone call with two of our grandkids. We each share our best and our worst (highs and lows) for the week, and we remind them that God is with us in the good times and the bad times. God has been with you as well, and it is important to remember how He sustained you in the bad times and blessed you with the good ones.

Our tough moments help build character and mold us into who God wants us to be, if we let Him. That doesn't make those moments easy or fun, but when we look back, sometimes the hardest trial was the same thing that brought out our best growth.

One of my toughest times a few years ago was when I found out our friends were leaving our church. I understood their reasons, but I went through a period of grief. Yes, they still lived just a few blocks away, and we could still talk on the phone or via texts. I was still sad that we wouldn't be doing ministry together in the same way we had previously.

God comforted me and helped me grow in this season. It made me more aware of others who might be living on the precipice of decision or who are just waiting for an encouraging word. It made me want to love better and empathize greater. God helped turn my sorrow into joy, my pain into purpose.

He wants to do the same for you! Reflect, remember, and be grateful for the goodness of the Lord.

January 2

"Your word is a lamp to my feet and a light for my path."
Psalm 119:105 (NIV)

We collect models of lighthouses, and Split Rock Lighthouse in Minnesota has always been one of our favorites. A few years ago, we were able to visit this iconic landmark. Walking on the grounds of the actual structure and learning some of its history reminded me of how important the lamp was to light the way for ships in peril.

God's word is like that. It shines our way to safety when we are in need!

- In our storms, God's Word anchors us and shines light on His character and love.

- When the fog of our culture tends to confuse us, God's Word breaks through the confusion with Truth.

- When darkness envelops us because of sin or sorrow, God's Word touches the deepest places of our souls and sheds light on our hearts and minds.

- When dangerous reefs of temptation or misdirection lie beneath the surface, God's Word warns us to avoid them.

Thank you, Jesus, for the gift of Your Word!

January 3

"There is no one holy like the Lord, There is no one besides You, There is no Rock like our God." 1 Samuel 2:2 (AMP)

Michael Todd wrote this in one of his devotionals:

"The answers to your question are not found in what you are believing for. They're found in who you are believing in."

We often limit God by trying to get answers to our prayers in the way we think they should be answered. We can't believe that God could allow this or would not allow that in our lives. When we focus on the character of God, who He is, our questions become less important and His purposes are magnified and glorified.

I've had my share of questions for God.

- "What is going on here?"
- "When are we going to get a break?"
- "How am I supposed to get through this?"

The prayer formula that has helped me is to ask my questions as I pour my heart out to God. Then I go to the Psalms and remember with David how God has been there in the past. I focus on His character, which never changes. I praise Him for how He is working and thank Him for being in control. I end with, "Not my will but Yours be done."

It's not easy…not one bit. It takes a lifetime of faith-building and reminding ourselves of the goodness and faithfulness of our God and the work that was accomplished on the cross. But when you shift your focus to your all-powerful, ever-loving, forgiving Savior, it puts things into perspective. As Hannah prayed in 1 Samuel 2:2, "There is no Rock like our God."

January 4

"Come to me, all you who are weary and burdened, and I will give you rest." Matthew 11:28 (NIV)

It wasn't a coincidence that during my morning quiet time, the same scripture verse was highlighted in the verse of the day and both on-line devotionals I was reading.

I needed the reminder, and I was getting a sweet repetition of the message.

Kathi Lipp reminded us that, "if you're not resting, you're not healing." In this passage Jesus didn't tell us to get over it or stop fixating on the problem. He just invited us to allow Him to share our burden.

Rick Warren reminded us that, "When you're yoked with Christ, you move together with Him. You move in the same direction at the same speed. You move in the right direction at the right speed. And you move with a lighter burden."

What burden do you need to take to Jesus so that you can leave your load, lean into Him, learn of Him, and lighten the weight of the problem on your shoulders? He is ready to give you rest.

January 5

"Also, seek the peace and prosperity of the city to which I have carried you into exile. Pray to the Lord for it, because if it prospers, you too will prosper." Jeremiah 29:7 (NIV)

We love to claim Jeremiah 29:11, "'For I know the plans I have for you;' declares the Lord, 'plans to prosper you and not to harm you, plans to give you hope and a future.'"

Without looking at the context of this promise, we miss out on some important truths. God was speaking to the Israelites while they were in exile. They were being told they would be there for seventy more years, yet God was telling them to pray for those who were around them.

In Lary Osborne's book, *Thriving in Babylon,* he reveals the many similarities of our world today and the Babylon in which Daniel lived and thrived.

It is so easy to get consumed by the world's problems, the news, the "crisis of the day." Osborne reminds us, "When we focus on the size of the problem, we forget the size of our God."

This is such an appropriate thought for me to repeat each day. Without sticking our heads in the sand, we need to monitor what and how much we are listening to throughout the day. We need to pray for those around us and be instruments of peace and love among them.

Remember that God is not unprepared for what is happening. He has a plan! His plan will not be thwarted. Pray for those around you, for your city, state, and nation. If they prosper, so will you.

January 6

"If you believe, you will receive whatever you ask for in prayer."
Matthew 21:22 (NIV)

I'm not sure why I'm surprised when God answers prayer. A few days ago, I woke up and breathed a prayer that was on my heart. It wasn't a huge, world-shattering request, but it was something important to me.

Within the next half-hour, God brought to mind the answer to my request. I was full of praise and joy.

We can get caught up in the fact that God didn't answer our prayer. We might even get angry at Him or beat ourselves up for not having great enough faith. Here are some things I have learned about prayer:

- He hears your prayer the minute you pray it. (Daniel 10:12)
- His answers may be yes, no, or not yet. By faith we need to pray as Jesus did in the garden, "...Nevertheless, not my will, but yours, be done." Luke 22:42 (ESV)
- Sometimes answers are delayed because of spiritual warfare (Daniel 10:13), so that God's glory might be displayed (John 11:4-6), or to give us a chance to grow in our walk with Him. The way to the Promised Land was through the wilderness.

I just want you to know, God cares about you. He cares about your needs and requests. He wants you to confide in Him, trust in Him, and believe in His love for you. Though our prayers are not always answered instantly, and sometimes the answer is not what we expected, God is in the prayer-answering business.

January 7

"And do not forget to do good and to share with others, for with such sacrifices God is pleased." Hebrews 13:16 (NIV)

I was motivated this week by a deep conversation I had with a friend. It wouldn't have happened without being intentional about keeping connected.

She came over for a cup of coffee, and we shared together, cried together, and laughed together for a couple of hours. I was motivated through her story to continue to choose joy, love others, and fix my eyes on Jesus. Now, that is some kind of friend and the kind of great motivation we all need more often.

We were never meant to do life alone. We need others as much as they need us. The sacrifice part is our time, our resources, or our strength, but the benefits far outweigh what we have to give up.

This verse also lets me know that God was smiling down on us. He loves us so much that He designed friendship and communication so that we could help each other. What an awesome God! What an awesome plan!

Maybe you need to call someone and get together. You might need their motivation. Perhaps they need to be spurred on by you!

January 8

"And Nehemiah continued...'This is a sacred day before our Lord. Don't be dejected and sad, for the joy of the LORD is your strength.'"
Nehemiah 8:10 (NLT)

He danced uninhibitedly around our living room. It didn't matter if he had the right moves. He didn't care what anyone thought. He was full of joy and had to express himself.

OK, he was a two-year-old, but it made me think of how as adults we are so worried about the right moves and what others think about us as we dance through life. The toddler's joy was contagious. All of those who watched were laughing and cheering him on. A few joined him on the "dance floor."

As believers in Christ, we should be the givers of joy in our world. We should draw people to the love of Jesus through our genuine joy, our pleasant disposition, and our happy countenance.

In our key verse today, Ezra and the other Levites had been reading and instructing the people from the Book of the law of God after they had returned from exile. The people were mourning and weeping as they were humbled by their sin and God's greatness.

Then, they were told, in essence, to stop mourning. The day was holy and sacred. They were to go out and celebrate, to dance and feast and share their joy with others.

Who can you surprise this week with your uninhibited joy? We have so much to be grateful for in the Lord. You may not dance for them, but maybe your joy will be contagious enough to elicit a laugh or a smile.

January 9

"Therefore do not worry about tomorrow, for tomorrow will worry about itself. Each day has enough trouble of its own."
Matthew 6:34 (NIV)

I recently saw a mug that said:

"Good morning. This is God. I will handle your problems today. I won't need your help. Have a cup of coffee and have a good day."

This is such sage advice. We typically start our day worrying about the unending tasks ahead. We get out of bed saying, "Oh, Goodness me!" When we should be declaring, "O, God, You..."

- You are in control.
- You can handle my schedule. Help me to prioritize relationships over accomplishments.
- You are the wisdom I need to handle the issues that may come up today.
- You know all and You are with me.
- You...

My college chaplain used to say that when you come across a verse that says, "Therefore," you need to find out what it is "there for." In our passage today, the previous verses explain why we have no reason to worry. God takes care of the birds of the air and the flowers of the field. We are just as important, if not more so, than all of these. And, worrying won't add one single hour to our life.

As you fill in your own blanks in the bullet point prayer above, may God's promises to take care of today motivate you! I hope you enjoy your coffee (or tea or whatever your morning drink might be), and are able to leave your day in God's hands.

January 10

"Your attitude should be the same as that of Christ Jesus: Who...made himself nothing, taking the very nature of a servant..."
Philippians 2:5-8 (NIV)

In my journal, I have a question that I come back to frequently: How can I be a servant today?

My desire is to hear God's voice and put aside my own selfish agenda so that I can show others His love. Kevin Harney in his book, *Organic Outreach for Ordinary People,* encourages us to pray a one-minute prayer before each part of our day: "Lord, who needs to experience your love today?"

- Before we go into the office or classroom
- Before we go into the grocery store or restaurant
- Before we open our front door to our home
- Before we go to our kids' sporting events
- Before we park the car in the garage and shut out the neighborhood

You get the idea. And the great thing is that God answers that prayer in surprising and wonderful ways. He will help you become more aware of your co-workers or classmates. He will give you an opportunity to share with your waiter or waitress or pray with a weary mama towing her toddlers. Your neighbors and friends will begin to open up to you. Your family will be blessed by your servant heart.

If we truly desire to be more like Christ, we need to have the attitude of a servant. The good news is that instead of feeling drained at the end of the day, you will be energized with doing the will of the Father.

January 11

> "The Samaritan woman said to him, 'You are a Jew and I am a Samaritan woman. How can you ask me for a drink?' (For Jews do not associate with Samaritans)." John 4:9 (NIV)

In the conversation between Jesus and the Samaritan woman at the well, Jesus was our perfect example of breaking down any walls or barriers with others. There was no reason for Him to be talking to a woman, much less a Samaritan, serving her living water.

Max Lucado says, "Neighborliness is not defined by where we live but how we love."

I have a group of friends who recently went into a not-so-safe neighborhood to help clean the apartment of a single dad who was struggling to keep up with work, parenting, and staying clean and sober. They broke down the barriers of financial status, the stigma of addiction, and the comfort of status quo.

Jesus wants us to love others. He came so that the wall of sin between God and man was demolished on the cross. He also came to break down barriers between His children. The Biblical example, as well as the current day illustration, remind us today, and every day, of the importance of treating others with love and respect, even if they don't look, think, or act like us!

Who is your Samaritan? Listen to God's call to you to be a neighbor.

January 12

"and Jesus and his disciples had also been invited to the wedding."
John 2:2 (NIV)

Did you know that God was the inventor of fun? We sometimes think of God only as a serious judge who is looking for ways to punish us. He is just the opposite!

God directed His people to have festivals, for days at a time. Jesus attended dinner parties and weddings. I don't think He even thought twice about whether to go to the wedding in Cana in Galilee, and, oh, did he have a fun time there. I can almost see his hidden smile when the master of the banquet declared that they had saved the best wine for the last part of the party.

Can you imagine a serious Jesus bouncing little children on his knees?

God delights in us, and we should be filled with joy in His presence. Take a moment today to just delight in God and His works. List them in your journal.

Here are a few of my joys:

- Enjoying the laughter of a child
- Basking in the uniqueness of each human being
- Taking in the beauty of each sunrise and sunset
- Serving a family in need by taking them some meals
- Receiving prayers and encouragement this week from my friends and loved ones

Have some fun today. Hug a kid. Eat dinner on the floor, picnic style. Memorize and tell a joke. Have a tickle fest with your grandkids. The sky is the limit, and God's love and delight in you is just as limitless.

January 13

"Delight yourself in the Lord and he will give you the desires of your heart." Psalm 37:4 (NIV)

We often work hard to get what we want. Setting goals and working toward them is a noble aim. The problem is we don't always see the big picture. What the desire of our heart really is, our deepest, in-most need, is to have a relationship with Christ. When we are spending time with Him each day, the desires of our heart fall into place.

Sometimes God changes our will to match His. Other times He gives us abundantly more than we ask or think (Ephesians 3:20). Either way His plan will knock our socks off.

As you revel in His character, love, and grace, you will sense a fulfillment of your desires because you recognize His part in your plan.

Try it...you'll like it!

January 14

"Then Jesus answered, 'Woman, you have great faith! Your request is granted.' And her daughter was healed from that very hour."
Matthew 15:28 (NIV)

In Max Lucado's *Ten Women of the Bible* study, he highlights the Canaanite woman in Matthew 15. This is not a woman typically studied or highlighted when we are looking at women who modeled great faith. We can gain some new insight through Lucado's interpretation of Jesus' interaction with her.

Jesus recognized her as a woman of great faith and granted her request (see Matthew 15:28). In the verses prior to His encounter with her, Jesus had been dealing with the Pharisees, who thought they were something because they followed all the man-made traditions and rules. Then, here was this woman who knew she deserved nothing, but was asking for everything.

Can you imagine the delight and relief it was for Jesus to be able to spar verbally with this woman and grant her desperate request? Her daughter was healed from demon-possession that very hour!

Jesus delights over us when we come to Him and humbly ask Him for help. If you need help today, do not hesitate to ask Him. If you just need to be reminded of how much He loves you, bask in the truth of Zephaniah 3: 17 which says ..."He will take great delight in you...he will rejoice over you with singing."

January 15

"If you, then, though you are evil, know how to give good gifts to your children, how much more will your Father in heaven give good gifts to those who ask him!" Matthew 7:11 (NIV)

I don't know about you, but I tend to get into a spiritual rut and forget that God wants me to seek His help and His answers. Maybe I've been discouraged from the seemingly unanswered prayers or the day-to-day needs. Regardless of my excuses, here is the thought that struck me this week:

"Jesus is delighted when we ask Him to do what He came to do: give great gifts to us, His unworthy children." Max Lucado

As a teacher, I was always delighted when a student asked for help. As a parent, I was always thrilled when my kids came to me for assistance. God knows our needs, but He desires relationship with us. He wants us to share and express our requests.

What is it that you need to ask for today? I will be praying with you as you learn to lay your needs and petitions at the feet of Jesus. Remember, He is waiting to give you great gifts!

January 16

"...if anything is excellent or praiseworthy—think about such things."
Philippians 4:8b (NIV)

I sat impatiently in the waiting room. I had been at the doctor's office since 7:30 AM and it was approaching noon. I had gone through the paper, read a few chapters of my book, and I was tired of waiting in my uncomfortable chair.

I took a deep breath, said a prayer, or two, and settled my mind on what was good and true, noble and thought-worthy.

In reality, the procedure I had for my basal cell skin cancer is quite the technological feat. They found a small spot on my skin that could have gone undetected if it wasn't for the diligence of checking every six months or so. Throughout the procedure, their on-site tech lab enabled them to check to make sure it was completely cancer free.

This minor inconvenience of my time, pride, and routine was NOTHING compared to what others were going through. I had a friend who was being treated with cyber knife treatments to try to thwart her cancer from settling into her brain and causing loss of sight. Another friend was facing a series of chemo treatments and an eventual bone marrow transplant in the next year for his recently discovered multiple myeloma.

I am grateful for technology, the ability of doctors to treat us, and the comfort and timing from the Lord in the middle of it all. By thinking on the good things, it gave me perspective and settled my mind.

Try focusing on the things that are praiseworthy the next time you are in a "waiting room" of life. It will help guard your mind from the hole of negativity.

January 17

"Simply let your 'Yes' be 'Yes,' and your 'No,' 'No;' anything beyond this comes from the evil one." Matthew 5:37 (NIV)

This verse is about keeping our promises and commitments, but it's also about prioritizing our lives.

Throughout your work week, whatever that may look like, consider being motivated by the fact that **Less is More**. Carey Niewhof put it this way, "Live in a way today that will help you through tomorrow."

We can't say "yes" to everything. We need to prioritize and set some boundaries in our work-life balance. Sometimes "no" is the right response. The one thing you should always say "yes" to every day is spending time with God. If something else needs to go by the wayside, so be it. More people will be served, more tasks will be accomplished, greater peace and joy will permeate your day if you can keep this discipline as your top choice.

What might you give up today so that your less can be more?

January 18

"Do everything in love." 1 Corinthians 16:14 (NIV)

I dread the thought of cleaning house a lot more than I dread the actual deed. Once I get started, it never takes as long as I anticipated. The end result leaves me feeling refreshed and accomplished.

I was reading 1 Corinthians 16:14 the other day. It simply says, "Do everything in love." Does that mean cleaning house? What if everything we did was motivated by love? I know my attitude would change about getting started if I considered who I am cleaning it for and how my acts of service show them I care about them.

So, whether you are cleaning toilets or managing a high-profile company, do everything in love! How will this change your perspective today?

January 19

"Wait for the Lord; be strong and take heart and wait for the Lord."
Psalm 27:14 (NIV)

I HATE to wait:

- in line
- on the phone
- for my husband to get the car started so I can feel the heat or air conditioning sooner
- for a text or email response to something

Yes, I am impatient in about every area of my life. YET, we are told to "Wait for the Lord, be strong and take heart and wait for the Lord" Psalm 27:14.

So, I'm trying to work on my waiting. If I put another word in place of "wait" it helps a lot. Instead of waiting, what if I think of it as "hoping." Hoping is looking forward to something with certainty and eager anticipation.

- I know I will eventually get to the front of the line. Who is around me that needs a little encouragement while we are standing there?
- I know with certainty that I won't have to listen to the elevator music on the phone for eternity. I will eventually receive the help desk or the person I need. What if I pray for that person who will eventually answer my plea for help and seek God's message for their life?
- I know the car will get started within seconds (yes, that is how impatient I can be). What if I breathe a prayer of gratitude that we have a reliable car with heat and a/c? What if I thank the Lord for my husband, who is always concerned with our safety?
- I know I will eventually get a response to my text or email. What if I sought direction and blessing from the Lord for when that text or email comes?

I don't know if you relate to my impatience, but maybe you can try waiting with hope this week.

January 20

"So the last will be first, and the first will be last."
Matthew 20:16 (NIV)

Our society certainly idolizes the super stars. We cheer the football team as they come onto the field. We secretly wish we could be the singer on stage who has "made it." We wish our meager contributions were more like those of a millionaire. We dream about our book being a best-seller (or at least I do)!

The thing is, Jesus honors faith as small as a mustard seed (and that is REALLY small). He says the last will be first and the first will be last. He turns our thinking and our world upside down by using our less-than acts for His greatness.

Our small conversations are bigger than the huge applauding crowds.

Our small gifts are multiplied like the loaves and fishes.

Our love-motivated efforts to ease the ache in others is beautifully used to ease our own ache.

You ARE God's super-star! He loves you and wants to use you right where you are. No one else can do what you are commissioned to do by Him. You are not in a competition or a pecking order in God's Kingdom. Allow Him to use you for His glory.

January 21

"And because we are his children, God has sent the Spirit of his Son into our hearts, prompting us to call out, "Abba, Father." Galatians 4:6 (NLT)

We got a great surprise text with video the other day. It was our youngest granddaughter proudly saying the words "Grandpa" and "Grandma." She had been working on them very hard, and it completely melted our hearts! It was an act of love that in her small way showed she desired relationship with us.

God's heart melts over you in the same way when you:

- Accomplish a task you have been working on for a long time (especially when it is for His kingdom)
- Say His name, calling Him "Abba, Father."
- Hide His Word in your heart

God is not surprised in the way we are surprised, because He knows all. He is just so pleased that you have chosen to share your life and relationship with Him!

Let God know today that you love Him, and bask in His love as well. He is smiling and singing over you.

January 22

"May the God of hope fill you with all joy and peace as you trust in him, so that you may overflow with hope by the power of the Holy Spirit."
Romans 15:13 (NIV)

Last fall and into December, I felt like I saw my theme verse, Romans 15:13, everywhere! Throughout advent, as we were anticipating Christmas and all that it means, hope was radiating throughout sermons, devotionals, and every gift and decoration.

The good thing about hope is that it is NOT seasonal. We can anticipate God's goodness every day. His mercies are new each morning. His hope fills us with joy and peace. It overflows into our hearts as we continue to learn to trust in Him.

If you're in the winter season of your life, remember that God's hope comes AS you trust in Him. It's an act of faith, even if we don't see the answers yet.

We're over half-way through the first month of this new year, but I want to encourage you to cling to God's abundant, overflowing hope. We all need it!

January 23

"Yet a time is coming and has now come when the true worshipers will worship the Father in spirit and truth, for they are the kind of worshipers the Father seeks. God is spirit and his worshipers must worship in spirt and in truth." John 4:23-24 (NIV)

My husband and I have always set Sunday aside as a day to worship. That usually means going to church for us. When we were recently in Hawaii, we worshiped at an outdoor church that overlooked the ocean. The Great Holy God always seems to meet me there! WOW!

A few weeks ago, I was drawn to two words: Worship and Worry. I decided they are opposites. Upon further word-study, I found some interesting things about their origins.

Worry—From the Old English means "Seize by the throat and tear; harass; cause anxiety."

Worship—From the Old English means "To revere, honor; give worth to something or someone." The word itself stems from the thought of "worth-ship."

When we give God honor and focus on Him, our worry lets go of our throats. The harassment and anxiety that we feel is lost in the reverence and worth we bestow upon our Lord.

You have a choice today: will you be torn apart by worry or overwhelmed with worship?

January 24

"When they saw the courage of Peter and John and realized that they were unschooled, ordinary men, they were astonished and they took note that these men had been with Jesus." Acts 4:13 (NIV)

When Peter and John answered accusing questions before the Sanhedrin, their Spirit-filled response went way beyond their unschooled and ordinary backgrounds. Upon hearing what they had to say, those listening "took note that these men had been with Jesus" Acts 4:13.

Karen Ehman (Proverbs 31 daily devotional contributor) reminded her readers that it is not enough to try to be LIKE Jesus. First, we must want to be WITH Him.

Let this simple truth resonate with you this week. We don't have to have titles before or after our name. We don't need to have a degree at a prestigious school. We can go about our ordinary lives being extraordinary because we spend time with Jesus each day. It is a discipline that is vital to our Christian walk and growth.

Think about whether others will see your behavior and recognize that you have been with Jesus.

January 25

"...give thanks in all circumstances, for this is God's will for you in Christ Jesus." 1 Thessalonians 5:18 (NIV)

It's interesting, though not surprising, that God's will for us is for our good. He is not trying to make us do something impossible when he commands us to give thanks. He is providing His loving plan for us.

There are a multitude of neuroscience research projects studying the effects of gratitude in our lives. One of the discoveries has been that writing down what you're grateful for—yes, with a pen and paper — has been linked in research to a multitude of health benefits:

- Increased happiness and positive mood
- Better sleep
- Being less materialistic
- Healthier relationships
- Greater resiliency
- Decreased depression, anxiety, chronic pain and risk of disease

From the small and material possessions, to my health and wellbeing, to the big, internal, and eternal things, I have so much to be thankful for.

You can start today. As a way to practice this concept, write down something that you are grateful for. Do this every day this week. Notice the difference. Your health may depend on it!

January 26

"May God be gracious to us and bless us and make his face shine upon us." Psalm 67:1 (NIV)

I was still waking up, just a little more than sleep-walking, as I made my way into the living room with my cup of coffee. I stopped suddenly, almost splashing some of the precious liquid onto myself. In the middle of the floor sat a purple Styrofoam "missile" from the grandkids' play things.

The thing that had me flummoxed was that we had not had grandkids over in a few weeks. I have no idea how this particular toy part could have landed in the middle of the floor.

I know it doesn't work this way, but it gave me a bit of comfort to consider that maybe our son in heaven had tossed it down as a practical joke.

My dad used to say that the angels threw coins down for him to find on his walks. He would always use them to pray blessings over his loved ones. He collected the coins he found each year in a jar. In December he would donate the change to the Salvation Army bell ringers.

We'll probably never figure out how these mysterious items are appearing, but I am choosing to use their discovery to remember to pray for and bless our friends and loved ones who are impacted by loss of any kind.

God is the inventor of fun, and I don't think He minds our little earthly antics. His face is shining upon us.

January 27

"For by him all things were created; things in heaven and on earth, visible and invisible, whether thrones or powers or rulers or authorities; all things were created by him and for him." Colossians 1:16 (NIV)

God created the world and all that is in it by the power of His Word. His Word has been given to us, and His creative power is still in His Word. When we speak God's Word out loud, we can trust and believe His desires in and for us will be accomplished.

That is amazing! Search for a promise that you need today. Speak/read it out loud. Post it on your mirror or car dashboard. Thank God for His Word and His Works!

Here are a few to help you get started:

- "I can do all things through him who gives me strength." Philippians 4:13
- "Have I not commanded you? Be strong and courageous. Do not be terrified; do not be discouraged, for the Lord your God will be with you wherever you go." Joshua 1:9
- "Peace I leave with you; my peace I give you. I do not give to you as the world gives. Do not let your hearts be troubled and do not be afraid." John 14:27

January 28

"And we know that in all things God works for the good of those who love him, who have been called according to his purpose."
Romans 8:28 (NIV)

I had recently started reading a new author, Davalynn Spencer. Her Christian romance novels take place during the turn of the 18th century in rural Colorado settings.

As I would read about the hard work the women of that era had to do just to get a meal on the table, I was forever grateful for my modern conveniences. It seems they were always making pies or cakes! I can't imagine doing so without a mixer and convection oven.

The other day, the main female character was making an analogy of her cake ingredients to Romans 8:28—All things work together for good. I have heard something similar in the past, but it is well worth repeating.

We love the taste of the final product—moist, rich chocolate cake, but the outcome is nothing like the original ingredients. Cocoa without sugar is bitter and dry. Flour without eggs is merely dust. Sugar by itself is soon to be too much. Raw eggs might have some nutritional value, but they are flavorless and slimy by themselves. However, when they are mixed together and placed in the proper heat, something beautiful and good is made.

God does the same thing with us. He takes our bitter dry experiences, the problems that leave us feeling like dust in the wind, the right amount of sweetness and nutrition, and the perfect time and temperature for everything to settle just right. The result is something beautiful and good—our lives redeemed for His purpose. Let God use the ingredients in your life to make something wonderful!

January 29

"Cast all your anxiety on him because he cares for you."
1 Peter 5:7 (NIV)

We were newlyweds. We were beginning to learn about each other and understand the differences in our personalities as well as the differences between males and females. My husband sweetly explained to me one day that if I wanted him to hear something I had to say, I needed to make sure his attention wasn't divided. Men, he explained, don't multi-task like women.

A few days later I needed to tell him something. I walked by the tv where he was watching a sporting event, and I let out a loud scream. Frightened that something terrible had happened, he immediately drew his attention to me to see what I needed. I let him know that dinner was ready.

Of course, this was an extreme response to his loving words the day before, but it worked! We have had many laughs over my dramatic comeback that day.

When we love someone, we pay attention to them. I recently read that God has never created anybody he doesn't love. So how does he pay attention to us? The list is endless:

- For starters, He gave His life up for us, taking our sin and our problems as His own
- He bottles our tears
- He laughs with us
- He knows the number of hairs on our head (and mine has to change by the minute, I'm always finding a stray blond lock)
- He knows each step we take
- He has our name written on the palms of His hands

God cares about you! He pays attention to you and your needs.

January 30

"Teach me your way, O Lord, and I will walk in your truth; give me an undivided heart, that I may fear your name." Psalm 86:11 (NIV)

Whenever I hear a reference to the story of Hosea, I immediately connect to Francine River's book *Redeeming Love*. If you haven't read this book, it is well worth your time. The book was recently made into a movie, which is also amazing.

God's people (and I am including myself here) are so prone, as was Hosea's wife Gomer, to go off on our own. We love and worship God while embracing other ideologies at the same time. These other idols can look like government, climate change, nature, television, spare time, technology, etc. These are not bad in and of themselves, they just have a tendency to divide our allegiances.

Here are a couple of truths from Hosea's story. 1) God never gives up on us. He does not give us what we deserve but chooses to pardon and restore us. 2) God desires a relationship of mutual love, fidelity, and intimacy from us.

I know I will occasionally stray from what is truly important, but my desire is that I will be quick to return to Christ alone, and that my tendencies to be a wandering sheep will be fewer and farther apart.

I pray that you will experience God's redeeming love in your life and that you will strive to live for and love Him with an undivided heart.

January 31

"For the Lord is good..." Psalm 100:5a (NIV)

Then, how could He let our son die? Why didn't He come through and answer our pleas?

To be honest, these are some of the emotions we have had to grapple with in the past few months. I still don't have the answers to those questions, but I do know that God has not left us during these difficult days. God has continued working in and through the sorrow and pain.

We have chosen to focus on the assurance of His love—that is good!

We have continued to look for and have found opportunities to share Jesus with others through this tragedy—that is good!

When we miss our son with tears and groanings, we cling to the promise of our inheritance and a home in heaven someday where we will be reunited—that is good!

I encourage you to:

- Learn about God's goodness through His Word.
- Experience God's goodness through worship.

Your choice to focus up rather than in will change your perspective and bring peace to your heart. One day at a time, one step at a time, let God's goodness fill you!

February 1

"That is why, for Christ's sake, I delight in weaknesses, in insults, in hardships, in persecutions, in difficulties. For when I am weak, then I am strong." 2 Corinthians 12:10 (NIV)

I was at a conference with a group of people I didn't know. The icebreaker question was, "If you could have a super power, what would it be?" I'm always uncomfortable with this question because I know it's not based on reality. I usually settle on being able to fly.

Romans 8:37 promises that "we are more than conquerors through him who loved us." Does that mean we can walk through walls or fly across the sky?

What this promise means for us is that we have Christ to help us complete the work He has started in us ((Phil. 1:6). Our spiritual super power to be a conqueror comes through the knowledge that nothing can touch us without God's knowledge, and that He is working everything for our good (Romans 8:28).

God is working in us. He is working for us. He is working through us, and He is working with us. His greatest plan is accomplished through my weakness, not my "super power." It's when I admit I am nothing without Him, that He can really begin to work.

It's God's power that gives us victory from our past, strength in the present, and vision for the future. Walk in God's super power today!

February 2

"Do not be anxious about anything, but in everything, by prayer and petition, with thanksgiving, present your requests to God."
Philippians 4:6 (NIV)

When I go through the Bible I use an acronym for CUP to help me decide what the verse is saying to me:

C – A Command to obey
U –An Unfailing truth to apply
P—A Promise to claim or a Praise to proclaim

Today's key verse is a command. It tells us what not to do (be anxious!). Then it tells us how to accomplish this—take everything to prayer, with thanksgiving.

We like to skip to the promises, but most promises have some condition of obedience attached to them. In this case, we would love to have the peace that transcends all understanding (Philippians 4:7), and it is available to us. However, we can't ignore verse 6.

When we need peace, we are often just one prayer away from receiving it. Remembering who God is and thanking Him for being loving, kind, just, patient, all-capable, all-knowing, forgiving, generous, and good, puts our minds at rest.

It's the perfect formula! The next time you are anxious and you crave peace of heart and mind, go to prayer! I've tried it, and it works!

February 3

"And pray in the Spirit on all occasions with all kinds of prayers and requests. With this in mind, be alert and always keep on praying for all the saints." Ephesians 6:18 (NIV)

The other day, a prayer request came across our Bible Study text thread. It was for a daughter's father-in-law who had been diagnosed with stage 4 cancer. The prayer need was so multi-faceted.

Of course, we wanted to pray for healing. We also wanted to pray for his comfort and peace through the process. We were praying for his wife and other family members that were affected. A few of us had been told that he had miraculously given his heart to Jesus a few years prior, but he was blaming his illness as punishment for his past failures. With this in mind, our prayer was for him to feel the love of Jesus completely surround him and take away the guilt that had already been redeemed. Ultimately, we wanted the Lord's will and for His glory to be revealed in this situation.

Sometimes, it's hard to know how to pray for someone else, so I wanted to share with you something I ran across regarding intercessory prayer. When we pray for someone else's needs, we need to GIVE it to God. Here is an acrostic that might help:

G Go into prayer with a focus on God's attributes
I Intercede for others by name, include what you know about their need
V View God's answer to prayer as His choice to express His glory
E End your time of prayer in praise

As you pray for those in your life who need someone to stand in the gap for them, come back to these principles.

February 4

"May the God of hope fill you with all joy and peace as you trust in him, so that you may overflow with hope by the power of the Holy Spirit." Romans 15:13 (NIV)

Grounds for Hope is not just the title of this book, but it is what I call my ministry and Facebook page. My tagline is "Stay Grounded, Keep Connected, One Cup, One Story at a Time." The "grounded" part means to remain in God's Word. Your life will be filled with more opportunities and purpose, more joy and peace, because you are grounded in God's Truth.

To have grounds for any kind of court order, certain requirements and actions must be fulfilled. Our grounds for hope requirements and actions have been fulfilled in Christ and His Word. His promises will not fail. His faithfulness and love are everlasting. His peace and joy are ever-present. He will never leave or forsake us.

If you are looking for that kind of hope, start by memorizing our key verse, Hebrews 15:13, this week. (There is more on this verse on January 22.) Write it on a note card and place it in a spot where you will see it throughout the day. Work on a short phrase at a time. Memorization is hard, but it is an important way to keep God's Word hidden in our hearts.

I'm praying for you to stick with this task!

February 5

"Come near to God and he will come near to you." James 4:8a (NIV)

It is so comforting to know that if we take a step toward God, He will be there for us (James 4:8a). We are promised that we can cast our cares on Him (1 Peter 5:7). He reaches out His hand to help steady us (Isaiah 41:10).

In truth, God is never "far" away from us like we may think. The reason He comes close to us when we come near to Him is because He never left our side in the first place. We're the ones that allow stress and circumstances to get between us. He's always ready and waiting.

In case you were wondering, dessert is stressed spelled backwards. I really don't recommend this as a relief from your stress, but sometimes a little chocolate doesn't hurt. But our true relief from stress is Jesus.

I wrote this little poem, more like a "ditty," to express these thoughts together:

When your heart is stressed
and ready for rest,
Jesus is ready
to hold you steady.

Whatever today holds, He holds your hand and is right beside you. Draw near to His comfort and care! Don't try to do it all on your own.

February 6

"Glorify the Lord with me; let us exalt his name together."
Psalm 34:3 (NIV)

Revering the name of God is important, but what does that look like? In the Old Testament, Jews took the third commandment, "You shall not misuse the name of the Lord your God," so seriously they didn't write or speak the name of God. They were so concerned that they might misuse God's name that they read Adonai in place of YHWH. They avoided writing any name of God casually because of the risk that the written Name might be defaced, obliterated, or erased.

Today's Christians capitalize the name(s) of God. I was taught to also capitalize the pronouns referring to God, to further show reverence to who He is. Growing up, we were not allowed to use the Lord's name in vain. We were not even permitted to say words that could be substitutes for His name, like, "Oh, my gosh!"

That may seem extreme, but it has helped me to have a healthy respect for the name(s) of God. Sometimes, our best form of worship might just be remembering and saying the names of God that are throughout Scripture and that reveal His character. Here are a few to get you started:

- Mighty God, Creator (Elohim)
- The God Who Sees Me (El Roi)
- The Everlasting God (El Olam)

February 7

"When Jesus spoke again to the people, he said, 'I am the light of the world. Whoever follows me will never walk in darkness, but will have the light of life.'" John 8:12 (NIV)

Darkness--It can be scary. Yes, the physical darkness of being in a place where you cannot see because there is no light, but also the emotional and spiritual darkness of not knowing what is ahead. Our trials heighten our fear of the unknown.

The good news, friend, is that God doesn't leave us in the dark. His light shines in us and on us when we trust in Him (John 12:46). His night is as the light of day (Psalm 139:12).

God created the patterns of light and darkness. He authored the winter and summer solstices for good purposes, and He gave us the sun and moon to guide us. We do not need to fear the dark!

Dr. Alicia Brett Chole, author of *The Night is Normal*, wrote, "Nights are invitations to grow our trust muscles, and trust--not answers--is what leads us further into love."

If you are going through a cold and lonely winter or a dark and dreary night, I would like to encourage you to keep walking toward the Light. Trust in Jesus, even when the answers aren't evident or the path is obscured.

February 8

"If any of you lacks wisdom, he should ask God, who gives generously to all without finding fault, and it will be given to him. But when he asks, he must believe and not doubt, because he who doubts is like a wave of the sea, blown and tossed by the wind." James 1:5-6 (NIV)

I read a quote the other day that challenged me. "Doubt is the enemy of imagination." You see, if we ask God for help with something, but ask with double-mindedness (doubt), we will be blown about like a wave on the sea, as our key verse states.

What if we stepped out in faith for God to lead us in ways beyond our imagination. I made a list of things I have thought about doing, but have let fear or doubt keep me from surging ahead.

One of those dreams is that I have felt like, for years, that we should host a block party in our cul-de-sac. I don't know why we haven't. Maybe I fear it will not be attended, I won't know what to say to my neighbors, they won't like our food. Dumb excuses, huh?

As I revisit this post, the weather is getting cooler. I am going to do it. I've already approached a neighbor about helping out. I believe if we ask God for wisdom, He will help us plan and execute this event to get to know our neighbors better. Hopefully it will be a pathway for sharing Christ's love.

What are you imagining? Ask God for wisdom, and believe Him for it.

February 9

"For my thoughts are not your thoughts, neither are your ways my ways, declares the Lord." Isaiah 55:8 (NIV)

When God closes the door to something, don't try to kick the door down. His ways are higher than ours (Isaiah 55:8-9), and He see things—past, present, and future—that we can't see. He always has our good in mind, and He is in control of the details (Jeremiah 29:11).

In the story of Jonah in the Bible, Jonah tried to run from God's plans. God used a huge whale to get Jonah's attention and reroute him back to Ninevah. Later in the story, God used a miniscule worm to teach Jonah a lesson about love and compassion.

In another Biblical account, the prophet Elijah saw God in a powerful fire that consumed the altar he had prepared. Later he heard from God through a gentle whisper as he hid in a cave in a rock.

The point is, God is going to accomplish His purpose. We can either be with Him or try to control things ourselves. The latter will never work out very well.

Are you kicking at a door? Leave it alone, and let God open a different and far better one!

February 10

"Teach us to number our days aright, that we may gain a heart of wisdom." Psalm 90:12 (NIV)

Along with this verse is this quote: "The greatest waste in all of our earth, which cannot be recycled or reclaimed, is our waste of the time that God has given us each day."

It made me think about the time I spend scrolling through Facebook posts with no particular intention in mind. I thought about the time I play games on my phone "to pass the time and exercise my brain." I thought about the moments spent in my recliner watching the latest show.

We are living in a society obsessed with waste. We are constantly being encouraged to "go green." Reduce, Reuse, Recycle. Save the planet...

While those things are part of good stewardship, we should not neglect the legacy that we leave. Will people remember us looking into their eyes and listening to them, or keeping our head down looking at our phones? Will they thank us for not littering and planting a tree (I'm sure those things will be appreciated), or will they remember our conversations and time spent together?

Set some goals today to be less wasteful of your time? Take a break from your phone. We can fast things other than food. Look at your calendar and fit in some time with your loved ones! Value the time each day brings to you, and use it for God's glory.

February 11

"But in your hearts set apart Christ as Lord. Always be prepared to give an answer to everyone who asks you to give the reason for the hope that you have. But do this with gentleness and respect..."
1 Peter 3:15 (NIV)

I believe there are 3 main types of people:

1) Those who leave chaos in their wake
2) Those who come along and try to fix everything (save the day!)
3) Those who just keep to themselves

We can probably have a combination of these traits, depending on the day. We may be good problem solvers or good problem creators, but ultimately our dependence for "fixing" must be on the Lord. He is the only Savior who can redeem us.

With this in mind, Jesus still called us to share the Good News of His life, death, and resurrection with our world. Because of Him we can keep befriending people, being generous, and sharing our redemption stories with others.

Even with this all-important mission, it is critical that we remember we are not the ones who save. "The accomplishment of the mission rests on God's faithfulness, not ours." (Amy Dimarcangelo).

Will you join me in being obedient to God's nudges and direction to share His message, then rest in His fulfillment of the calling? Who is your one(s) you are praying for? God knows and desires that no one should perish.

February 12

"[God] alone is my rock and my salvation; he is my fortress, I will never be shaken." Psalm 62:2 (NIV)

God is our Rock. He steadies us when the earth shakes beneath our feet. He is our defender, Father, friend, our fortress, and refuge. In a recent study of the Psalms, Meredith Houston Carr gave us this acrostic to help us establish our feet on Christ, the Solid Rock:

R -- Remember what God has done

O -- Open yourself to what God is trying to teach you

C -- Cry out to Him with honesty

K -- Keep the faith by putting one foot in front of the other

I have heard so many stories of how God established believers' footing when they were going through an earth-shattering trial...So many stories, in fact, I wrote a book about them. It's called *Solid Ground*.

We have all either had, are in the middle of, or will experience a trial that shakes the ground we stand on. God is our Rock. He will be the anchor throughout life. Trust Him alone!

February 13

"You have laid down precepts that are to be fully obeyed."
Psalm 119:4 (NIV)

When you ask your kids to do something, you want to be fully obeyed. A partial obedience is no obedience at all. Completing 50% or even 75% of your request would be considered a disregard of your authority.

Let's say you ask them to take out the trash. They take care of 80% of the task, but leave the kitchen trash untouched. Soon you will smell the stench of their disobedience.

How much more should we **fully** obey God. He has given us a complete set of instructions on how to live a blessed life in Him. If we only do the parts we like or the parts that make sense to us, we are not partially obeying Him. We are disobeying His precepts. Soon our lives will emanate the "odor" of that disobedience, and it won't be pleasant.

It's important to study God's Word, look into the context of the culture and setting of His words, and strive to understand and apply what they say. It's not always easy, but it's worth it!

February 14

"Surely goodness and love will follow me all the days of my life, and I will dwell in the house of the Lord forever." Psalm 23:6 (NIV)

We are blessed to have GPS apps on our phones and in our cars. It's pretty easy to get somewhere. We just have to type in the location, choose the "directions" button, and we receive the best possible route to our destination. Wouldn't it be nice to have the capability of having a life map--to be able to pull up directions to navigate us through our current situation or to give us the best path for our next step? Unfortunately, our life doesn't come equipped with a map like that.

What we do have is God's promise that His goodness, love, and presence will follow us all the days of our lives. Our plans may shift and our future may have more questions than answers, but we can rely on the Good Shepherd who holds our past, present, and future.

On this Valentine's Day, thank Him for His unconditional, eternal love.

February 15

"Be joyful in hope, patient in affliction, faithful in prayer."
Romans 12:12 (NIV)

We like to pair things like mac and cheese, peanut butter and jelly, shoes and socks, Batman and Robin, pen and paper. They flow together and roll off our tongues.

The Biblical pairings in Romans 12:12 are thought-provoking and interesting. I'm not always naturally joyful when I am waiting and hoping for something, especially if I can't see God working. I really don't like the patient and affliction pairing. Really? Faith and prayer make a little more sense, but sometimes my prayers are just a long list of complaints or desires, rather than listening to what God has to teach me.

These pairings are for a reason. It's not what they do for me but in me.

- Being joyful in hope showcases our trustworthy God.
- Being patient in affliction builds my empathy toward others and develops my faith.
- Faithfulness in prayer teaches me to trust God fully. Another translation says "persistent in prayer." To pray continually, believing for God's best, over time, brings me to a point of total submission.

As you work to apply these Biblical pairings, I invite you to enjoy one of your favorite pairings. I think today I'll settle on coffee and cream.

February 16

"Consider the ravens: They do not sow or reap, they have no storeroom or barn; yet God feeds them. And how much more valuable you are than birds!" Luke 12:24 (NIV)

Some of you have heard my story of how God showed up during the biggest trial of our lives. We watched our son leave this world, and our hearts were broken.

Through our sorrow, God kept showing up. He brought us people, finances, prayer, scripture, songs, and love and peace beyond human understanding. It was often in the little things that we noticed or "considered" God's presence. It was the way the sun shone through the clouds. It was hearing just the right advice at the right time from a godly friend. It was the tender care of the hospital staff.

We must make a habit of considering God's faithfulness. He is there. We just have to be looking for Him.

Look around you today. See the people and nature that God has provided for you. Think of all your conveniences and provisions, and know that God considers you so valuable.

February 17

"Your hands made me and formed me; give me understanding to learn your commands." Psalm 119:73 (NIV)

I'm sure you are familiar with this scenario: You have been burning the candle at both ends. Your husband comes home from work and wonders why the dishes are still in the sink. You snap. You take it out on the kids. They take it out on each other or the dog. The dog cowers under the bed.

We have to maintain self-care. It's hard to love when we are tired. Small issues become big issues. Our physical state effects all other parts of us—our emotions, reactions, our mental and spiritual state.

God made us to need rest and rejuvenation. He tells us to sleep (Psalm 127:2). He reminds us to eat a balanced diet (Ecclesiastes 3:13, 1 Corinthians 10:31). He encourages regular exercise (1 Corinthians 6:20). He commands that we be still and know Him (Psalm 46:10).

Make sure you are taking care of yourself so you can be the best possible tool in God's hands for your family and friends.

February 18

"...The prayer of a righteous man is powerful and effective."
James 5:16b (NIV)

At my mother-in-law's Celebration of Life, her prayer life was recognized in a couple of ways:

1) Her "prayer board"—she kept a chalkboard "chalk-full" of names of people she prayed for consistently, persistently, and sincerely. As a tribute to her, we had people put their name on a large chalkboard if they had ever been prayed for by Carol. It was totally filled by the end of the afternoon.

2) The pastor mentioned how she would not ask, "How can I pray for you?" She would say, "Let me tell you how I've been praying for you." She was so in-tune with the Holy Spirit. He guided her prayer time to specific needs for the person she was praying for.

I think most of us left motivated to have a better prayer life. I know I did. One of the most meaningful things that others do for me is to not just say they are going to pray, but they stop and pray (or text a prayer) right then and there. I have tried to repeat this practice for others.

Sometimes we feel like "all we can do is pray." My friend, the best thing we can do is pray!

February 19

"Do not swerve to the right or the left; keep your foot from evil."
Proverbs 4:27 (NIV)

Oh, how easily I can get distracted. I will go to my phone to look something up or to do some task. When I look at my phone there will be a notification that I open. By the time that notification has been clicked, I will have completely forgotten why I came to my phone in the first place—PATHETIC!

I can laugh about my "squirrel" behavior, but it is not so funny if we swerve to the right or left spiritually (Proverbs 4:27). It is important to keep our eyes on Jesus, the author and finisher of our faith, to keep from being distracted by the things the devil puts in our path (Hebrews 12:1).

If you can relate to me in any way, I encourage you to pray this prayer with me:

Dear Father, my Guide, help me to keep my eyes on You. When I am tempted to look left or right, I know I will stumble. Thank You for picking me up and setting me back on the right path. Help me to be persistent in finishing the race for You. Amen.

February 20

"Rest in the Lord; wait patiently for him to act. Don't be envious of evil men who prosper." Psalm 37:7 (TLB)

The first time I ever snorkeled, I was determined to not go home until I saw a sea turtle. It seemed like just as I would come in from the water, those still in the ocean spotted one. On our last day, I finally glimpsed the prize. I was in awe. I could watch sea turtles all day. It's as if they don't have a care in the world. They just float through the ocean, feed on the reef, and when they are ready, they move gracefully and slowly through the water.

I have seen many sea turtles since that day. I STILL love watching them. When I am at home or at work and I start sensing myself getting agitated or irritated, I go to my "sea turtle place." That image helps me settle down and take things in stride.

Another image I go to for resting my spirit is a quiet stream. There are apps that allow us to hear the sound of a babbling brook or gentle ocean waves to help us rest or sleep. Our good Shepherd, Jesus, leads us beside quiet waters and restores our soul.

The imagery is helpful, but the promise is certain. When we trust Him, hope in Him, wait on Him, or rest in Him, He will help us (Psalm 37:5). He is working and we must learn to be patient.

February 21

"I will refresh the weary and satisfy the faint." Jeremiah 31:25 (NIV)

When I am hungry, I often bypass the healthy protein or vegetable and reach for the empty calories. These are the things that satisfy for the moment, but don't fulfill the need—chips, cookies, candy.

When I am empty spiritually, I tend to bypass the Bible and reach for the meaningless—video game, tv, news bites. Nothing is inherently wrong with these things, but they will never replace or fulfill our deepest longings.

Jeremiah 31:25 promises that God will satisfy the weary soul. Paul, in Phil 4:12, tells us that he has learned the secret of being content.

- Do you live satisfied?
- Do you live with contentment?
- Do you live as if you are loved?

Whatever you are doing right now, stop and thank God for being everything you need. Thank Him for loving you and dying for you. Thank Him for what He has given you rather than focusing on what you don't have or wish you could achieve.

February 22

"Holy, holy, holy is the Lord God Almighty, who was, and is, and is to come." Revelations 4:8b (NIV)

On January 23, I referred to our favorite church and worship experience when we go to Maui. A few years ago, we attended their morning service in a park overlooking the ocean. They had moved from the oceanside restaurant to this setting because of Covid restrictions in 2020.

The whales had been pretty active all weekend, but this particular morning we were seeing an amazing amount of motion They were spouting, splashing, and breaching. We were mesmerized at God's wonders.

While singing "Holy, Holy, Holy," we came to the verse that says:
"All Thy works shall praise Thy name, in earth and sky and sea."

At that time, as if in tune with our praise, a whale in the distance shot up out of the water, creating a huge splash, putting an exclamation mark on the holiness of God. It was a moment of worship I will never forget.

All God's works include the whales, the ocean, and you and me. We need to rise each morning exclaiming His holiness. You may or may not make a huge splash in your day, but God enjoys the ripples of our praise any way we express it. Look around you this week to see how God's holiness is displayed in earth or sky or sea.

February 23

"He makes me lie down in green pastures, he leads me beside quiet waters." Psalm 23:2 (NIV)

As our kids and grandkids have come through toddlerhood, there has been a common thread we have noticed. The more tired they get, the more frenetic their energy becomes. It's almost as if they are fighting the sleep and rest (nap time), and are doing everything possible to keep themselves awake.

We adults are not much different. We run around at a frantic pace, trying to keep up with our appointments and schedules. The more exhausted we are, the more desperate we are to keep our wheels spinning.

That's why our Good Shepherd has to make us lie down in green pastures (Psalm 23:2). It is why He blessed the Sabbath day and made it holy (Exodus 20:8-11). He made us in His image, and even God took a day to rest from the work of His creation.

We know, as parents and grandparents, that our toddlers need to slow down and rest. God knows that about us, too. Think about ways you can rest today. Here are a few:

    A.   Take a nap
    B.   Read
    C.   Sit outside (somewhere in nature) and take in the sights and sounds (even if it means sitting at a park on your lunch break)

February 24

"Remember the Sabbath day by keeping it holy." Exodus 20:8 (NIV)

Exodus 20 records the Ten Commandments that were given to Moses on Mount Sanai. The majority of the commands are stated in a sentence. The Sabbath Day command takes up four verses. It seems to me that this one needed some extra attention, though they are all equally important.

That being said, I hope you schedule a Sabbath each week. It may not be on Sunday, depending on your career or work situation. Regardless, the principles of God's laws are there for a reason.

During the French Revolution, government leaders abolished Sunday as a day of rest. They later restored it because the health of the nation had collapsed. They learned the hard way what God had made clear centuries before.

You need to recharge your emotions and refocus your spirit each week in some way or another. Your mental, physical, and spiritual health depend on it.

February 25

"For our light and momentary troubles are achieving for us an eternal glory that far outweighs them all. So we fix our eyes not on what is seen, but on what is unseen. For what is seen is temporary, but what is unseen is eternal." 2 Corinthians 4:17-18 (NIV)

I have stopped taking my Bible to church. It's big and bulky, and it's very convenient to pull up the verses being referenced on my phone.

The problem is, I am not highlighting, underlining, or making as many notes in the margins as I used to. I came across our key passage the other day that I had underlined as a teenager.

As I reflected on my "momentary troubles" of five decades ago, they were worries about the latest pimple on my face or the boy I liked who didn't seem to pay any attention to me. They were still real issues, but they were probably more on the "light" side.

Today, my troubles weigh a little more. I've known some great sorrow in the past few months. More than ever, I have had to fix my eyes not on what is seen, but on what is unseen and eternal (2 Corinthians 4:18).

I showed my marked-up Bible to a group of high school girls the other day. I encouraged them to use their physical Bibles as much as they could. They actually talked about taking their Bibles to school to read during their silent sustained reading time. I hope they really do it. Who knows what treasures they will uncover.

February 26

"**Remain** in me, and I will **remain** in you. No branch can bear fruit by itself; it must **remain** in the vine. Neither can you bear fruit unless you **remain** in me." John 15:4 (NIV-Emphasis mine)

It's amazing that the word remain is used four times in this short verse. Teachers tend to repeat something that is important, so this must have been very important to Jesus.

To stay grounded, we must "remain" in God's Word. It isn't a one and done affair. We must search the treasures of the Bible every day. It's more than just seeking knowledge. It is learning to cherish the depths of God's truths.

Our youth pastor recently said that "remaining" is the easiest yet the hardest thing you will ever do. He gave us a prayer to pray every morning: "Jesus, I love You, I trust You, I surrender all to you."

Another word that is used for "remain" in other translations is "abide." My mom recently shared that abiding in Christ is not a feeling or a belief, but it is something we DO!

With all of these thoughts in mind, let's live abiding and obedient lives to our True Vine!

February 27

"Do not conform any longer to the pattern of this world, but be transformed by the renewing of your mind. Then you will be able to test and approve what God's will is—his good, pleasing and perfect will."
Romans 12:2 (NIV)

God gives us transforming wisdom to stand up in this world by being "different" from the culture around us. Yet, we can also stand out in our circles of influence by loving others wholly and uniquely. We are not to love the value systems of this world, but we are to love the world as God so loved the world (the people God created).

This can be tricky at times, finding a balance between loving people while not conforming to the cultural norms and values. We are called to be transformed by the renewing of our minds, and that happens with staying in God's Word, using it as a filter for all of our choices and attitudes. His Word transforms what we love!

I don't know about you, but I need prayer each day to get this right.

Lord, give me the wisdom I need for being in the world but not of the world. I want others to see Your love through me. That will happen because I am not molded to this world's philosophies and values, and because I show love and compassion to others. Thank you for renewing my thoughts and mind. Help my words and actions to be acceptable in Your sight. Amen.

February 28

> "And if the Spirit of him who raised Jesus from the dead is living in you, he who raised Christ from the dead will also give life to your mortal bodies through his Spirit, who lives in you."
> Romans 8:11 (NIV)

A couple of Sundays ago, we were singing "Mighty to Save" in church. The chorus says:

> "Savior, He can move the mountain
> My God is mighty to save, He is mighty to save.
> Forever, Author of Salvation,
> He rose and conquered the grave,
> Jesus conquered the grave."

As I often do when I am singing a worship song, I began praying for those I know who need the redeeming salvation of Jesus. Sometimes when I think of these people, their situations seem impossible. It would be like moving a mountain to get them to accept Christ.

Then, we sang that Jesus conquered the grave. We have the same power in our lives that raised Jesus from the dead. My mustard-seed faith begins to look a little more like mountain-moving faith when I think about this power.

I know you have friends and loved ones you want to see come to Jesus. Boldly pray a prayer to the Author of Salvation for your loved one today.

February 29 (a bonus devotional for Leap Year)

"You prepare a table before me in the presence of my enemies. You anoint my head with oil; my cup overflows." Psalm 23:5 (NIV)

Are you feasting or fasting? God has a banquet table filled with food He has prepared for you, but you must sit at His table to fully taste it. Snacking, grabbing a bite here and there, or only sitting down one day a week (say, Sunday?) will not give you the full benefit of His nourishing spiritual food. Unfortunately, that is what we tend to do.

Are His words sweet to your taste? Do you need to change your "eating habits?" Take this mental survey—I partake of God's table by:

A. Feasting every day
B. Eating once a week
C. Nibbling here and there
D. Dessert only (partaking only in the things that make you happy)
E. Other or a combination of the above

Determine to fill up on Him each day. It's the only way you will be satisfied.

March 1

But as for you, be strong and do not give up, for your work will be rewarded. 2 Chronicles 15:7 (NIV)

Don't give up staying grounded and keeping connected! Don't give up praying for others. Don't give up doing good. We wait for the harvest with trust and obedience, but God is the one that brings about the harvest in His time (Galatians 6:9).

I recently read of two people who had recently come to accept the Lord as their Savior. Sue made a connection with the church clothing distribution center because she was in need. The women from the church showed her God's love. Their discipleship and caring for her brought her fairly quickly to a decision for Christ. Six months later she was involved in leading the clothing ministry and building the kingdom for God.

The other person was a self-proclaimed atheist. Over time, he became curious about the gospel and was well educated on all religions and tenets. He just "wasn't ready" to commit to becoming a Jesus follower. Forty-three years after his own children had begun praying for him, he recognized his need for a Savior.

Whether it takes 6 months or 60 years, we cannot give up praying and coming alongside others. I just returned from a retreat where over half the women had come to know Jesus in the latter years of their lives. May this encourage you to persevere in praying for and ministering to the lost.

March 2

"Be still and know that I am God; I will be exalted among the nations, I will be exalted in the earth." Psalm 46:10 (NIV)

We seldom enjoy silence. There is always something going on around us. Take, for example, a restaurant. It is very difficult to have a conversation due to the music, TV screens, crying kids, or the robotic tones of the kids on their games.

We need to cultivate a quiet heart in a loud and restless world. Even when things are crazy around us, we can settle our hearts by whispering a prayer. Using breathing techniques are becoming a cultural norm to settle heart rate or anxiety. We can add to this physiological practice by breathing in the Spirit of God and breathing out the chaos of this world.

We also need to build into the discipline of our day a quiet time with the Lord. That may look like getting up fifteen minutes earlier than the rest of the family. It might be finding a moment after the rest of the household has been put to bed. It might mean shutting yourself in the bathroom for a few minutes. I remember being a mom of little ones-- desperate times call for desperate measures!

Whatever it looks like for you, be still and know that He is God!

March 3

"On the evening of that first day of the week, when the disciples were together with the doors locked for fear of the Jews, Jesus came and stood among them and said, 'Peace be with you!'"
John 20:19 (NIV)

Have you experienced locked-behind-the-door kind of fear? We all had a little taste of that when Covid-19 was first announced. No one really knew what was going on, but we were hunkered down, especially in those first few weeks, to see what would unfold.

When Jesus appeared to the disciples after His resurrection, His first words to them were very intentional. He didn't reprimand them for hiding away. He didn't give them a rally speech to get them to move on. He didn't talk about His grueling experience on the cross. He simply said, "Peace be with you!"

John's account places an exclamation point after Jesus' words. He wasn't just giving them a casual greeting. He was emphatic and deliberate, knowing what they needed most at that moment. His very presence brought peace and joy to their hearts.

Jesus says the same to us. "Peace be with you!" In essence He is saying, "I am with you. I am peace, in the absence of trouble and in the presence of trouble."

When you face trials or troubles, you are not alone. Jesus is with you. He wants you to replace your fear with His presence.

March 4

"Each one should use whatever gift he has received to serve others, faithfully administering God's grace in its various forms."
1 Peter 4:10 (NIV)

As our Women's Ministry team at church was planning our spring retreat, it was a joy watching the ladies work together. Each person had strengths that they brought to the table—finances, graphic arts, décor/hospitality, organization, communication. There is no way one person could have done it all and done it well.

There is a standing joke among our women's team. They know NOT to give me anything that has to do with crafts. I am terrible at them, though sometimes I really do try, but I am in such awe of those who are natural leaders in this area. Others feel the same way about doing the music or being up front. When we put all our gifts to use, something beautiful happens.

Jasmine Williams speaks about being good stewards of the gifts God has given us. We are designed to be in community. She comments, "We get to feel more complete when we thrive alongside others, filling each other's gaps when needed." By being connected to God, we are also connected with the greatness He has put in others who follow Him. What an ingenious plan!

We don't have to do it all ourselves! You can fill in the gaps for others, and they will fill in the gaps for you. Together you will be administering God's grace! What a deal!

March 5

"So give your servant a discerning heart to govern your people and to distinguish between right and wrong. For who is able to govern this great people of yours?" 1 Kings 3:9 (NIV)

I needed to make a tough decision. I wanted to support my friend, a person whom I love very much, but I didn't agree with her unbiblical point of view.

I thought about how to approach her. I could make an excuse and technically avoid the situation. That just didn't feel right. If I spoke the truth, I wanted it to be in love.

The very day I was contemplating my choices, I read about King Solomon asking for wisdom. The question was posed to me: "Why not ask God for the wisdom of Solomon?"

Of course, that was the reminder I needed. I asked God for wisdom and felt a great peace about my course of action. I communicated with my friend, letting her know I loved and supported her, but I needed to stay true to my heart and convictions. She totally understood, and our relationship remains intact.

God is more than able to grant our request for wisdom. He was pleased with Solomon and He will be pleased with you.

March 6

"Do not be afraid, little flock, for your Father has been pleased to give you the kingdom." Luke 12:32 (NIV)

Are you filled with fear these days? There are certainly things to worry about all around us.

God totally understands that we will have fears. That's why He has said, "Do not be afraid," in a variety of forms all throughout the Old and New Testaments.

- Fear no evil (Psalm 23:4)
- Fear not, for I am with you (Isaiah 41:10)
- Be strong, do not fear (Isaiah 35:4)
- Do not be afraid, do not be discouraged (Joshua 8:1)
- Do not let your hearts be troubled (John 14:27)
- Do not worry about tomorrow (Matthew 6:34)

I've heard it said that "Do not be afraid," in one form or another is in the Bible 365 times, one for each day of the year. I have never been able to substantiate that claim. However, the accuracy of the number is not as important as the concept. Jesus wants us to trust Him with our fears every single day!

I think it's important to understand that Jesus isn't promising a safe life. He's promising His kingdom. We can replace our fear with faith, believing that He is present with us. As we seek His kingdom in our lives, He gives us His vision and His desire to love and encourage those around us. It's exciting, adventurous, and totally fulfilling to follow Him. Instead of fear filling your life, let God's presence fill you!

March 7

"'Though the mountains be shaken and the hills be removed, yet my unfailing love for you will not be shaken nor my covenant of peace be removed,' says the Lord who has compassion on you."
Isaiah 54:10

I read the verse of the day and immediately wanted to paraphrase it a bit. We were camping just yards from the ocean to the West, and we had the central California coast hills to the East. My thought was that though the ocean waves crash and the riptides are strong, His love is my anchor and His covenant of peace will not be swept out to sea.

I spent a few moments looking to the ocean and acknowledging my need for calling on God for help and recognizing His unfailing love. Here were a few of the things on my list. His love was evident in:

- His beautiful creation
- My precious family
- Friends who care deeply about me
- The Lord's help and salvation
- God's constant presence in my life
- His peace that passes all understanding

What is on your list? How do you recognize His love? As you view the hills, or mountains, or ocean, or sky, or desert, or anything that the Creator God has made, let it remind you that you can rely on God's unchanging character, love, and peace.

March 8

"Be kind and compassionate to one another, forgiving each other, just as in Christ God forgave you." Ephesians 4:32 (NIV)

We were walking back to our vehicle after having lunch at one of our favorite diners. On the way, we had to pass by three gentlemen who were sitting on a grassy knoll to the left of the sidewalk. They were surrounded by bags, blankets, and other collected paraphernalia.

They were obviously homeless. Previously when we passed by, they were being spoken to by a couple of police officers, probably just checking on their well-being.

We got eye contact and greeted them. They all said, "Hi," and one of the men said, "God bless." I was touched. It was just a simple smile and greeting. We acknowledged them as opposed to ignoring them or passing on the other side. We made eye contact, and it elicited a response and a blessing from them.

I would love to tell you that we stayed and chatted. We did move on, but we pondered how we are all God's children and He loves us all!

It can be as simple as saying "hi" to a homeless person or going the extra mile to help someone in need. As Christ followers we need to be conduits of kindness.

March 9

"In his heart a man plans his course, but the Lord determines his steps."
Proverbs 16:9 (NIV)

Proverbs 16:9 has always been one of my favorite verses. Loosely translated, it tells us to set goals, make plans, but rely on God to direct the details and the detours. If He wants you to go in a different direction, He'll let you know, if you are depending on Him to show you.

I shared this verse with a young lady who was one of my employees, but who I also was mentoring. We were having coffee, and she was sharing some of her dreams and plans for the near future. She was at a crossroad, trying to figure out if she should keep working at her current job (with me) or quit so that she could pursue the next step in her schooling for her career.

My encouragement to her was to go after her goals, make plans, and begin to implement steps. I also let her know that God wanted to be a part of all of it, and she should be aware of closed doors and redirection from Him. His way would always be the best way.

Later in the day, my friend found an illustrated path with the verse I had shared with her written at the top. I knew she was listening and beginning to "get it."

God is there to help you with every decision and goal. Let Him lead!

March 10

"I in them and you in me. May they be brought to complete unity to let the world know that you sent me and have loved them even as you have loved me." John 17:23 (NIV)

This verse is part of Jesus' prayer for all believers. He prays for unity among believers to be a sure sign to the world that God has fatherly love for them.

We let the world know about Jesus' love when we are unified. Why would anyone want to get to know Christ if His people were always disagreeing and unhappy with each other? I know it goes deeper than that, but it is such a profound thought.

There are a lot of things that are divisive these days. It makes Satan very happy when the church fights and bickers. We don't all have to think alike. We don't all have to look alike. We just need to unite in the things that are important—the love of God for His children.

Don't let Satan win!

Work at being united, loving each other, showing each other the love of Jesus so it spills out to those who don't know Him.

March 11

"Finally, brothers, whatever is true, whatever is noble, whatever is right, whatever is pure, whatever is lovely, whatever is admirable—if anything is excellent or praiseworthy—think about such things."
Philippians 4:8 (NIV)

When we meditate on God's Word, we are transformed from the inside out. Our actions and what we say are reflections of what we study and think about the most.

That's why I love this acronym, and I remind myself of it often. I used it in my classroom as a reminder of how to respond to each other, but it is certainly appropriate for adults as well! Before saying something, THINK! Is it...

True?
Helpful?
Inspiring?
Necessary?
Kind?

If the answer to any of these questions is "no," whatever you were about to say is probably best left unsaid.

THINK about those things that are lovely and true, pure and noble, excellent or praiseworthy. Let your words uplift and bring life to others. (See August 24-27 for a break down of these terms.)

March 12

"The Lord is close to the brokenhearted and saves those who are crushed in spirit." Psalm 34:18 (NIV)

I sat and listened. It was just about all I knew to do as my friend poured out her grief over the loss of her husband. Yes, his passing had been over a year ago, but she was still processing her life without him by her side.

I prayed the key verse over my friend, that her broken heart would draw her closer to the Lord and that she would feel comforted in His presence. Little did I know that we would be needing this promise to cover us during our days of grief just a few months later.

Our Lord knows and understands sorrow. He is brokenhearted alongside us as we mourn our losses. I'm convinced that we can't dictate how we are going to grieve, or when a song or memory will trigger the hurt all over again.

We can't determine how many weeks, months, or years we will feel the ache in our spirit. But we can know that God is right by our side as we walk this road.

For anyone who is in need of this promise today, I am praying for you!

March 13

"Above all, love each other deeply, because love covers over a multitude of sins." I Peter 4:8 (NIV)

"If it is possible, as far as it depends on you, live at peace with everyone." Romans 12:18 (NIV)

These two verses go hand in hand with a quote I came across the other day: "Harmony and empathy go together."

This is a simple yet profound thought. Without caring and listening and having love for others, we can't expect to have peace in our relationships. This is true in our homes, in our work places, in our society, and in our churches.

The verse from Romans 12 actually showed up twice in my morning devotions. When that happens, I ponder whether it is a mistake or a message. I tend to believe there is purpose and meaning behind the things that come across my path repeatedly.

Then, in Sunday's sermon, we were taught that the exiled people were called on by God to pray for peace in their city, the place of their exile (Jeremiah 27:9).

We need to pray for peace and prosperity, even for your potential enemies. Love and extend grace to those who you are closest to. Put yourself in someone's shoes. Empathize and harmonize.

March 14

"I waited patiently for the Lord; he turned to me and heard my cry. He lifted me out of the slimy pit, out of the mud and mire; he set my feet on a rock and gave me a firm place to stand. He put a new song in my mouth, a hymn of praise to our God. Many will see and fear and put their trust in the Lord." Psalm 40:1-3 (NIV).

I often stop to question why I do what I do? Why do I continue to interview people and write their stories? In case you didn't know it, I have written three books in this format of sharing God's Work through amazing testimonies.

I used to think I was writing the books for my audience. However, when we experienced one of the toughest seasons in our lives, I knew God had me write these books for myself as well. I am so encouraged in my personal faith when I hear of what God is doing in other's lives. Their joy in relating how God was at work has helped to build my own "trust bank."

Similarly, in our Bible passage for today, David's experience of God's help during his times of trouble moves him to praise, and it bolsters the faith of others.

You have a story. You most likely have many stories, testimonies that can help point people to Jesus. Think about when He heard your cry. Ponder the moment you came to Christ and He pulled you out of the muddy pit. Look back in your journal to the times He gave you a firm place to stand or put a new song in your mouth. Pray about someone with whom God might want you to share your story.

March 15

"Rejoice with those who rejoice; mourn with those who mourn."
Romans 12:15 (NIV)

I love March for many reasons, not the least being that it is the beginning of spring. Another reason, a rather big deal in our family, is the NCAA basketball tournament, better known as March Madness.

It is amazing how many games come down to the wire. There is always such elation by the winning college that their team is moving on in the brackets. It's also interesting to watch the team who didn't come out on top this particular time. Their crowd often stands in stunned silence as the others are jumping and screaming around them.

I have to admit I'm a little, no make that a lot, competitive. Sometimes it is hard to watch "my team" lose, and I hate to admit that I don't always feel like celebrating with the winners.

That's why I find this passage so intriguing. I think it's easier for us to weep with each other, feel each other's pain, than it is to rejoice in someone else's victories. Too often we wonder why God didn't bless me with that job or that answer to prayer. We are happy on the outside, but maybe a little jealous on the inside.

We were put on this earth for relationship. We are meant to comfort each other in times of sorrow. We are also supposed to celebrate with each other in times of success.

Whether we are meant to congratulate the "winner" or empathize with someone who has "lost," may God grant us His heart!

March 16

"Jesus replied, '"Love the Lord your God with all your heart and with all your soul and with all your mind." This is the first and greatest commandment. And the second is like it: "Love your neighbor as yourself."'" Matthew 22:37-39 (NIV)

Do you need some motivation today? Do you need to know how you are going to make it through your week? Here's the answer in two parts:

1. Love the Lord your God with all your heart soul, mind and strength.

2. Love your neighbor as yourself.

Loving God, staying grounded in Him, puts all our issues, petty and significant, into perspective.

Loving others helps you live out your purpose. We were created out of relationship (God the Father, Son, and Holy Spirit) FOR relationship. When we are living out our purpose, we will find fulfillment.

I'm not saying that it's easy, but it's a start! Begin today! You are already seeking God through His Word by doing a devotional like this. Good job! Now, pray about who God may want you to love today. You are on your way to making it through the rest of your week.

March 17

"Whatever you do, work at it with all your heart, as working for the Lord, not for men." Colossians 3:23 (NIV)

I am a bit of a perfectionist. It gets me into trouble at times, because NO ONE is perfect, right?

Whether it's being a parent, a writer, a wife, a teacher, a mentor, a Bible study leader, or anything else, I want to exhibit excellence. There is nothing wrong with striving to do your best, but it can lead to doubt or guilt or frustration when we are not careful.

The good news is that we can rest in the fact that God is perfect, and we are not. He is in control, and we can live surrendered to our loving Creator.

Go ahead and work as unto the Lord. It is built within us to want to do a good job! But let His goodness and mercy motivate you to keep moving forward.

March 18

"Be completely humble and gentle; be patient, bearing with one another in love." Ephesians 4:2 (NIV)

We had to wait for a long time before anyone came to get our drink order. It was morning, for Pete's sake, and we needed our coffee!

It was one of our favorite local breakfast restaurants. The last couple of times we were in for our usual omelet, they were extremely busy. It appeared that management was understaffing for the Saturday morning rush.

Instead of showing our frustration, especially when the people who came after us were served ahead of us, we chose to speak kindly to our waitress. We know them all by name, and we let Lindsay know we had noticed how busy it had been lately.

She was appreciative, and she seemed to need a little time to vent, so we leant her our ears for a few minutes.

Later, when we received our bill, we noticed she didn't charge us for our coffee. We knew it wasn't an oversight but her way of saying thank you. We didn't expect anything in return for our kindness, but it sure made me glad we had responded positively toward her. We tipped her generously, as we always try to do, and went on with our day.

We never know what others are dealing with. It's so easy to judge quickly or to demand immediate attention to our needs. Instead, let's take a deep breath, try to stand in their shoes for a few seconds, and spread love and joy.

Even if we don't get a free cup of coffee, we will get a smile from Jesus!

March 19

"He cuts off every branch in me that bears no fruit, while every branch that does bear fruit he prunes so that it will be even more fruitful."
John 15:2 (NIV)

We were hiking a familiar path. The area around Lake Tahoe is called the Tallac Estates. It is a series of three historical homes that have been preserved throughout the years for tourists to visit. They are beautiful homes with spectacular views of the lake and surrounding snow-capped mountains.

The surprise on this day was that we were stopped in our tracks by the forest department. They were getting ready to cut down a tree that was leaning dangerously toward the path. They had discovered and marked it as a tree that needed help coming down before it created a disaster on its own.

We were allowed to stand back and watch their handiwork. First a back cut was made at the base of the tree. Next, they used their brand new, formidable Stihl power saw and cut through the opposite side. Yes, they yelled, "Timber," as it began to slowly lean farther toward the lake. It came down with a loud crash and cheers from all of us.

Sometimes we need something that is in our lives to be cut out. It is becoming a dangerous entity that could lead to potential destruction. Maybe it even started out as something good, but it has become an idol or a distraction keeping us from being God's best version of ourselves.

The Master woodcutter might need to take His time cutting through our cracked or diseased character weakness to allow light to shine on the rest of our path. It might feel painful or seem unnecessary, but it is for our safety and for our good.

The next time God is doing a work in your life, it may be hard or uncomfortable, but let Him do His "tree surgery" so that you can continue living out His purpose in and through you.

March 20

"As the heavens are higher than the earth, so are my ways higher than your ways and my thoughts than your thoughts."
Isaiah 55:9 (NIV)

Have you ever been at a place where you just need a different perspective? Maybe you are so entrenched in the daily grind that you just can't see any relief. Rising above our circumstances is tough, even scary at times, but it is important for us to be able to see things from God's point of view.

As we took a 2.4-mile Gondola ride up the side of Heavenly Mountain at Lake Tahoe, we found out that one of our passengers was deathly afraid of heights. She white-knuckled it most of the way, but she knew the end result would be worth it.

When we got off at the observation deck, the panoramic views left us breathless. We could see the entire valley, the vastness of the lake, from shore to shore, and the majestic snow-capped mountains all around us.

As we reveled in the beauty, I thought about how God takes what we are doing each day. Our faithfulness in showing up at work every morning, in spite of our tough boss or our menial tasks, is honing us for something bigger down the road. We may not be able to see it now, but we can get a glimpse of what God wants to do when we look at some of the Bible stories.

When Moses was tending smelly sheep in the arid desert, he probably never envisioned sitting at the top of Mount Sanai receiving God's tablet of Ten Commandments that would live on through history. When Peter left his fishing business to follow Jesus, I don't think he imagined being the conduit of God's plan of salvation to the Gentiles

Take a minute this week to catch your breath and give your daily routines to Jesus. You never know what He is preparing you to do in the future.

March 21

"For the word of God is living and active. Sharper than any double-edged sword, it penetrates even to dividing soul and spirit, joints and marrow; it judges the thoughts and attitudes of the heart." Hebrews 4:12 (NIV)

We were on the elevator having a good chuckle at the way God works through His Word. I had just read my Grounds for Hope post for the day (which I had written a couple of weeks in advance). It was about rejoicing with those who rejoice and mourning with those who mourn.

The "joke" was on me. I had NOT been happy that my husband had beaten the socks off us in our card game the night before. The next morning, reading my post, made me realize how silly my attitude had been. I congratulated him, gave him a sincere kiss, and apologized for my poor sportsmanship.

I know it's a bit ridiculous, but God worked in me over my pathetic competitive spirit. God's Word is such a sharp tool. His timing is impeccable. Even in a trivial thing like winning or losing a game, God shaped me a little bit more into His likeness.

I am grateful for His Word that judges my thoughts and attitudes. May we be pliable and willing to allow God to penetrate our heart when He knows we need it.

March 22

"'How may loaves do you have?' [Jesus] asked. 'Go and see.' When they found out, they said, 'Five—and two fish.'" Mark 6:38 (NIV)

Our pastor gave a sermon recently about the feeding of the five Thousand. He made a statement that stuck with me:

"Jesus did this miracle to teach the disciples to depend on Him."

Jesus is the Bread of Life. He didn't really need the disciples to help find five loaves and two fish to feed all those people. He could have done it without them, but He chose to involve them. He wants to use me and you, and He wants to build our faith in Him by using our meager efforts and mustard-seed faith.

I have always thought it was interesting that at the end of the story they collected twelve baskets of left-overs (Mark 6:43), one for each disciple. They started with nothing and ended up with a full belly, enough food for several more meals, and hearts full of awe and wonder.

In what area of your life do you need to depend on Jesus today? Give Him what little or much that you have. He will fill your cup to overflowing! He will work beyond your wildest imagination (see Ephesians 3:20).

March 23

"Pleasant words are a honeycomb, sweet to the soul and healing to the bones." Proverbs 16:24 (NIV)

I was getting in my car after shopping at Costco. A loud voice caught my attention, and I looked over to the source of the sound. A mother was yelling at her children, berating them, and letting them know how worthless they were.

I'm sure I didn't have the full picture, but my heart broke for those kids. They appeared to be trying to please her. They were helping bring the full cart to the trunk of the car to get unloaded. Maybe they weren't doing what she said fast enough. Maybe the mom was having a terrible day. I didn't know what else to do but pray for her and for the hearts and spirits of those young lives.

We are called to live and speak with grace. I KNOW I have not always done this perfectly. That's why it is important to fill my mind and heart with His Word every day. "Words sweetened with grace will only overflow from a heart overwhelmed by God's grace." (Beth Knight)

Will you join with me in praying for gracious words to flow from our mouths?

March 24

"A happy heart makes the face cheerful, but heartache crushes the spirit. Proverbs 15:13 (NIV)

On my daily Facebook blog, each Friday I try to post a coffee joke or something that I hope will make you chuckle. I'm not just trying to fill up a day of the week. I do it because I have always believed the Proverb that says "A happy heart makes the face cheerful" (Proverbs 15:13).

A few months ago, the paper had daily heart health tips. One of the article's headlines was that "A Happy Heart is a Healthy Heart." It went on to site that laughter relaxes the whole body. Laughter boosts the immune system. Laughter releases endorphins, the body's natural feel-good chemicals. Laughter reduces stress and protects the heart.

Pretty amazing. Wise Old Solomon was given this tidbit of wisdom long before the science supported it. Even in the middle of your most stressful ventures, a moment of comic relief can change your outlook.

Enjoy a good laugh today. Look up a joke, or tell one you know already.

March 25

> "I will fear no evil, for you are with me; your rod and your staff,--they comfort me." Psalm 23:4b (NIV)

I love alliteration, so I loved these reminders:

**Replace your panic with prayer
your worry with worship
your anxiety with adoration**

I want to add one more alliterative phrase. As we consider our Good Shepherd and the 23rd Psalm, Jesus came to give us life to its fullness. The shepherd's rod symbolizes that He is guarding, protecting and guiding us. The staff is used to rescue us. His goodness and compassion lift us up, unlike the world around us that has a tendency to pull us down.

Jesus doesn't beat us up because we got off the path or fell in a ditch. He urges and guides us to keep going to safe waters and green pastures. So here it is. Our thought for today. (Cue drum roll)

Jesus doesn't **hassle** you
He **heals** you!

I pray that you will feel His loving, healing touch in your life today.

March 26

"But the wisdom from above is first of all pure. It is also peace-loving, gentle at all times, and willing to yield to others. It is full of mercy and the fruit of good deeds. It shows no favoritism and is always sincere."
James 3:17 (NLT)

How can we be agents of God's mercy? How can we be more like Jesus and full of His wisdom? We must value relationships over rules. We need to practice building bridges rather than digging ditches. We have to be willing to give second chances and offer forgiveness.

Oh, baby! It's hard at times. It takes studying God's Word, imitating Jesus' life, and lots of prayer. It's a whole lot easier when we remember the mercy God has bestowed upon us.

Worship the God of Mercy and Grace today! Notice the number of times you run across those words in Scripture, in worship songs, and in your daily devotionals/inspirations. Draw on God's mercy, AND extend His mercy to others in your life.

March 27

"Then the man said, 'Your name will no longer be Jacob, but Israel, because you have struggled with God and with men and have overcome.'" Genesis 32:28 (NIV)

If you are struggling as you start your day, you are in good company! You are not alone!

Many of us start our days or our weeks already feeling a bit defeated. We wrestle with stamina and patience. We fight with the alarm clock, spill coffee on our fresh outfit, and start the day in a bad mood. Mondays can be hard! Every day can be hard!

Oh, I know our trials are more than an early morning alarm or a stained shirt. We have dreams and goals that seem unattainable at times. But, what if those struggles were just the thing that God uses to build our stamina, deepen our patience, and increase our resilience. If we can hold on to Him and wait for His blessing and anointing as Jacob did when he wrestled with God (see Genesis 32:22-28), we will come out on the other side having overcome whatever it is that is weighing us down.

Don't give up the fight. Live as an overcomer. God has a new name for you, "Overcomer."

Claim His promise to you by placing your name in the blank, and actually say it out loud, "I, _____, have overcome!"

March 28

> "The thief comes only to steal and kill and destroy; I have come that they may have life, and have it to the full." John 10:10 (NIV)

Do you want to live a full life overflowing with good things? I know I do. The good news is that God's Word tells us how we can be that vessel, full and spilling out.

First and foremost, we must accept Jesus into our lives. Without His saving grace, we are prey for the enemy who wants to steal our joy, kill our dreams, and destroy our relationships.

With Christ in control, we can live with an attitude of thankfulness. First Thessalonians 5:18 says, "Give thanks in all circumstances, for this is God's will for you in Christ Jesus."

We often make life so complicated. When simply put, we should just start each day by being grateful. Make a list, sing a song of praise, pray that you will see the world through fresh eyes each morning.

It is scientifically proven that gratitude produces chemicals in your brain such as dopamine, serotonin, and oxytocin, that make you feel peaceful and happy.

So, if you want to start filling up with peace and joy, begin today by voicing one thing you are thankful for, and do it as soon as you wake up.

You can add as many as you want as you head to work or continue through your day! Crank up the worship music in the car. Surprise yourself, and thank Him in the middle of your trial today. Be blessed, my friends!

March 29

"Therefore put on the full armor of God, so that when the day of evil comes, you may be able to stand your ground, and after you have done everything, to stand." Ephesians 6:13 (NIV)

In a recent Bible study on Ephesians, I read this: "Motivations push us toward something. They give us a reason behind our actions." I immediately thought of my "Motivating Monday" posts on my Grounds for Hope Facebook page. My goal is always to motivate us toward good works for the Lord, not for ourselves.

The study text went on to say that our best motivation is when: "Our motivation is Christ. We work like we are working for Jesus. We lead remembering we are accountable to Jesus. We stand firm against our enemy because we have strength and victory in Jesus. We put on our armor every day, which means we put on Jesus! And then we pray, pray, pray, in the name and power of Jesus..."

With Jesus by your side each day, acting as your motivation for everything you do and face, you will experience love and grace and peace!

What a difference it will make if we are willing to put Jesus in front of every decision and effort that we make.

March 30

"Commit to the Lord whatever you do, and your plans will succeed."
Proverbs 16:3 (NIV)

Are you a planner? I certainly am. I like to know where I'm going and what I'm doing each day. I'm a ducks-in-a-row kind of gal.

Making plans is good. It's Biblical. It's even godly. But, as our pastor recently preached, "we must hold loosely to our plans and hold tightly to our purpose."

Things will not always go perfectly, as planned. That's why it is so important to commit the plans to God. When our course seems to get interrupted, looks to be left unfinished, or appears to have failed completely, we need to remember our purpose. Those unfulfilled plans are often pathways to God's greater purpose. He is wanting to bring us to a place of success.

Go ahead and make your list for today. Set your goals, both short-term and long-term. Just remember that God is in control. He will determine what is best for you in the long run. Lean into Him, surrender to Him, and let His purpose prevail.

Pray over your plans. Give them to God. Enjoy your day!

March 31

"...a time to weep and a time to laugh, a time to mourn and a time to dance," Ecclesiastes 3:4 (NIV)

We were laughing so hard as we walked through the art gallery that we were doubled over. We were trying to be quiet and respectful, but that just made it worse. My friend and I look back on that moment, and we can't even remember what we were laughing about. We do remember that we were trying to keep the tears of laughter from running down our legs, if you get my drift.

Friends are important! We laugh with them and cry with them. Jesus was a perfect model of being a friend. He shared many moments with His disciples and others, just getting to know them, joining in their joys and sorrows.

He wants to be your friend as well. He hurts when we hurt. He rejoices with our successes. He is moved to laughter and tears with us.

As we strive to be more Christ-like, we need to be vulnerable with our friends. Be sensitive to what they need at the moment. Enter into their problems with them by being present. They don't always need our words of advice. Give them a shoulder to cry on or a memory to laugh about.

Pray about that friend who might need you to share life with them today. Call or text them to set a date on your calendar to go to coffee or lunch. Be the type of friend that Jesus demonstrated for us.

April 1

"But Moses said to God, 'Who am I, that I should go to Pharaoh and bring the Israelites out of Egypt?'" Exodus 3:11 (NIV)

My husband and I retired from teaching several years ago. God made it clear He was not finished using us for Him. We volunteer at church in a variety of capacities. We supervise college students who are working toward their teaching credential. God has laid His message on my heart, and I have been able to write a few books.

Like Moses, I have wondered who I am, that God would give me a particular task. Moses was eighty when he began his journey with the children of Israel into the wilderness, but with God a day is like a thousand years, and a thousand years is like a day.

When my dad's twin brother turned ninety-three, we were able to celebrate with him over the weekend. I'm sure my dad was looking down from Heaven and celebrating with us. At that time, my uncle played prelude music for a gospel concert in the Pismo Beach area every week. This "First Friday" event was one of the things that kept him going.

In *Common Ground* there is a story about a man named Larry who started ministering at his local Starbucks after retirement. He still meets with the group of prayer warriors and loves on people who enter the doors each morning.

On the opposite end of the spectrum, at our church's baptism services, the candidates share their testimonies. The eight and nine-year-olds share the sweetest ways God is using them in their schools or with their families.

It doesn't matter if you are eight, thirty-eight, or eighty-eight, God intends to use you for His glory as long as you are willing. God's response to Moses' question (and to yours as well) was, "I will be with you." (see Exodus 3:12). Even up until your ripe old age, He has purpose for you. Are you seeking His plan for your life right now, whatever your age or stage of life? Let God surprise you with how he chooses to use your gifts!

April 2

"Commit your way to the Lord; trust in him and he will do this."
Psalm 37:5 (NIV)

When I began to feel frustrated about the timing of my third book, I committed the project back to God. After that rededication of my efforts to Him, the final stories began to come to my attention. My last interview, which kept getting delayed, revealed God's perfect timing. The weekend before finally getting together over dinner with this couple, the final piece of their story fell into place. They were able to share the total picture. If we had met earlier, the story would have been incomplete.

When we hand over our works to the Lord, He shows us what to do. Our heart becomes more in tune with His heart and mind in the matter at hand. We soon find success, maybe not in the way we had anticipated it at first, but in the way God directs it.

Our key verse is a promise from God that He will make your righteousness shine (Psalm 37:6). Our goals will be reached in His timing, in His wonderful way. However, we must do our part by committing what we are doing to the Lord. We must give Him our to-do list. We must surrender our life dream. We must trust Him to direct our paths, even if it takes a different turn than what we expected.

Are you having trouble with something you are trying to achieve or finish? Maybe it's cleaning house. Maybe it's a work project that is looming? Try committing it to God, and see what He accomplishes.

April 3

"They took palm branches and went out to meet him, shouting, 'Hosanna!' 'Blessed is he who comes in the name of the Lord!' 'Blessed is the King of Israel!'" John 12:13 (NIV)

Each year Easter falls at a slightly different time on the calendar. Holy week always begins with Palm Sunday. Palm Sunday takes my mind back to being a little child, waving a palm branch in Sunday School, and shouting "Hosanna!"

I was not surprised to learn that "hosanna" is a phrase that was used to express praise, adoration and joy. I was surprised to find out that it also has a Hebrew translation that means "please, save!"

When Jesus rode through Jerusalem on the donkey, people were shouting praise and adoration for what they had heard and seen Jesus doing. He had healed, spoken words of wisdom and peace, and had "stood up" to the legalism of the Pharisees.

The people's shouts were also a plea for salvation. They were hoping for victory over the political hold that the Romans had on them, but Jesus had come for a much greater victory. He had come to save them from eternal death.

There needs to be a balance in our worship of Jesus. We should express adoration for who He is and what He is doing. We also need to humbly seek, even beg for, the salvation that only Christ can give.

As you sing and proclaim "Hosanna" this season, let it be a reminder that the One who died so that we might live deserves all the honor and glory!

April 4

"Jesus Christ is the same yesterday and today and forever."
Hebrews 13:8 (NIV)

The Monday after Palm Sunday was full of dramatic moments. Walking back into town with His disciples, Jesus cursed a fig tree for not bearing fruit, and it withered on the spot. Upon entering the Temple, seeing the corrupt dealings of the money changers, Jesus began turning over the tables and clearing the courtyard.

Knowing that it was getting close to His suffering and death, Jesus probably figured it was past time for negotiating. It was time to drive home the point that living faith must bear spiritual fruit and living worship could not be inundated with thieving hypocrisy.

I can almost see brazen Peter doing a silent "Yes" fist pump when He saw Jesus' action sending the coins flying in every direction. Maybe Andrew or John's jaw was agape at the extraordinary wilting of the fig tree. If they had only known what was to come, they may have seen and understood the intensity of Christ's messages.

In Matthew's account (see Matthew 21 – 22), Jesus continued throughout His day telling parables and answering the attempted traps from the religious leaders. His teachings were consistent and true. He never contradicted His character of being a loving judge.

His message has not changed. He still wants us to be bear fruit and to love and worship in truth and spirit. He still extends His mercy and grace to those who ask and receive His gifts in order to be free of the curse of sin and death.

I am grateful for the unaltering character of God. Thank Him today for His mercy and grace that never changes.

April 5

"But God demonstrates his own love for us in this: While we were still sinners, Christ died for us." Romans 5:8 (NIV)

At some point during Holy week, Jesus and His disciples were probably hanging out with Mary, Martha, and Lazarus in Bethany. Maybe this was the day Jesus just needed to rest from the exhausting and tumultuous events of the previous days. He also was aware that Judas had already negotiated with the Sanhedrin to betray Him.

I can almost envision it now. Mary is sitting at Jesus' feet. Martha is bustling in the kitchen, expressing her love language through hospitality. Lazarus is still in awe that he is alive, and doing better than ever. The disciples are milling about, some enjoying the break, while others are restless and antsy, needing something to do.

What extravagant love Jesus had for His followers. He knew they were going to doubt, deny, betray, and abandon Him, yet He continued to fellowship and live life with them.

Jesus did that for us as well. He didn't wait until we were all cleaned up and perfect before He went to the cross. He died while we were still sinners. His love knows no bounds.

Breathe a prayer of gratitude. Write a sentence or two in your journal thanking Christ for His exquisite and extraordinary love!

April 6

"Do this...in remembrance of me." 1 Corinthians 11:25b (NIV)

When Jesus directed His disciples to the Upper Room, they were to prepare and partake in the Passover Feast. That night Jesus washed their feet, demonstrating how believers should love one another with humble acts of service.

As Jesus then shared the feast with this motley crew, He explained how He was to be the fulfillment of the meaning of Passover. His broken body and shed blood would free them and future generations from sin and death. He established the Lord's Supper, or communion, telling us we should continue sharing these elements in remembrance of His sacrifice.

Jesus was soon to be handed over to the Sanhedrin. His anguish was so great, the Bible tells us He even sweat drops of blood while praying in the Garden of Gethsemane.

Even in His last moments Jesus was thinking of us by giving us:

- A final illustration of humble service
- A legacy and tradition to remember Him by
- An example of submitting His will to the Father (in spite of the agony He was experiencing)

We can follow Jesus' modeling through humble service, passing on a rich legacy, and submitting to the Father's will in the middle of trials. These are tangible ways to honor and live for Him. He deserves nothing less!

April 7

"I can do everything through him who gives me strength."
Philippians 4:13 (NIV)

Since September 2021 I have been practicing intermittent fasting. What that means is that most days I eat between a seven to eight-hour period (between 11:30 AM and 6:30-7:30 PM) and fast for a 16-17- hour period (between 7:30 PM and 11:30 AM the next day). I did quite a bit of research, and felt like it was a very healthy and safe approach to trying to lose some unwanted pounds as well as bringing some of my other health issues under control.

The only thing that has been hard about it is that I had to learn to drink my morning coffee black. I usually take it with half-and-half, but that would break the fast too early in the day to be completely effective. Other than that, I don't really deprive myself of anything food related. I don't go overboard on calories or sweets, of course.

The exciting news is that my pandemic 20 pounds have been dropping. The other day I got out my skinny jeans, and they actually fit again! I'm not saying this to brag, and I am not completely where I want to be yet. I'm just feeling better and I wanted to share a couple of things that have motivated me in case you are thinking about trying to lose weight or are in the middle of a plan.

1) Remember, it takes time! My pounds were added gradually over the course of 2020-21. They are coming off gradually as well.

2) I don't weigh myself every day. In fact, I weigh about once a month. I read that if you feel you must weigh every day, take a weekly average. Too many things can affect our daily weight (especially as women), and not seeing the scale numbers drop can feel discouraging.

3) When you get off track, just get back on as soon as possible. Don't punish yourself for it and spiral even further off course. I

have blown it during some vacation and holiday moments, but I try to give myself a little grace.

4) Find a fun way to exercise. My go-to is a 20-30 Pilates routine in the morning and 30-60 minutes of walking three days a week (at minimum).

I hope this encourages you! Often, we lose the inches before the scale number goes down, so find a reasonable outfit that you can use as a goal. Mid-way through, I still couldn't snap my jeans, but it was less hard to pull them up over my hips. Every step can be considered a little win.

Most important, bring God with you on your goal journey. He wants you to be healthy and whole, and He will give you strength.

April 8

"The Lord replied, 'My Presence will go with you, and I will give you rest.'" Exodus 33:14 (NIV)

Occasionally we enjoy an amazing stretch of weather here in Bakersfield. It may be in mid- spring or fall when residents say, if it would just be like this more throughout the year, they would have no problem living here!

One particular spring, the skies had been blue, spotted with a few clouds. The temperatures remained in the 70's. The air quality was at its finest. Even when a few of the days rose into the upper 80's, the evenings cooled down with a slight breeze.

That's when it is perfect to sit outside on my patio and read or work. Trust me, I'll enjoy it while I can!!!!

The good weather also spurs me on to planning and pursuing some spring-cleaning projects. Letting as much light in as possible helps me see some of deep corners of rooms to get where there is some unwanted dust and grime.

As I write this, however, it's Sunday. It's 78 degrees. The sun is shining, and I think I'll just bask in God's goodness. The chores will still be there tomorrow.

God can give us Sabbath rest any day of the week. Sometimes we catch it in a five-minute increment. Other times it might look like a 30-minute nap. I especially enjoy the snuggling-on-the-couch-with-my-grandkids moments of rest.

Whether today is Sunday, or any other day of the week, take time to enjoy His presence! In His Presence we will find rest.

April 9

"They devoted themselves to the apostles' teaching and to the fellowship, to the breaking of bread and to prayer." Acts 2:42 (NIV)

A few months ago, I was scheduled to meet a friend for a walk and to catch up on life. You can imagine my disappointment when we had to meet for coffee because it was raining (wink, wink).

Truly, either way would have been fine. I just needed the connection with her. We shared about our business pursuits, our families, our personal successes, and our individual struggles. There was no judgment, no pretense, just intimate conversation and genuine fellowship.

We decided on a book we would mutually read and discuss, giving us an "excuse" to schedule some more meetings. We prayed together before going about the rest of our day.

Friends, we need each other. We were created for fellowship. At Grounds for Hope I encourage you to "Stay Grounded, Keep Connected, One cup, One story at a time." It is so important to keep the "connected" part in your life.

The early church got this concept. They were together often, had everything in common, and shared with those in need. As a result, others were drawn into the fellowship, and the Lord added to their numbers.

I encourage you today to pick up your phone and plan to meet with a friend you haven't connected with in a while. It will be worth your time, and God will use it to build His Kingdom.

April 10

"By wisdom the Lord laid the earth's foundations, by understanding he set the heavens in place." Proverbs 3:19 (NIV)

I have worn corrective lenses since I was in about 3rd grade. I remember when I sat in the optometrist's chair for the first time and heard the doctor telling my parents I was almost legally blind in my right eye. No wonder I was having to squint at the chalkboard to read in class.

I am thankful for glasses, contact lenses, and prescription sunglasses that have helped me see more clearly. Even the best lenses, however, aren't perfect. They must be kept clean for a clear view. They have to be updated as vision needs change from year to year. Aging adds a new dimension to "seeing" as you have different prescriptions for things that are up close and far away. The tiny print seems more and more elusive.

Even with the perfect pair of spectacles, there are limits. But one thing that gives a clear view of life and is boundless in its wise counsel, is God's Word. If our life's perspective and our view of who God is gets clouded with doubt, pain, or unanswered prayer, God's Word reveals the truth. God is inexhaustibly compassionate, always near, and unlimited in His care for us.

What unchangeable truth do you need to be reminded of today? Choose one of these, or one of your own favorites, and hang onto it. Here are a few of my go-tos:

He is wise (Proverbs 3:19)

He is good and merciful (1 Chronicles 16:34)

He is in control—I do not need to be afraid (Philippians 4:6-7)

April 11

"...let us run with perseverance the race marked out for us, fixing our eyes on Jesus, the author and perfecter of faith."
Hebrews 12:1b-2a (NIV)

When being trained for running a race, it is crucial that you don't waste time and effort looking over your shoulder to see how the other runners are doing. The best strategy is to keep your eye on the goal, the finish line. Along with that, you need to tune your ears to your coach to hear what he/she is telling you to do, how your times are compared to previous trainings and races (your own PR-personal record), and how to proceed in the current race.

It is the same with our spiritual lives. We have been given a particular race that God has set before us. It is counterproductive to look over our shoulders and try to see where others are in their race. Your race is different from anyone else's and it's important to keep your eyes on the finish line. You need to listen to God's voice as He coaches you to do the things that are best for your race. Whatever He tells you to do, He has your good in mind and will get you closer to the goals and purposes He has prepared for you.

If you need motivation today, take these steps:

1) Don't compare yourself or your race to anyone else's. In John's gospel, chapter 21, Jesus was calling Peter to follow Him and feed His sheep. Peter sees John and asks Jesus about John's future. Jesus says, "What is that to you? You must follow me." (v. 22) We can't get caught up in what someone else is doing or not doing. We need to persevere in the race God has marked out for us.

2) Believe in your Coach. Listen to His voice and heed His directions. John 10 describes Jesus as the Good Shepherd. We are to stay close to Jesus, our Shepherd. As His sheep, we will recognize His voice and follow Him!

3) Keep your eyes on the finish line (eternal hope). At the finish line Jesus awaits, urging us on to complete the race. He's the author/pioneer and finisher of our faith. He starts us off on our journey with Him and He will be there through eternity with us.

4) Remember why you are doing step 1-3---because God loves you, knows better than you, and has good plans for your life. "'For I know the plans I have for you,' declares the Lord, 'plans to prosper you and not to harm you, plans to give you hope and a future.'" Jeremiah 29:11

If you are having trouble with one or all of these steps, claim the scripture verses for your own life. Reach out to a pastor or a friend who can pray for you. Lean into God's training and listen for His voice.

April 12

"You hem me in—behind and before; you have laid your hand upon me." Psalm 139: 5 (NIV)

Have you ever felt like you were between a rock and a hard place? I'm sure the Israelites felt this way as they were facing Pharoah's army behind them and the Red Sea in front of them. They were between a sand dune and a body of water!

The only thing that gave them a little bit of peace in the midst of this impossible situation was that they had the presence of God with them. He was visibly present as a pillar of cloud in the day and a pillar of fire at night. They may have felt trapped by the enemy, but they were enwrapped on all sides by the God of Creation.

You have that same privilege. No matter what you are facing, God is leading you, shining His light in your darkest nights, and reminding you that His presence and power is with you. He hems you in, going before you and behind you. What an awesome promise!

Trust His presence!

April 13

"And he said, 'I tell you the truth, unless you change and become like little children, you will never enter the kingdom of heaven.'"
Matthew 18:3 (NIV)

The teacher was doing a great job with the kindergarteners. The day had been windy and rainy, and the students were in need of a little revisiting of the expectations. She gently reminded them of the rules and procedures. I observed the lesson and made my notes, then I started looking around the room at the students.

One of the things I noticed made me smile. Some of the students were dressed to the nines with bows in their hair and everything in place. A couple of others had obviously dressed themselves-- matching floral tops with striped leggings, and a plaid shirt dress with star-studded sweat pants. Nobody was judging them for their sense of style, and I loved it.

We should be more like children. Even Jesus said, "Unless you change and become like little children, you will never enter the kingdom of heaven" Matthew 18:3. I believe He was making a heart statement rather than a fashion statement, but both apply here.

Of course, we need to follow our work dress codes and employee expectations. But try enjoying work with a child-like care-free spirit this week. Wear what makes you feel comfortable. Don't judge those around you. Do your best without being overly concerned with how the other person is doing.

I hope to see a few flowers and stripes this week!

April 14

"Since we live by the spirit, let us keep in step with the Spirit."
Galatians 5:25 (NIV)

The first thing my husband wanted to do when we retired was take a river rafting trip. We signed up to go down the Kern River with a guided group. It had been a particularly wet spring, so the water levels were healthy, the rapids exciting (and a little dangerous), and the entire experience exhilarating. It was important for us to have a guide that could show us how to nose into the sections of turbulence in such a way that kept us from capsizing. If we did what we were told, and didn't fight against the waves, we were fine.

Galatians 5:25 says, "If we live by the Spirit, let us also keep in step with the Spirit." The same principle of heading downstream in a raft applies to our rapids of life. If we choose to listen to our guide (God's Word and the Holy Spirit's still small voice), and do what He says, we can stay afloat. We might even sense some exhilaration as we watch His truths work in our tumultuous circumstances.

We have a choice each day. We can either walk in the flow of God's power, or we can resist and fight against it. Our resistance will eventually end in capsizing. Which will it be for you?

April 15

"But because of his great love for us, God, who is rich in mercy..."
Ephesians 2:4 (NIV)

I don't know what I did before GPS. When I need to go somewhere new, I just put the address into my phone's app and off I go. Prior to this wonderful technological tool, I would write down the directions, study a map, wander a bit, or even get lost.

Our spiritual GPS stands for God's Perfect Solution. When we do not see a way through our problem, He creates roads unknown to any humanly created Global Positioning System. He knows just what to do. In the Old Testament, He was able to split the rocks in the wilderness to give His people the water they needed (see Psalm 78:15-16). In the New Testament, Jesus provided living water to the woman at the well (see John 4:13-14).

God doesn't intend for us to wander without direction. Without His love and grace, I would be lost, cut off from His presence. Ephesians 2:4 begins, "Because of His great love for us..." We could fill in the rest with a myriad of things His love has provided for us. I will start with my list.

Because of His great love for me...

- I have been brought to life from the death of my transgressions
- I have perfect peace in Him
- I have a wonderful counselor and guide
- I know where I am going to spend eternity
- It's your turn now! Fill in the blank with how God has provided and shown His love for you.

April 16

"When the day of Pentecost came, they were all together in one place."
Acts 2:1 (NIV)

The people of Israel were waiting for their Messiah. They didn't know He was already with them, teaching radical love and showing them how to live for God with all their heart, soul, and mind. A few days later, the disciples were hiding in a house, waiting for the other shoe to drop. They didn't know God was working and they were about to witness His resurrection power.

A month or so after that, Jesus' followers were waiting in an upper room as they had been instructed. In no way did they anticipate the infilling of the Holy Spirit in their lives and how it would impact their ministries (see Acts 2).

We are awaiting Christ's second coming. We have a very limited understanding of what it will be like. In the meantime, we wait with expectancy.

Sometimes we feel fortunate to just make it through to the next day. We are living in the middle of our stories, and sometimes the answers seem so far away. But God is working on your behalf (Romans 8:28).

Know that God is at work. While we are waiting, we can have confidence He will see us through.

April 17

"Will you not revive us again, that your people may rejoice in you? Show us your unfailing love, O Lord, and grant us your salvation."
Psalm 85:6-7 (NIV)

It was so exciting to follow the break-out of revival at Asbury College in the spring of 2023. The Holy Spirit was alive amongst His people, and the young adults who were able to experience the powerful presence of Holy God will never forget it!

Revival is a funny word. It has so many meanings and connotations. I always think of a tent with nightly services, much like the Billy Graham gatherings in the 60's. By definition, a revival is a renewed attention to or interest in something, a period of renewed religious interest.

God wants to revive us, again and again. He wants us to become more and more aware of His presence. He wants to show us His unfailing love and salvation.

This renewal does not have to happen in a church building, a school, or a tent. It can happen in your living room, in your heart, as you earnestly seek God's will for your life. It starts in you and me! I am praying for your own spiritual awakening and revitalization as we seek the new thing that God wants to do in our personal souls.

April 18

"For I am convinced that neither death nor life, neither angels nor demons, neither the present nor the future, nor any powers, neither height nor depth, nor anything else in all creation, will be able to separate us from the love of God that is in Christ Jesus our Lord."
Romans 8:38-39 (NIV)

Before church one Sunday morning I read Romans 8:38-39. It tells us that NOTHING can separate us from the love of God. I sensed that God wanted me to share that Word with someone at church, so I watched and listened for His prompting. I knew when I saw her, that I was to share what I had heard from the Lord. She had gone through a tough week with her young toddler son ending up in the hospital with a fever and unexplained illness. Through great prayer across the church body, this little one turned a corner and was sent home late in the week.

As I shared this verse with my friend, I quoted some words and paraphrased others. It sounded somewhat like this:

"Sarah, neither death nor life, neither your little one being in the hospital or coming home, neither the present nor the future, whether 50 or 500 attend the upcoming women's retreat (which she was in charge of), nothing in all creation can separate us from the love of God that is in Christ Jesus."

She shared that this very verse was in the front of her mom's Bible which she received after she came back to the Lord from a life of being a prodigal child. We hugged and rejoiced at the confirmation God was giving of His goodness to us throughout different periods of our lives.

Who do you know who might need a Word from the Lord today? You can use this verse or a different one that God lays on your heart. Do not hesitate from being obedient!

April 19

"Dear friends, since God so loved us, we also ought to love one another. No one has ever seen God; but if we love one another, God lives in us and his love is made complete in us"
1 John 4:11-12 (NIV)

What a verse. So many don't believe in God because they can't see Him. Jesus told Thomas those that believed, though they had not seen Him, would be blessed (see John 20:29).

According to the verse in 1 John, however, I believe we see God all the time as His love shines through others. I have watched Pastor Debbie at our church reach out to the homeless and underprivileged in our community. I see God through her.

My husband and I witnessed such an outpouring of love from fellow-believers all over the nation when we went through our sudden loss last fall. We saw God through them.

Our friend, Chris, has taught Sunday school, even throughout his cancer treatments. His love for the kids is so evident. I see God through him.

I'm sure you all have examples of someone through whom you have seen God. Let them know this week. It will bless them and you to share how God's love is evident!

April 20

"Even though I walk through the valley of the shadow of death, I will fear no evil, for you are with me; your rod and your staff,--they comfort me."
Psalm 23:4 (NIV)

I have noticed that I often see familiar passages of scripture in a devotional, a sermon, a Christian novel, or a note someone sends.

At first, I had a tendency to just kind of passing over these verses. I almost had the attitude that I really didn't need to read them carefully since I was already acquainted with them.

Then, it hit me! Reading these verses and digesting them thoroughly was like visiting with an old friend. No, they weren't brand new, but in the current context they provided companionship and comfort. If a long-time friend came by for a visit, I would totally embrace them, invite them in, and spend quality time with them over a cup of coffee.

I now welcome these verses as a reminder of God's love and grace. I spend quality time with them over a cup of coffee and embrace them fully. It has enriched my life.

I'm just going to use Psalm 23 as an example. What a comfort this Psalm has been to me, in an entirely different way this year than ever. We walked through the "valley of the shadow of death." Our Good Shepherd was right there comforting us with his presence.

I hope you can see the Scriptures as a "friend" you can love to wrap your mind, soul, and heart around. Let it speak to you in fresh and new ways.

April 21

"He [Jacob] had a dream in which he saw a stairway resting on the earth, with its top reaching to heaven, and the angels of God were ascending and descending on it." Genesis 28:12 (NIV)

When we go to Hawaii or Newport Beach or Tahoe, or any scenic place, we always request the highest possible room with the best possible view. We love to step out on our balcony and see the vast ocean or the majestic mountains. Taking the steps (or elevator) up is all worth it when we can look out the windows.

Charles Spurgeon said, "Faith goes up the stairs that love has built and looks out the window hope has opened."

In Jacob's dream, The Lord was at the top of the stairway. He spoke to Jacob, confirming His covenant blessing with His people through Jacob. He promised to be with Him wherever he went.

It was God who built the stairs of access to His throne through the love of Jesus. Jesus himself is the bridge between heaven and earth, the only mediator between God and heaven. When we access the stairway, we gain relationship with God, by faith, and our view is always hope.

Do you need a new view today? Start up the loving ascent of faith. God will love you every step of the way and will offer you hope for whatever you are facing in life.

April 22

> "For he chose us in him before the creation of the world to be holy and blameless in his sight. In love he predestined us to be adopted as his sons through Jesus Christ, in accordance with his pleasure and will—"
> Ephesisans 1:4-5 (NIV)

I was thinking about the phrase from Ephesians 1:4 this week that says, "He chose us in him before the creation of the world." Before God even created the world for me to live in, He was thinking of me. He knew I would exist, and He had a plan for my life.

It's really quite mind-boggling. If you ever played with your dolls or stuffed toys as a young child, you probably imagined what it would be like some day to have a family of your own and be the mom or dad. You practiced your love for these objects in ways that had been modeled for you. If you are a parent or plan to be, you have probably prayed over your children, even before they were born.

That's only a small picture of the love God had for us. He planned for us to be a part of His family before time came into being.

Live loved today! I hope you realize how much God treasures you.

April 23

"For I am the Lord, your God, who takes hold of your right hand and says to you, 'Do not fear; I will help you.'" Isaiah 41:13 (NIV)

When we are with our grandkids, we always grab their hand, especially when we are walking through a parking lot or across a street. Sometimes they try to squirm away from our grip because they want their independence, but we know better than to let go. We know what keeps them safe and headed in the right direction.

God is like that with us. He takes our hand to guide and help us. We often try to squirm out of His reach because we want to be independent and in control. We have no idea what dangers may be heading our way.

We are secured, not because we hold tightly to Jesus, but because He holds tightly to us. My independence and stubborn will sometimes want to let go, but Jesus knows what keeps me safe and heading in the right direction. His loving grasp is accompanied by the assurance that I am not alone and that He will help me.

I pray this is a comforting thought to you. God is not trying to make your life miserable. He is trying to keep you safe!

April 24

"Whoever believes in me, as the Scripture has said, streams of living water will flow from within him." John 7:38 (NIV)

God's love is multi-faceted. At any given time, we may need to draw on one of these aspects of love.

God's fountain of love—The headwaters of the Sacramento River are found In Mt. Shasta City Park. It is a site worth visiting. Crystal clear water that flows through the park begins its journey high on the snow-covered peaks of Mt. Shasta, makes its way through underground lava tubes, and finally gushes forth into the City Park's headwaters area. We can't see where God's love originates, or comes from, but we know there is a constant fountain of it flowing over and through us (John 7:38).

God's motivation—God loved me, while I was still a sinner (Romans 5:8)! If He loves me just as I am, before I'm fixed and cleaned up, it should motivate me to love others in the same way—to treat them as my neighbor and forgive them as I was forgiven. I have a friend who recently picked up her brother who had been living on the streets. When he got in the car, they had to roll down the windows because of his stench. He hadn't showered in weeks. She chose to love him and take him to a place where he could get help. She continues to pick him up for appointments and help him get on his feet. She is motivated by God's love. This isn't the first time she has had to lift him out of a bad situation. God never gives up on us. What a motivation for us!

God's pinnacle of love—No mountain is high enough to surmount God's love. He reaches to the highest height and bends to the lowest depth to find us and wrap us in His arms (Psalm 103:11).

These are just a few ways God shows us His love. Which dimension of love do you need to draw from today?

April 25

"'Everything is possible for him who believes.'" Mark 9:23b (NIV)

God is the God of the possible! There are a lot of things in my life that seem impossible. When I start to list them, I can easily become discouraged.

I have people in my life that have wandered from God or have never invited Him into their hearts. It feels like their change will never happen.

Our world is a mess. Inflation, politics, world tragedies and wars. Peace seems impossible.

My goals and dreams even sometimes feel unreachable. Things aren't happening fast enough or in the way I want them to go.

Then, I read of Abraham and Sarah giving birth to a son in their old age. I revisit the children of Israel and Moses parting the Red Sea. I consider what the disciples must have felt when Jesus was crucified and their world had fallen apart, but He rose from the grave! I think of the highly unlikely prospect of Saul of Tarsus becoming a missionary for Jesus when he was persecuting the Christians. But it happened!

You see, "God extends His hope to us. He promises abundant life, and then, when the world is ready to give up and throw in the towel, He comes through." (Higher Ground, p. 15)

Let God be the God of your impossibilities today!

April 26

"He who covers over an offense promotes love, but whoever repeats the matter separates friends." Proverbs 17:9 (NIV)

Here's a fun topic—GOSSIP!

If I asked any of you what you thought about gossip, you would probably all say it is a bad thing. We can agree about that in theory, but it isn't as easy to keep juicy tidbits of information to ourselves as it may seem.

When we hear something a little nefarious about someone, maybe it gives us a momentary pleasure to know we aren't as bad as them. Maybe we even present gossip off-handedly as a prayer request.

It's okay to pray for others, but we need to be careful because the thing about gossip is that is never little or harmless. It destroys relationships and separates friends.

The opposite is also true. When we turn gossip around and build someone up it promotes love.

Our key verse reminds us of how we need to live wisely and lovingly when it comes to retelling the chin-wagging or finger-pointing.

Are you a repeat offender? Or are you a peacemaker? I was thinking about mending fences and building bridges when I read this verse. Maybe we can be an "of—fence" mender. Let's do what it takes to love by only speaking in an uplifting way about others.

April 27

"We demolish arguments and every pretension that sets itself up against the knowledge of God, and we take captive every thought to make it obedient to Christ." 2 Corinthians 10:5 (NIV)

On the first day of Lent, a Christian radio host threw out a challenge. He spurred the listeners to think about giving up not just things like coffee or chocolate, but to give up a negative attitude of the heart.

I immediately thought about my reaction to a friend the night before. I didn't say anything, and hopefully I kept my body language under control, but I had some really negative thoughts. It dawned on me that "gossip" doesn't have to be verbalized to be harmful. Even if the other person never gets wind of your thoughts and you don't share them with anyone else, it is still breaking down the relationship.

I actually did share a few things with my husband. In his godly wisdom, he chided me for my harsh words toward her. I realized that even in my thought life, I need to bring those negative biting words into submission before Christ. I do love that friend, and I would never want anything to come between us. I began to pray for her and her circumstances, and God changed my heart.

Yesterday we looked at being peace makers and fence menders (Proverbs 17:9). My new exhortation for today is that we cover that offense even before it takes root in our thought life. We need to bring every thought captive to Jesus, asking Him to help us not harbor evil in our heart (2 Corinthians 10:5; Matthew 15:19).

April 28

"And Mary said, 'My soul doth magnify the Lord, And my spirit hath rejoiced in God my Saviour.'" Luke 1:46-47 (KJV)

One of the best activities for a curious child is to give them a magnifying glass and let them discover the world from a different lens. The little creepy-crawlies suddenly become a science investigation. The blades of grass and samples of soil are seen in a whole new light!

What we magnify is what gets our attention. In our lives, our magnifying glass is often pointed towards our problems. Everything seems to revolve around the minutia of the issues we are facing, and we get bogged down and overwhelmed.

If we point our spiritual magnifying glass to who God is and what He promises us, our problems become smaller and less significant. We honor the One who is worthy, rather than worshiping the thing that brings worry.

If you need a shift in your focus today, join me in magnifying the Lord. List some of His names or qualities in your journal or in your prayer time that help you take your mind off your problems and onto Him. I'll start:

1) He is Creator, therefore He can make a miracle of my mess
2) He is Love, therefore He knows what is best for me and it is always good
3) His presence never fails, therefore I know I will not be alone in what I face
4) Your Turn! Go!

April 29

"'Here I am! I stand at the door and knock. If anyone hears my voice and opens the door, I will come in and eat with him, and he with me.'"
Revelation 3:20 (NIV)

I sat across the lunch table from my friend. She was so close to giving her heart to the Lord. He was knocking. I know she heard it! I even asked her what was holding her back from opening the door. Her response was that she knew what she would have to give up.

Funny she would say that since our lunch date was motivated by her wanting to share with me about a horrendous set of events in her life. These issues had dominoed from some of her poor decisions regarding things she didn't want to give up. Her indiscretion and lack of self-control at a bar had landed her in jail overnight. The jail time created issues at work and in her home.

I wanted to say, "Really, you don't want to give that up?" Instead, my reply was, "But how much more you will gain!" My life experience with Christ has been so rich and full of hope and peace. I shared with her how God had enriched my life in so many ways. I don't miss the things of this world, and I knew she wouldn't either.

She didn't make the decision to accept Jesus that day, but I'm still praying for that day to come. He is waiting to sit down and eat with you and share His wonderful table of blessing. I hope you have a relationship with Jesus. If you don't, all I can say is, "What are you waiting for? Open the door!"

April 30

"Enoch walked with God; then he was no more because God took him away." Genesis 5:24 (NIV)

The story of Enoch in the Bible is intriguing. He was walking with God, and then was gone from the face of the earth.

I wonder what that looked like. Was anyone else around to see him just vaporize or swoosh up into the sky? I imagine it being a little like the Star Trek series where they would step into a capsule and be "beamed up" to another location.

I would love to go to heaven like that, but more than how I go is how I travel before that time comes. I want my legacy to be as simple yet profound as Enoch's: "She walked faithfully with God."

This is more than just a "holy duty." It is a friendship cultivated by:

- Walking and talking
- Sashaying and praying
- An attitude of gratitude
- Sharing life, love, and laughter
- Basking in His creation

I pray that our friendship with God is so intimate that others will take note when we are not around.

May 1

"May God himself, the God of peace, sanctify you through and through. May your whole spirit, soul and body be kept blameless at the coming of our Lord Jesus Christ. The one who calls you is faithful and he will do it."
1 Thessalonians 5:23-24 (NIV)

I love a good track meet. The start of the races is so exciting as the runners get on their marks, get set, and then take off as the starting gun goes off and the crowd begins to cheer.

In life, we tend to take off each day like that. But I like to do it a little differently. My method is: "Ready, Set, Wait!" I get up, set up my coffee, and then wait on the Lord as I comb through verses and listen for His direction. I wait for the peace that only He can bring to my whole spirit, soul and body, no matter what else may be going on around me.

Try to build some wait time into your daily routine—quietness before your Maker (and your coffee maker). You will be amazed at how those moments with the Lord in prayer and in His Word will give you perspective for your time, your problems, and your relationships that will help you navigate the curves and straight-aways of the track.

Wait—for hope to appear, for peace to manifest itself, for love to motivate your actions. He is faithful and will do it!

May 2

> "The Lord would speak to Moses face to face, as a man speaks with his friend. Then Moses would return to the camp, but his young aide Joshua son of Nun did not leave the tent." Exodus 33:11 (NIV)

Moses spent time with God daily. He made the trek each day to the tent of meeting outside the camp. The Lord would actually speak to him face to face, as a friend. It must have been amazing!

What if Moses had decided throughout his week that he just didn't have time on certain days to go to the temple and have his communion with the Heavenly Father. I'm sure he felt like the children of Israel were demanding more time from him than he had to give, so giving up time in the temple would have made sense (in an earthly realm). The Hebrew word for friend in Exodus 33:11 (rea) indicates intimacy, companionship, a reciprocal relationship. Moses had to reciprocate, do his part in the friendship.

We must do our part as well. God desires time with us each day. We must actively participate with Him. It's a reciprocal relationship of intimacy and companionship.

It would be easy to let other things get in the way. Work is looming. Our to-do list is non-ending. On a temporal level, it may not seem to make sense to take time out of our schedule for God. However, when we make time with God a priority in our life, we will come away changed and renewed each time. Maybe, like Joshua, we will want to linger just a little longer.

Let's not neglect our quiet time with the Lord each day.

May 3

"Peace I leave with you; my peace I give you. I do not give to you as the world gives. Do not let your hearts be troubled and do not be afraid."
John 14:27 (NIV)

This has always been one of my favorite verses. Probably because it carried me through some of the noisy, crazy times when my kids were young. They would get in the car and start arguing before we even backed out of the driveway. I began to quote John 14:27 to myself on the way to work.

The peace Jesus is talking about here isn't the absence of troubles. It's a tranquil state of the soul, independent of external circumstances. Peace isn't a process, it's a Person.

My days and car rides began to be better and more peaceful. The noise level wasn't what changed, but the state of my heart felt God's presence.

Many of you would say that loud children are the least of your worries. The chaos in your world revolves around tough, adult-led problems. You are facing divorce, abuse, financial woes, loss, and/or any other plethora of problems.

That same peace is available no matter what you are going through. Jesus isn't promising to make things go away instantly. But He is promising to be with you. He is the Peace! Cling to Him!

May 4

"Your statutes are my delight; they are my counselors."
Psalm 119:24 (NIV)

Duty vs. Desire: Sometimes we do something because it is our duty, not because we want to do it: Cleaning the bathroom; reporting to work (some days); returning the grocery cart to its proper place (OK that's a personal one that I feel strongly about).

When I received a jury summons a few months ago, I knew I would dutifully call in and show up when beckoned. I made it through Wednesday before I had to report to the jury services building. By three o'clock, I thought we would probably be done for the day. Lo and behold, in walked a bailiff, ready to muster the next group.

As the names were called, I waited while they went through the names alphabetically. When the T's were done, I fully expected to hear "Janice Unfried" next. To my delight, they were already onto the V's! It was a pleasant surprise! A few minutes after this group left the building, the rest of us were dismissed. They let us know that our duty had been served for the next twelve months. Phew!

I may not WANT to report for jury duty, but I see it as an important part of citizenship, a duty. Similarly, for years I woke up early to read God's Word because I knew I needed it, not necessarily because I enjoyed the pre-dawn hours and loss of a few extra moments of sleep. Over time, it has become less of a "duty" and more of a "desire." I cannot wait, most mornings, to see what God has to teach me.

As we stay grounded and keep connected, it's important to know that sometimes the duty has to precede the desire. It will be worth it in the long run. His words will become our delight.

May 5

"Taste and see that the Lord is good; blessed is the man who takes refuge in him." Psalm 34:8 (NIV)

Awhile back, I had the privilege of sharing treats with a couple of seniors. Our life group took pie and ice cream to a gentleman who recently moved to an assisted living facility. We were the ones delighted, as he regaled us with stories from his past. The wisdom from his life and experiences was soothing and challenging at the same time. His spiritual insights, as he awaits seeing Jesus face-to-face and joining those who have gone before him, were inspiring.

Later in the same week I took chocolate chip cookies to my mother-in-law. She was residing at a skilled care facility. Though her mind was very confused at this stage of her life, her tastebuds still enjoyed a sweet morsel, and her heart had not forgotten her Savior.

Both of these saints lived long lives and remained faithful to God. They loved the Lord and had been blessed by Him. They not only tasted the sweets we brought them, but they reminded us of the sweetness of walking with the Lord.

I don't know about you, but I want to live like that. I want to continue serving my Savior and tasting His goodness. I'll keep taking treats to others, and maybe someone will treat me some day. I hope I will bring honor and glory to His name!

May 6

"For it is God who works in you to will and to act according to his good purpose." Philippians 2:13 (NIV)

At first, I didn't put two and two together. In talking to my husband and later to one of my sons, I was excited to hear that one of my boys was making some healthy eating choices. The other son was sharing some future work-related goals that he was considering. I later realized that these were two specific things I had been praying about.

My ladies' Bible study was going through Stormie Omartian's *The Power of Praying for Your Adult Children*. We had been focusing our prayer on helping them understand God's purpose for their lives and experiencing good health. Here were two specific answers to my prayers!

There is nothing more powerfully motivating than answered prayer, but we have to recognize that God is the One working His mighty hand through our humble efforts of prayer. When we pray, we should be watching and waiting for the answers.

Are you praying about something specific? It may be that God has already begun to answer. He is working and acting according to His good purpose. Look for the signs, little and big, that show He is at work!

May 7

"He got up, rebuked the wind and said to the waves, 'Quiet! Be still!' Then the wind died down and it was completely calm."
Mark 4:39 (NIV)

As I sit here typing this, in the shelter of our RV, the wind is whipping around us in huge gusts. We have had perfectly gorgeous sunny days for the last couple of mornings, but around noon the wind has raged until about 6:00 PM. It stops just as suddenly as it starts, and all is peaceful once again.

I imagine it was a little like that on the Sea of Galilee when the disciples followed Jesus' directions to go to the other side (see Mark 4:35-41). The seas were calm and everything was going along fine until the evening breezes turned into dangerous gusts. The disciples were beside themselves with fear. They woke Jesus up and expressed their despair, "Teacher, don't you care if we drown?"

Jesus got up and rebuked the winds. Just like that, with His words, "Quiet! Be still!" the wind stopped and it was completely calm.

Life can be like that. One minute everything seems to be going along just fine. The next minute we find ourselves in gale-force conditions:

- Covid-19
- A car accident
- Financial disaster
- Report of a dreaded physical condition

We must remember that Jesus is the calm in our storm. He can speak peace to the circumstances, but even more importantly, He can speak peace and comfort to our very souls. Just like we were in the safety of our 5th wheel while the winds were howling, we can rest in the shelter of our Savior, even when the storms of life surround us. Jesus loves you and He ultimately controls the winds and waves.

May 8

> "Say to those with fearful hearts, 'Be strong, do not fear; your God will come...to save you.'" Isaiah 35:4 (NIV)

I don't get why people are so obsessed with horror movies. Maybe you are one who likes to be scared out of your mind, but it's not for me.

I feel like there are three types of horror films:

1) Those that are so ridiculous that they are more laughable than scary.
2) Those that try to be scary through being gory and gross.
3) Those that build suspense and really have you on the edge of your seat, biting your nails, and having nightmares for days.

In my mind, there is enough fear in this world without having to conjure up extra. God gives us multiple reminders (actually commands) to fear not.

I read the other day that the reason we fear is because we focus on the problem and forget who God is. The antidote is to "remember." Remember who God is. Remember how He has come through for you in the past. Remember His promises.

Whether you enjoy horror movies or not, let's face our real-life fears by focusing on remembering who God is and that He comes to save us.

May 9

"Yet the Lord longs to be gracious to you; he rises to show you compassion. For the Lord is a God of justice. Blessed are all who wait for him!" Isaiah 30:18 (NIV)

For her eighth birthday, my granddaughter wanted a spy kit, complete with night-vision goggles, an invisible ink pen, motion alarm, and a voice disguiser. It was interesting to see what type of espionage she used to make sure her younger sibling didn't bother her "treasures."

I suppose it is natural for her, as the oldest child in her family, to want to be able to "protect" her stuff or to maintain her privacy, making sure younger brother doesn't mess with it. It gives her a sense of power and fortification to play "spy."

Some people have a misconception that God is a Spy in the Sky, watching our every move, waiting for us to trip us so He can strike us with lightening. Nothing is further from the truth. He never leaves us nor forsakes us, but it isn't so He can sneak up behind us and catch us "in the act of sin." He already knows all our thoughts and motives. He sees all our deeds, good and bad (Psalm 139:4, 8).

God stays near to us, so that when we do repent and turn back to Him, we can see that He was always close at hand. He is waiting for us to surrender to Him so that we can have the benefit of all His promises. He wants the best for us!

Lean into God today. Know that He loves you enough to give you freedom of choice, even when it means hurting Him. He is always there, ready to forgive and start anew!

May 10

> "But I tell you the truth: it is for your good that I am going away. Unless I go away, the Counselor will not come to you; but if I go, I will send him to you." John 16:7 (NIV)

A friend moves away.

Your principal changes you to a new grade-level.

Your church gets a new pastor.

Your travel plans get delayed or rerouted.

CHANGE! We don't like it. We want things to stay the same—familiar and comfortable. I'm sure that is what the disciples were thinking in John 16. They were full of grief and angst at Jesus' words. He was talking about going away. Then Jesus said these words: "... it is for your good that I am going away."

Can change really be for our good?

Though we may initially be lonely for our friend, it can open our hearts up to new friends.

Changing grade-levels can help you grow you as a teacher and give insight into the scope and sequence of student learning.

A new pastor brings opportunities for the congregation to grow in new and unique ways.

Thwarted travel plans might save you from an unforeseen accident or teach you patience and grace.

Without Jesus going away, the disciples wouldn't have received the Holy Spirit. The Spirit was about to breathe new life into them and give them access to God in exciting, life-altering ways.

Are you resisting or dreading change? Take a moment to thank God for what He is going to do for you and in you as you adapt to this new thing. Frustration can turn to fresh renewal; worry to a wealth of life-experience; loneliness to leaning; change into challenge.

May 11

"...I have loved you with an everlasting love; I have drawn you with loving-kindness." Jeremiah 31:3b (NIV)

Do you feel like giving up sometimes? Here is what my self-talk sounds like:

"My house needs to be cleaned. I have a hundred things on my to-do list. Dinner, at best, will just have to be Taco Bell tonight. My faith is floundering. I'm a mess!"

Here is what God-talk says back to me:

"I have loved you with an everlasting love; I have drawn you with unfailing kindness." Jeremiah 31:3 (ESV)

You see, friends, God is part of our "messy" as much as our polished moments. He understands our pain and treats us with kindness and grace. As the words to the song *My Story Your Glory* say, He wants to turn our mess into His message. He is able.

Will you just rest in that today? The house will eventually get cleaned. The to-do list will someday get checked off (or you may realize the to-dos weren't a reason for a crisis moment). Be assured that there are few wives and moms who place gourmet meals in front of their families every night. Take just five minutes to refresh your mind with Scripture, worship music, or breathing out the day's busyness while breathing in the Everlasting Love of God (also known as prayer).

Let Him draw you to Himself today.

May 12

"He cuts off every branch in me that bears no fruit, while every branch that does bear fruit he prunes so that it will be even more fruitful."
John 15:2 (NIV)

Some of the best advice I have ever heard was in regards to pruning. It wasn't about pruning my plants (although I need to learn how to do that better). It was about pruning my activity branches.

You see, I have a little---no a lot---of trouble saying "no." I want to do it all, be it all, and experience it all. Here's the wisdom that was given:

When you sprout new activity branches, you must also cut things out. Some of those cut-out activities may be good, but to remain healthy, effective, and fruitful in the Kingdom, you must allow some pruning to be done. You'll actually accomplish more in life by doing less.

It is rather freeing to realize that it's okay to cut some things out of your life in order to be more productive in others. News alert: We can't do it all! We were not made to do it all. That's why there is a body of believers with different strengths and abilities.

Take stock. Is there something you need to cut out of your activity tree this month?

May 13

"He has showed you, O man, what is good. And what does the Lord require of you? To act justly and to love mercy and to walk humbly with your God." Micah 6:8 (NIV)

As I was reflecting on my journal, I realized that I was receiving a similar message through a variety of sources. One of my devotionals focused for several weeks on setting healthy margins. A sermon was preached entitled "From Burnout to Balance." Yesterday's devotion was about learning to prune our activities (especially as we add more things to our plate). Today's message is similar. Simplify your life!

We tend to make life so complicated, thinking we need to solve all the world's problems, much less our own. Instead, we need to disentangle, clarify, streamline, reduce (as in simplifying a fraction). How do we do that? I'm glad you asked.

- In your speech, be honest, and open with people and with God.
- In the way you act, there are only a couple of things you need to remember—love the Lord and love your neighbor.
- In the way you live, make alone time to be with Jesus and to rest amidst your busy schedule.
- In the way you believe, develop a child-like faith and trust.
- Act justly, love mercy, walk humbly with God.

I know, easier said than done, but we all must start somewhere. What part of simplifying do you need to concentrate on today?

May 14

"Take my yoke upon you and learn from me, for I am gentle and humble in heart, and you will find rest for your souls. For my yoke is easy and my burden is light." Matthew 11:29-30 (NIV)

When Jesus said these words, He was painting a word picture of two or more oxen sharing the load by being yoked together, thus lightening the load. He was driving home the point that He wants to help us carry our burden!

Why do we try to bear our burdens alone? I suppose we want to appear self-sufficient, but it really is border-line pride. One author gave this frank reminder. "We are not general managers of the universe!"

That quote made me smile. Now, I need to start listening to that message!

Thank you, Jesus, for helping me carry my load. You've got the whole world in Your hands! What makes me think I can "help" You hold it together? Thank You for your wonderful promise! Amen.

May 15

"Jesus answered, 'I am the way and the truth and the life. No one comes to the Father except through me.'" John 14:6 (NIV)

I remember when one of my sons shared with us the discovery he had made through this verse. He was in his second month of a drug rehab program. In one of our rare calls, he recognized the fact that Jesus didn't say, "I am **A** way, truth, and life." He said, "I am **THE** way, truth, and life."

The world wants us to believe that there are many paths to happiness and well-being. We can create truth if it is true to us. Everything is relative to the individual.

Jesus came to show us the only way to the Father. He wasn't being exclusive to anyone. He was including ALL who believed in Him to share in the joy of salvation. He paid a tremendous price, His very life, to ensure that it was available to the world.

Do we really believe Jesus is **THE** only way? Do we really believe His truth is **THE** truth? Do we live like He has given us **THE** life that all mankind longs for?

What we believe about Jesus is really a decision about everything else. I pray that our lives as believers in Jesus Christ would be so attractive to those around us that they would desire to know not just our way, but THE way, truth and life.

May 16

"Father, if you are willing, take this cup from me; yet not my will, but yours be done." Luke 22:42 (NIV)

We were talking about answers to prayer in Bible study the other day. Sometimes we don't believe God answers our prayers because we don't get what we asked for. Our discussion went deep into those places of unrealized expectations.

One of our young moms had lost two of her young-adult brothers. Another had lost her teen-aged brother. We had just lost our 40-year-old son. Another had a dad who had struggled with alcoholism as long as she could remember. Yet another was praying for both her parents who were fighting two different types of cancer.

Sometimes it seems like it is futile to pray when God is just going to answer how He deems best anyway. But then we talked about Jesus' example of submitting His will to the Father's will. He didn't want to go to the cross. He knew it was His path, but He still asked the Father to take the cup from Him.

God is interested in our needs and desires. He wants us to ask and trust Him. God always answers. Sometimes it's yes. Sometimes it's no. And sometimes it's wait. Oh, how we get impatient in the waiting (or is it just me?).

I saw this quote the other day. "God's 'no' is not a rejection. It's a redirection." Sometimes He has to close a door so that we'll go through a different one.

Bring your requests to God. Leave them at His feet. Know that He hears you and will answer in the way that will bring glory to His name.

May 17

"—just as the Son of Man did not come to be served, but to serve, and to give his life as a ransom for many." Matthew 20:28 (NIV)

I long to bring glory to God. I think in my mind this means it has to be through some major feat. Do a big job for Jesus and He'll be glorified.

Then I read this: "Jesus is glorified when a need and my servant-heart intersect."

WOW! The lights don't need to flash. The fanfare can keep still. We just need to look for those who have a need and then let our hearts for Jesus take over, intervene, assist, or come along side that one who needs a special touch. That sounds like an everyday thing, not an isolated accomplishment.

Who needs your servant-heart today?

- Your neighbor?
- Your co-worker?
- The homeless person by the roadside?
- A weary mom or dad?
- An elderly shut-in?

The list is endless. Open your heart to Jesus. He was our perfect example of servanthood. Obey His nudging to be His hands and feet to someone around you. God WILL be glorified.

May 18

> "Come, let us bow down in worship, let us kneel before the Lord our Make; for he is our God and we are the people of his pasture, the flock under his care." Psalm 95:6 (NIV)

Our problems can feel overwhelming at times. The solutions seem far away, and the time we are awaiting an answer can feel like eternity. But here's the deal with our problems. We are supposed to give them to God. How do we do that? Through prayer and supplication, with thanksgiving (see Philippians 4:6).

Charles Stanley said, "We must remember that the shortest distance between our problems and their solutions is the distance between our knees and the floor."

Even if your knees are creaky and you can't get in a kneeling position, we can position our hearts to bow before God. Either way, He is just waiting for us to ask!

He doesn't promise to take away the problem instantaneously. He does promise to give us peace beyond understanding (Philippians 4:7). He does take care of us, His flock.

Do you have a need? Give it to Jesus today?

May 19

"In the beginning God created the heavens and the earth."
Genesis 1:1 (NIV)

In April, 2024, the world was watching the sky for a remarkable, once-in-a-lifetime event. A full solar eclipse was to arc its way through North America. I wasn't able to be physically present in one of the locations, but I did watch the crowds on television as the moon shadowed the sun in several locations over the course of time.

Whether the person was the reporter or a spectator, most were brought close to tears as they watched this amazing phenomenon. Several spoke of how it puts our significance in lieu of the vastness of the universe into perspective. It was definitely an emotional experience, but I kept wondering how anyone could view such a sight and still not believe in the God who created it all.

The same God that put the sun and moon and all the stars into space cares personally and supremely about each of us. His power is greater than our seemingly insurmountable problems. Our desperate dependence needs to be in the One who tells the planets to keep spinning and orbiting AND who knows the direction we need to go.

Our help comes from the Creator, not the creation. We can be in awe of what He has made, but we need to remember where our help comes from, the Creator of Heaven and Earth (Psalm 121:1-2).

May 20

"Put on the full armor of God so that you can take your stand against the devil's schemes." Ephesians 6:11 (NIV)

This may come as a surprise to you, but our enemy is NOT our unreasonable boss, our unfaithful spouse, our malicious friend, or even our snarky teenager. Our enemy is Satan.

With that being said, we need to remember who should be feeling the brunt of our attacks. In Jesus' name Satan must flee. We are no match for Satan in and of ourselves, and he certainly doesn't play fair. Therefore, we must call upon God and His heavenly army to fight the battles that rage all around us.

With the armor of God, which includes the sword of the Spirit, the Word of God, we can lance Satan to the core by claiming God's promises. Our helmet of salvation, breastplate of righteousness, and belt of truth keep our enemy from getting into our heads or hearts. Our faith shield and our shoes of readiness that come from the gospel of peace help us to stay strong and persevere whatever fiery trials are coming at us (see Ephesians 6:10-18).

The next time you want to lash out at your boss or your spouse, your friend or your child, remember who your real enemy is. Make yourself ready to face him. He doesn't have a chance against God's power in your life!

May 21

> "Stand firm then, with the belt of truth buckled around your waist, with the breastplate of righteousness in place..."
> Ephesians 6:14 (NIV)

For most of the world, Monday means it is time to wear our work hats and accomplish much.

Here's my question for you whether you are starting your week or finishing it: Do you live throughout the week with integrity? Or do you say one thing and act one way on Sunday, but do the opposite throughout the rest of the week?

It's a simple question, but it takes some introspection and letting God uncover our motives and actions. The belt of truth (Ephesians 6:14) holds our pants on. Without it, they will fall down to our ankles as we embarrassingly try to hold things together. Let's strive to live as God would have us live throughout the week, not just when it's convenient. Let's allow God to search our hearts so that we can avoid those moments of being exposed before others.

Buckle up, my friend!

May 22

"Now you are the body of Christ, and each one of you is a part of it."
1 Corinthians 12:27 (NIV)

It would be pretty horrible to live in a world of cookie-cutter people and personalities. Most of the time, I'm okay with myself, but I wouldn't want everyone to be like me. God knew what He was doing when He made us unique and gave each of us special abilities. We were designed to help each other, to use our talents for something greater than ourselves.

Though I wear several hats, part of my God-given work right now is to encourage you each day. I hope it is helpful to you, but I know God has the right person reading these devotionals each morning or evening.

I am so grateful that you are doing what God has tasked for you today. We need nurses, teachers, artists, musicians, engineers, trash collectors, and grocery store managers and clerks. My life is so enriched by whatever it is that you are doing.

If we are going to be the "same" in any way, it is to be unified in sharing the gospel of Christ. You have a unique set of people you are surrounded by each day. You are the one to reach them with the love of Jesus. Your pastor or Bible study leader can't be where you are each and every moment.

Thank the Lord for your special talents and abilities and for the opportunities to share Him with others today.

May 23

> "But be sure to fear the Lord and serve him faithfully with all your heart; consider what great things he has done for you."
> 1 Samuel 12:24 (NIV)

I was working on my notes for an upcoming retreat. I had worked really hard at developing their theme, seeking God's direction, and preparing my words and my heart. At some point it dawned on me that there would be less than thirty women there, but I was putting in the same amount of work and hours for thirty as I would for three hundred.

This thought did not discourage me. I wanted to be faithful and trustworthy with whatever was put before me. As I pondered these things, I ran across a devotional that spoke to my heart. It talked about how Joseph was faithful for forty years as a slave and a prisoner before he rose to prominence. God developed Joseph's character during those mundane years of service.

In the same way, God uses us where we are at to sow patience and plant seeds of joy, love, and peace in our heart. He uses our tears and faith to fertilize the seeds so we can grow into the person He has planned for us to be all along.

I love speaking to women's groups and sharing the things God is teaching me, and I will keep doing it as long as God provides opportunities. My expectations are not that I would reach a place of prominence, but that God can continue to use me, however He sees fit.

As you strive to remain faithful in your day-to-day job(s), even when you don't feel like it, remember that God is more interested in your character than in your career. Work for the Lord with all your heart!

May 24

"So then, be careful how you walk, not as unwise people but as wise, making the most of your time, because the days are evil.
Ephesians 5:15-16 (NASB)

It feels like we never have enough time to accomplish all that we need to get done. Giving our time to God somehow expands our time. Our college chaplain, Reuben Welch, used to say we need to use our "five minuteses." In other words, We have lots of wasted time in the day, moments that we should use wisely, asking God to help and guide us.

This isn't to say you shouldn't take a break now and then. That's important too! Maybe that is how you need to use your five minutes right now. I'm working on my 25-5 plan today. I type for 25 minutes, then get up and walk or do something for 5 minutes. After 4 cycles of that, I take a 30-minute break, then come back and repeat four more cycles. I end up being so much more productive, and it doesn't feel like I've written for 4 hours.

Author Ginny Ytrupp says it this way, "When we entrust our moments to the Creator, he provides all we need to accomplish his will."

Do you have a never-ending list to get through today? Use the time God created for you today!

May 25

"In addition to all this, take up the shield of faith, with which you can extinguish all the flaming arrows of the evil one."
Ephesians 6:16 (NIV)

Doubts are thrown at us by Satan—part of his fiery darts. We are to protect ourselves with the shield of faith. I was talking to a friend the other day, and she told me that she often advises Christians struggling with their mustard seed faith to doubt their doubts.

Attacking our doubts by realizing there is no substance to them is a good way to face them. Satan wants us to doubt Jesus, but who we really need to doubt is the doubt thrower.

As I was reflecting on that, I thought of another way I throw off those flaming arrows. I claim Scripture, reminding myself of what I know is true. My friend and I added to this wisdom that you should also believe your beliefs.

When we focus on who God is and what He has done, when we revisit Scriptures that focus on God's character and goodness, those fiery darts are deflected.

So here it is, my friends: "Doubt your doubts. Believe your beliefs."

May 26

"A cheerful heart is good medicine, but a crushed spirit dries up the bones." Proverbs 17:22 (NIV)

"Good humor and laughter are far too wonderful not to come straight from the heart of God." (anonymous) I wish I knew who said this. I bet they are a lot of fun!

I love to laugh. It is good for the soul and is proven to be good for our health. I believe that God has a sense of humor. We are created in his image, so I'm sure He has had some real hearty laughs. Maybe he cracked Himself up when He created the aardvark or the giraffe. Maybe He chuckles tenderly each time a new baby is born. Perhaps He gets tickled when humans finally discover some of His scientific properties like gravity, the shape of the earth, or how to land on the moon.

Take some time to laugh today. Read a funny joke. Have a tickle session with your kids or grandkids. Celebrate each other's accomplishments with joy and laughter. It is better than medicine!

May 27

"I delight in your decrees; I will not neglect your word."
Psalm 119:16 (NIV)

"If you see a Bible that is falling apart, it probably belongs to someone who isn't!" This quote was written in the front of the Bible of one of my dear friends, written by her father when he gave it to her as a gift. What a true statement.

As my husband's siblings were going through their deceased parents' possessions, they decided that they would take turns keeping their mom and dad's Bibles for a year before passing them to the next brother or sister. We had the privilege of having them the first year after their mom passed away. Both Bibles are worn at the edges, practically falling apart, with highlighted passages and notes written all throughout in the margins. When reading a passage, often we will find our names or the names of our kids as we were brought to the Lord in prayer over a specific promise or truth. What a blessing!

Their lives were so full and rich in the Lord. It is not surprising that their Bibles are falling apart. I have started using my Bible app on my phone for convenience, but there is nothing like getting my physical Bible out and leafing through the pages. Our pastor recently did a sermon series on the Bible—the Best-Selling Book of all Times. He encouraged us to bring our physical Bibles to church. I love seeing the things I have underlined and highlighted. I have found promises I have claimed for myself or for others.

What does your Bible look like? I hope it is not sitting on a shelf somewhere collecting dust!

May 28

"So do not fear, for I am with you; do not be dismayed, for I am your God. I will strengthen you and help you; I will uphold you with my righteous right hand." Isaiah 41:10 (NIV)

My husband is an amazing example of living out his faith. The other day he lost his keys...In The OCEAN! I was dismayed. How could that have happened? We had a spare key to get into our trailer (we were camping), but the truck keys were gone. As I fumed a bit, he prayed. He knew God would lead him to the right locksmith. After several calls, we got a decent price for having the keys to the truck made. His brother was able to drive him into town to pick them up which saved another big chunk of money. Oh, that I would learn to react better to apparent disaster.

God's promises are sure. They steady us when our world is turning upside down. We can wait with hopeful expectation for His help.

Notice the "I am" and "I will" statements in the Isaiah 41 passage. He doesn't say, "I'll be with you when I finish up all my other duties for the day." He doesn't say, "I might strengthen and uphold you, if everything falls into place at the right time." NO! He says:

> **I AM with you.
> **I AM your God
> **I WILL strengthen you
> **I WILL uphold you

He is present. He is everything we need! We can depend on Him—even for key replacements. What a comfort that good news is!

May 29

"May the words of my mouth and the meditation of my heart be pleasing in your sight, O Lord, my Rock and my Redeemer."
Psalm 19:14 (NIV)

This has become one of my daily prayers. It is the prayer I pray before I speak to a group. It is the prayer I pray when I wake up. It's the prayer I pray when I want to give someone a piece of my mind. It is the prayer I prayed before I wrote this book.

When we keep our foundation in Christ, our Rock and Redeemer, He lives in us and can sanctify our words and thoughts to be pleasing to Him. If they are pleasing to Him, they will also be a blessing to others.

As our Rock, God can anchor our thoughts to His true and steady Word. He never wavers or moves with the changing tide of life. As our Redeemer, He forgives and by His grace transforms us into His vessel. I need my "vessel" to be anchored to His secure position.

Did you know that ungodly thoughts don't like to share space with Christ? With Christ being the focus of our thoughts, those ungodly things get bumped out. That's the way I want to live! Help me, Jesus!

May 30

"You, dear children, are from God and have overcome them, because the one who is in you is greater than the one who is in the world."
1 John 4:4 (NIV)

Good versus evil is the theme of many exciting action movies. The bad guys attack the good guys. There are battles and conflicts, but in the end good prevails.

We were born into a cosmic battle of good versus evil. We know who is going to win, but we still have to decide whose side we are on. Satan can't hurt God, so he goes after His children. He isn't afraid of you, but he's afraid of Who is in you.

The heroes in the movies appear to have no doubt that they will win, or they will die trying. They brave the enemy with courage and determination. They may come out of the fight a little beat up, but they are victorious.

We don't have to try to conjure up our own courage. We can rely on the victory of the One who has already won. Jesus defeated death and plans to return some day to set things right once and for all.

Live today with the knowledge that God is fighting our battles because He has victory in mind.

May 31

"Great peace have they who love your law, and nothing can make them stumble." Psalm 119:165 (NIV)

I hopped out of the truck in my flip-flops so that I could push the button to activate the green light. We were at the beginning of a construction zone. It was early in the morning, and a little foggy. There were obviously no cars coming the other direction, but for some reason we had not tripped the sensor when we drove up. As I became impatient, I decided to do something about it. When I landed on the gravelly shoulder of the road, my foot slipped one direction, and my knee went the opposite way. I tweaked it pretty bad, and paid for the poor footing for the next couple of weeks.

We stumble when we lose our footing. We often lose our footing because we are not wearing the proper footwear. We are supposed to wear the Good News of peace on our feet (Ephesians 6:13) to help us stand strong.

Part of the Roman soldiers' armor was their shoes that had hobnails on the bottom for grip to keep them from sliding during battle. We can't go shoeless into our battles with Satan. Without the proper footwear, we get out of sync with relational peace (with God, ourselves, or others).

Maintaining peace starts with loving God's Word. Hiding His promises and truths in our hearts help us to stand on solid ground and keep from stumbling.

June 1

"So also is my word. I send it out, and it always produces fruit. It shall accomplish all I want it to and prosper everywhere I send it."
Isaiah 55:11 (TLB)

In this passage, God is comparing His word to the rain and snow that come down from heaven. It waters the earth and makes it bud and flourish. It yields more seed for more growing, and it provides bread for people to eat. The King James Version says, "it shall not return unto me void." That's the version I learned as a little girl. It means that His Word is not empty and useless. It has a purpose that will be accomplished.

Occasionally someone will surprise me with a text out of the blue. It might simply be a quote from one of my books or a thank you for a chapter that they read that touched them. It blesses me that perhaps something I had written spoke to their heart.

As a parent, it means a lot to us when we hear our child repeat something we have said, perhaps over and over again. When the words come from their mouth, it makes us smile. We think, "OK, they're starting to get it."

How much more God loves it when we use His truths and His promises as we pray and claim His words. Maybe we are allowing a verse to soothe our hearts. Perhaps we are spurred to action by something God's Word teaches us. At times, we may just repeatedly whisper His assurances to affirm His love for us and dispel Satan's lies.

Get to know His Word. Repeat the words of Scripture over and over. They will accomplish God's purposes and will produce fruit in your life.

June 2

"For where two or three come together in my name, there am I with them." Matthew 18:20 (NIV)

I attended a memorial service a couple of years ago of an acquaintance from church who passed suddenly and peacefully while talking on the phone. She had a heart attack, and the Lord took her in a quick moment, leaving her family and friends in a state of shock.

As her life was remembered at the service, it was clear that she lived a life of loving Jesus and others. One of her sons shared some humorous and endearing memories, but a particular part of his story stuck out to me.

His business requires him to do the vast majority of his work in the months of March, April, and May. During those months, he makes his money for living expenses for the remainder of the year. March of 2022 was such a dismal month of business, that he expressed to his mom that he was uncertain of his future. He thought he might have to pick up extra work or give up some things.

His mom promised to pray for him and told him that her care group would also lift him in prayer. Though he forgot her words initially, he was amazed at how April's business month picked up. It wasn't until May's numbers came in that he realized he had the most successful month of his career.

When he asked her if her group had also prayed for him, she replied in the affirmative. His comment was, "Prayer still works!"

Yes, it does! God's Word tells us, "For where two or three come together in my name, there am I with them" (Matthew 18:20). If you have a prayer need, bring it to others who you know will pray for you. PRAYER WORKS!!!

June 3

"For all have sinned and fall short of the glory of God, and are justified freely by his grace through the redemption that came by Christ Jesus."
Romans 3:23-24 (NIV)

Our pastor was doing a series on the book of Romans. The first three chapters were tough. Each week the pastor prefaced the sermon by saying he would be sharing the bad news before we could get to the good news. It was hard, but important truth about our depravity as humans, not so we could dwell in that depressing space, but so we could understand the extravagance of God's mercy and grace to us.

Sometime during my thirties I was freed by this concept. Even though I had not lived a terrible life (by some people's standards I was probably a bit of a goodie-two-shoes), I recognized that I was still a sinner. Nothing I could do would be good enough to save me.

As I recognized my helplessness, I was able to revel in God's goodness. I spent several weeks expressing my deep gratitude to God for his love for me. One morning, as I prayed in a spirit of thankfulness, I was overcome with the need to bow before my Savior, literally face-down on the floor. It was a powerful moment before Him.

I was glad when we got to the "good news" section of Romans, but I am forever grateful that I don't have to rely on my own righteousness to gain eternal life.

Friend, give up your striving and rely on the only One who can redeem you! Recognize the "bad news," and accept freely the "good news" that can save your soul!

June 4

"For to me, to live is Christ and to die is gain." Philippians 1:21 (NIV)

Our society has developed a negative connotation of the term "surrender." We are told not to surrender our rights. We are encouraged to never give in or give up. We are not to be held captive by anything or anyone.

Biblical surrender, on the other hand, is about freedom. Scripture talks about at least two types of surrender:

1) Surrendering your life to Christ. In Philippians 1:21 Paul says, "For to me, to live is Christ..." Nothing else we live for—success, money, pleasure—deserves the place of the One who gives us life.

2) Surrendering our circumstances. 1 Peter 5:7 reminds you that you can "cast all your anxieties on Him because He cares for you." Releasing the need to know the when, why, and how of our circumstances to the care of God's hands is sweet surrender.

When we surrender lordship of our life to Christ and surrender our anxious hearts and minds to Him, we are free of depression, isolation, anxiety, and so much more!

So, remember, when you surrender to God, you are not giving up, you are gaining hope and joy.

June 5

"For we are his workmanship, created in Christ Jesus for good works, which God prepared beforehand, that we should walk in them."
Ephesians 2:10. (ESV)

I have several notes in my Bible around this verse. A couple of them are in the published study notes. The others are things I have written as I have listened to sermons or worked on my personal meditations of God's Word.

1) "Workmanship" in its Greek connotation, denotes a work of art. You are a work of art that God has created.

2) "Prepared beforehand" matches the theme of God's sovereign purpose and planning that is seen in Ephesians 1. You can rest assured that God has a specific purpose for your life.

3) Nothing brings more glory to God than doing what you were created to do. Your good works are not for your benefit, but as a way to point others to Christ.

4) Your works are not limited to your service in the church. Your good works are prepared daily for wherever you go.

As you move through your day and your week, remember that you are a work of art! God has a specific purpose for your life that will bring glory to Christ. You can count on these truths each and every day!

Go put God's art work on display!

June 6

> "What is more, I consider everything a loss compared to the surpassing greatness of knowing Christ Jesus my Lord, for whose sake I have lost all things. I consider them rubbish, that I may gain Christ."
> Philippians 3:8 (NIV)

Paul had such a deep and intimate relationship with Christ. He compares a life of not knowing Christ to rubbish, garbage. I have seen the word rubbish translated as "dung." Any way you look at it, all of our human achievements are a huge loss compared to knowing Jesus Christ and the power of the resurrection and the fellowship of sharing in His sufferings (Philippians 3:10)

Think of someone you know and love well. Did your relationship grow by accident? Maybe your meeting was by chance, but to develop a deep friendship you most likely had to work at it.

The same thing is necessary for us to get to know Jesus better. It should be our primary aim at the beginning of each day, to get to know Him more. That takes time and effort. It takes intentionality. The good news is that Jesus is just as interested in spending time with you. He makes an effort each day, whether you are on board or not. He was intentional in loving you by dying on a cross for you.

Stay grounded in Him! Get to know Him more and more deeply. It surpasses greatness!

June 7

> "The Sovereign Lord is my strength; he makes my feet like the feet of deer, he enables me to go on the heights.'" Habakkuk 3:19 (NIV)

Prior to Habakkuk 3:19, Habakkuk is declaring his joy in the Lord in spite of seeming calamity and injustice. God has made it clear that the wicked will eventually be destroyed, but that the people of Judah must rest in His timing.

When you have had to do without something for a period of time, it seems unfair. Waiting for relief is hard. For years we anticipated taking our kids and grandkids to Family Camp with joy. This is an annual event with our church that we have been attending since our boys were little. The pandemic shut things down for a couple of summers, so we had really missed it.

This isn't a glamorous spa vacation with all the amenities. This is a rustic cabin with ten bunk beds, a sink, and a toilet. For showers we head up to a common restroom facility. Sometimes the week is very hot, but the pool and creek water are freezing! There are mosquitos by the gazillions. We tolerate the camp food. So why do we keep going back?

We have generated so many memories there. We discover and rediscover capturing the ladybugs, catching fish, feeding the ducks, and NOT feeding the bears! We relive and experience anew God's Spirit meeting us around family prayer time, camp services, and kids' choir performances. We build relationships, play afternoon games, and compete in the Saturday obstacle course race.

The week is exhausting, but we keep going back because we know the Lord will be our strength!

June 8

"...My child, don't make light of the LORD's discipline, and don't give up when he corrects you." Hebrews 12:5b (NLT)

As a teacher and administrator, I did a lot of training. I trained young minds to focus on academics. I trained after-school employees with best practices for working with children. Part of training involves correction. There were times when students would need to be redirected. Sometimes they would need to do a task over again, to gain a more complete understanding of the concept. When I observed employees, I would sit down with them and give them three to "glow on" and one to "grow on." In other words, I would point out things they were doing well. Then I would give them something they could work on until I came to watch them again.

There is a difference between punishment and correction or discipline. Punishment is a penalty for the past. Discipline is training for the future. God trains us by pointing out how we are getting off the path He has laid out for us and guiding us back on the right path. We may feel like we are being punished, but Christ has already taken all the punishment for our sins. We need to cooperate with him.

"God is not mad at you. He is mad about you!" (Rick Warren) He guides and disciplines you because you are His child.

June 9

> "See, I am doing a new thing! Now it springs up; do you not perceive it? I am making a way in the desert and streams in the wasteland."
> Isaiah 43:19 (NIV)

The use of a rearview mirror and its origins is quite fascinating. As early as 1909, **Dorothy Levitt** in her book *The Woman and the Car* noted that women should "carry a little hand-mirror in a convenient place when driving" so they may "hold the mirror aloft from time to time in order to see behind while driving in traffic." Her revelation came a little more than a decade before the rearview mirror was patented for street-going vehicles.

I use a journal for looking back on my spiritual journey. It helps me to remember God's faithfulness in my past. This is a healthy looking back, not a dwelling on my past. Just like constantly looking into your rearview mirror when driving would eventually cause a crash, we need to be looking ahead to the new things God is going to do. We are products of our past, but being a prisoner of our past will cause us to "crash."

Strive for what God has in store for your future. Occasionally look back in the mirror to remind yourself of how He has worked in the past, but know that His desire is for you to live in the present and allow Him to shape your future.

June 10

> "For God so loved the world that he gave his one and only Son, that whoever believes in him shall not perish but have eternal life."
> John 3:16 (NIV)

I must admit, I don't really "get" this age of technology and the generation of social media influence. A young kid will post a video on social media, it goes viral, and the next thing you know he/she has millions of followers. They make a living from their continued following, and they are known as "influencers."

I would love to have that kind of following, but when I wonder if I am making any difference in the lives of others, God reminds me the importance of the influence of one—your ministry and mine, right where we are. There are valuable souls in our neighborhood that need our "influence." Our pastor has had us pray for our "One" this year—someone in our lives who needs God's touch, and we may just be the one who shows them who He is.

A ministry started in our church called "Influencers." It has nothing to do with anyone's social media presence. It has everything to do with connecting with God through studying His Word and mentoring others who are just beginning their faith journey.

Be the one for your "one" this year. If your videos go viral, good for you! But the true success will come when a life is transformed by Jesus Christ through your influence.

June 11

"The Lord is my shepherd, I shall not be in want..." Psalm 23:1 (NIV)

Are you going through a valley today? Jennifer Dukes Lee writes (in response to Psalm 23), "He doesn't guarantee we'll avoid valleys, but He guarantees we won't walk through them alone. The valley we dread often becomes the exact place where we come to experience God's presence most."

When we look at Psalm 23:1-3, the Psalmist is speaking **about** God. He is grateful for being guided by the Good Shepherd. He takes care of His sheep by meeting their needs, making them rest, and restoring their soul. He makes sure His sheep don't veer off the path into dangerous territory.

In verse 4, the text shifts to talking **to** God. "Even though I walk through the darkest valley, I will fear no evil, for **you are with me, your rod and your staff, they comfort me**" (emphasis mine). The Lord becomes very personal when things get hard. His presence is exactly what we need, even more than answers to our questions of why we are going through our particular valley.

If you are in the middle of your valley today, be assured that God's presence is with you. He cares deeply and is there to comfort you. He is your Shepherd, and you will not be left wanting.

June 12

"Why are you downcast, O my soul? Why so disturbed within me? Put your hope in God, for I will yet praise him, my Savior and my God."
Psalm 42:5 (NIV)

I spoke to a group of women, women much like you and me, encouraging them to ask God their questions as they invite Him into their struggle.

- Why did this happen to me?
- Where are You, Lord?
- How can I get through this?

The Psalms are filled with examples of this type of heart-wrenching emotion and lament. The Psalmists also model for us the pattern of turning our why's into worship. The step between lament and worship is to remember God's goodness and faithfulness. As we reflect on God's character, we are reminded that He is in control, and we are not. Our cries of sorrow and anguish become confessions of trust. Our petitions become praise.

If we stay stuck in our "why's," we can become blind to His presence, goodness, power and hope. We must surrender our "why's" so that we can have spiritual sight. Our questions of lament may never be answered on this side of heaven, but in response, Jesus comes near to us and helps us to see spiritual potential and purpose in our brokenness. Lysa Terkeurst put it this way: "Instead of answers, He's given me Himself. I don't have to have His answers to have His comfort."

Be honest before God. Let Him enter your space of grief. Accept His presence. Put your hope in Him!

June 13

"As the Father has loved me, so have I loved you. Now remain in my love." John 15:9 (NIV)

I smiled as I watched two of our grandkids, ages 5 and 7, wrestle on the floor with my husband. With the loss of their own father, this first Father's Day without their own daddy was especially tough for them. They giggled and squirmed for their turn to come at grandpa from a different angle as they tried to avoid his tickling, while inviting it at the same time!

As we said good-bye later that afternoon, grandpa asked them, as he always does, who loves them. They went through the litany of relatives—mommy, daddy, grandpa, grandma, aunts and uncles. Then, he teased: "Who else?" Even though they had heard it before, grandpa filled in the blank: "JESUS! Don't ever forget that Jesus loves you!"

The godly leadership of our husbands and dads is so appreciated. Their playfulness and willingness to wrestle on the floor with our kids is a precious gift. The reminder that Jesus will always love them is priceless.

I don't know if anyone has ever counted the number of times Jesus reminded the disciples of His love for them, but I'm sure it would be quite a few! Important words bear repeating, and Jesus didn't want them to ever forget this part of His message. He doesn't want you to forget it either.

June 14

"O afflicted city, lashed by storms and not comforted, I will build you with stones of turquoise, your foundations with sapphires. I will make your battlements of rubies, your gates of sparkling jewels, and all your walls of precious stones." Isaiah 54:11-12 (NIV)

One of my granddaughters loves jewelry. She was known in her toddler years to "borrow" her mom's wedding ring because she was drawn to its beauty. Then she wouldn't remember where she had put it. They had to build in some strict rules to keep her from permanently losing this precious piece.

Another one of my granddaughters has become obsessed with collecting gems. She loves to go to rock stores and pick out pieces for her collection. She could spend hours looking through the piles of stones for the perfect treasure.

Have you ever wondered why we are drawn to "bling?" In Isaiah 54:11-12, God tells us through the prophet that He will rebuild our "destroyed" city with stones of turquois, lapis lazuli, rubies, sparkling jewels, and precious stones. As you can see, Our Creator loves beautiful stones as well.

We all have a void in our lives that is unfulfilled without Christ. He promises to fill that void with redeeming beauty that will outshine anything we could ever try to accomplish for ourselves. Spend some time looking up these beautiful gems. (Do you know what lapis lazuli looks like?) They are a picture of God's everlasting love for us. He values you more than the beautiful jewels and stones He is preparing for us.

June 15

"In the same way, the Spirit helps us in our weakness. We do not know what we ought to pray for, but the Spirit himself intercedes for us with groans that words cannot express." Romans 8:26 (NIV)

I typically read from several different devotionals each morning. I'm often surprised by the fact that even though the Scriptures are different and the key thoughts are separate, a common truth will run through them like a thread tying it all together.

One such morning, the theme that struck me was "surrender." The first devotional shared from Romans 8:26 how the Spirit helps us in our weakness. When we choose daily to hand our emotional trauma to God, He draws near to us and cares about our despair—past, present, and future.

The next reading was from Psalm 62:7 declaring that God is my mighty rock and my refuge. As we surrender our lives in God's hands, He brings glory and honor to Himself and helps us as we achieve our goals. God, alone, is our true success.

The final passage focused on Proverbs 4:23, which admonishes us to be careful about our thought life. We need to surrender (take captive) our thoughts to Jesus.

Surrender to Christ brings freedom and purpose to our lives. We need to surrender different areas of our lives depending on the day or the moment—our emotions and weakness—our actions and successes—our thoughts and motives.

My prayer today is: *Lord, I surrender all to You! Thank You for interceding for me throughout the day because You know best what I need to surrender. Amen.*

June 16

"Be joyful always; pray continually." 1 Thessalonians 5:16-17 (NIV)

It seems like 1 Thessalonians 5:17 might simply be a literary metaphor or an impossible command. It says to "Pray without ceasing" (ESV). REALLY? How does anyone do that?

First of all, NOT with your eyes closed all day! We need to keep our eyes open, seeing anything and everything as a prompt to pray. There are countless opportunities for us to present requests before the throne of God.

- Do you hear a siren? Pray for the first responders, the victims, and the lives of those involved.
- Are your neighborhood kids playing outside, making noise while you are trying to take your Sunday afternoon nap? Pray for their hearts to come to know Jesus.
- Did you just lose your glasses or your keys? Pray for God to help you find them. (He really cares about that stuff!)

I'm not being trivial here. We have limitless intimacy with the God who hears us and helps us. We don't have to wait to go through someone else to mediate for us. We can come boldly before Him because of the work that Christ did on the cross.

Don't think of praying as a chore. Think of it as a precious privilege! Do it continually throughout the day!

June 17

"If you obey my commands, you will remain in my love, just as I have obeyed my Father's commands and remain in his love."
John 15:10 (NIV)

If you know me at all, you know that I love word plays—acrostics, alliterations, puns, etc.

When I read John 15, I am struck by the number of times Jesus says the word "remain." I circled eleven times "remain" was used in ten verses. That's a lot of remaining.

So, I've been working on an acronym for REMAIN. In John 15, Jesus says we are to remain in Him as He also remains in us. So here it is:

R – Read God's Word in the morning

E – End each day with Scripture

M – Memorize (or meditate) on God's Word

A – Adore Christ (Praise Him)

I – In between, pray without ceasing (see June 16)

N – Notice what God is doing and be grateful

That's a start. You might want to play around with your own acrostic, but whether you use mine or create your own, I hope you understand the importance of remaining in Christ!

June 18

> "Anyone, then, who knows the good he ought to do and doesn't do it, sins." James 4:17 (NIV)

This passage in James is referring to us making plans as if we were in control of life. We can say we will do this or that, but we do not really know what will happen today or tomorrow. We should make our plans prefaced with, "If it is the Lord's will…" (see James 4:13-16).

I saw this statement a while back: "A year from now you will wish you had started today." That can be a hard quote to swallow. Procrastinating can cause regrets down the road because time has now passed that you cannot get back.

I randomly get these posts on my phone that will bring up past memories. Sometimes they are fun adventures, but other times they are projects that we have worked on.

The other day the photos were of our remodel in 2019. I'm glad we are on this side of all the mess and chaos of those days. I'm glad we started and finished that project, so I don't look back and wish we had.

It's good to look back and be pleased with what we've accomplished. It's not so good when we see that we have not done anything toward our goals.

Set some goals. Break down some steps that you can do to start working toward those goals. But most importantly give them to God.

June 19

"But blessed is the one who trusts in the Lord, whose confidence is in him. They will be like a tree planted by the water that sends out its roots by the stream. It does not fear when heat comes; its leaves are always green. It has no worries in a year of drought."
Jeremiah 17:7-8 (NIV)

I love to look at trees. When we go to the mountains, the pines and Sequoias tower above us. In Hawaii, there are different types of trees and foliage with a variety of green hues that are incredible. One year we took a special trip to see our kids in North Carolina during the fall, with the express purpose of capturing the changing colors of the leaves. Trees are incredible.

Pastor Richard of Kaanapali Beach Ministries remarked on this passage of Scripture with these words: "We stand at the end of an incredible stream of God's work. We can look at history and know Him to be profoundly faithful to His people. We can launch out into the future with boldness because we know God is already there!"

Live in the confidence of the Lord today. Plant your roots by the stream. You can move forward today knowing that He has your back!

June 20

"For to us a child is born, to us a son is given, and the government will be on his shoulders. And he will be called Wonderful Counselor, Mighty God, Everlasting Father, Prince of Peace."
Isaiah 9:6 (NIV)

We always chuckle when the beauty pageant contestants' answer to any question can be summed up by saying, "We need world peace."

"Peace" in the Bible is an interesting word. When used in Mark 4:39, Jesus was telling the waves, "Peace, be still." In this context, peace means to keep silent!

The greater use of peace throughout Biblical times was the Hebrew word, "Shalom." This was a greeting which wished tranquility and harmony in the person's life.

The peace which passes all understanding as described in Philippians 4:7 takes shalom to a deeper place. It is a restoration of all things to their original intent. Peace is more than emotional stability. It doesn't depend on what is happening in the world around us. It is a peace in the midst of the storm. Our emotional waves can be stilled by Christ's presence. We are filled with incomprehensible rest in our spirit because we are filled with peace.

Peace is a person! Peace is Jesus! He is the Prince of Peace!

Invite His peace into your life today. Invite Him into your life!

June 21

"When you pass through the waters, I will be with you; and when you pass through the rivers, they will not sweep over you. When you walk through the fire, you will not be burned; the flames will not set you ablaze." Isaiah 43:2 (NIV)

Notice this passage doesn't say "if you pass through the waters…" It says "when." We should not be surprised by our trials. We were never promised that they would not come. We were promised that God would be with us when we suffered hardships.

Sometimes that seems hard to fully comprehend. I know it in my head, but I don't always feel it in my soul. I believe that is partly because in the middle of our angst, we want God to give us all we ask for. When He doesn't answer our prayers the way we want, we allow doubt and fear to creep in. We forget it isn't about what we want but what we need. All we need is Him.

Nicki Koziarz says, "His presence doesn't eliminate what is hard, but it does illuminate what is holy." We may feel close to drowning or being consumed by fire, but the waters will not overtake us. The fires will not set us ablaze. As we wait to see God's plan unfold, while we are between what was and what will be, we are with God.

Thank Him for His holy protection and presence today.

June 22

"It was good for me to be afflicted so that I might learn your decrees."
Psalm 119:71 (NIV)

I just heard from my doctor this morning that I need to be on a more powerful drug to rebuild my bone density than the one I am currently taking. Apparently, I have osteoporosis. His words to me, with a little chuckle behind them, was to make sure I didn't go skiing this winter.

Funny thing is, I did fall last year skiing. It wasn't pretty, but it wasn't bone-breaking, thank goodness. I was in pain for a month or so as my knees and shoulder tried to get back to normal. Since the fall was on the first morning we skied, we didn't go back. Looking back, I can see that God was directing my path, putting me in pain, so I wouldn't go back on the slopes for the possibility of a more serious injury.

You see, I'm working to be where the Psalmist in our key passage was. I don't like pain, so I don't see it as "good." However, I am seeing the second part of the verse as good. I can learn through the pain. I can seek God's Word and His counsel and comfort because of my trial.

C. S. Lewis "God whispers to us in our pleasure but shouts to us in our pain." When we are down and out, God is just trying to get our attention because we hesitate to listen otherwise.

Make this your prayer with me today: *Lord, may I always be willing to hear and learn from You! Amen.*

June 23

"Therefore, as God's chosen people, holy and dearly loved, clothe yourselves with compassion, kindness, humility, gentleness and patience." Colossians 3:12 (NIV)

I fuss about what I am going to wear each day. I go through my closet and look at the same shirts, pants, and dresses that I have had for a while. I don't "need" anything new, but I do wish to be in style. I might try on a couple of outfits before heading out the door. This garment fits too snuggly, that one is too wrinkled... When I do buy something new, I'm learning to get rid of an article of clothing so my closet doesn't continue to get cluttered.

I would never consider going outside without being dressed. I may or may not grab the paper from the driveway in my pajamas on occasion. But to truly go out into the day for work or errands, I want to be properly attired.

This passage in Colossians encourages us to put our Jesus on each day. What if we made sure we didn't leave the house without compassion, kindness, humility, gentleness, and patience. Wow! That could potentially be earth-shattering, world-changing clothing. Ephesians 6:11 admonishes us to put on the full armor of God. Romans and Galatians tell us to clothe ourselves with Christ. Repetitions like these in the Bible highlight something important is going on.

When we clothe ourselves with God's wardrobe, we are never out of style or having to sort through clutter. His clothes are the Ultimate Designer Collection, also known as "character."

Make sure you put your Jesus on today!

June 24

"But we have this treasure in jars of clay to show that this all-surpassing power is from God and not from us."
2 Corinthians 4:7 (NIV)

When our son passed, he was an organ donor. He had indicated on his driver's license that his desire was to give a second chance to someone else in the event of his death. The process for finding a match was very thorough. It took a couple of days to measure and test his organs and find a viable recipient.

His heart went to a 50-year-old man. His liver and kidneys helped a couple of young people. We have reached out to the recipients, but have not heard anything back, but I did meet a donor recipient at a retreat a few months back. We shared and cried together about God's goodness. She had never met the family of a donor, and we were both blessed by the chance meeting.

In 2 Cor. 1:4, it says that God comforts us, and He wants us to comfort others who may be going through trouble.

This passage, along with our key verse for today, indicates that our pain can be redemptive. God can work in and through us because we live in fragile bodies and in a world of heartache. Redemptive pain means that you may just have the right story (blood type or life-giving donation) to help someone else during their time of need. Sharing your story, with His surpassing power working through us, might just be the second chance on life they are looking for.

Pray today about who you need to share your story with.

June 25

"Though one may be overpowered, two can defend themselves. A cord of three strands is not quickly broken." Ecclesiastes 4:12 (NIV)

When we take up the shield of faith (Ephesians 6:16), we are protecting ourselves from Satan's attacks. He cannot take away our faith, as long as we remain defended. Our faith is even stronger when we join forces with others. Now the safeguards are really difficult to break through.

At the time that Paul wrote to the Ephesians, he most likely was in prison at Rome. The Roman shield covered the entire front side of a soldier. When in battle, the soldiers would stand side-by-side and form a wall with their shields to deflect the attack of the enemy. Some would stand behind the line of soldiers and place their shields over the heads of their fellow warriors to provide protection from arrows that might come over the top.

We are not meant to do this life alone. When we take up our shield of faith, we can gather others of faith around us to create an even greater wall of protection. Keep connected!!!! And when you are in need of prayer support, rally those other "shields" around you! Two or three (or more) with faith will not be overpowered.

June 26

"Don't let anyone look down on you because you are young, but set an example for the believers in speech, in life, in love, in faith and in purity." 1 Timothy 4:12 (NIV)

Our ladies' ministry team planned a Spring Brunch which was a perfect combination of good food, fun, and fellowship.

One of the greatest things about it was the involvement of multi-generations. We had some of the teen girls serving, young moms leading worship and helping with décor, and every age in between helping out in some way. There was a mix of people seated at each table.

I love seeing God using the younger generations. They are not waiting to lead. They are starting now!

Some of those same young ladies and their male counterparts can be seen helping in children's ministry on Sundays or during Vacation Bible School in the summer. They take food to the homeless, and go on mission trips to aide other churches and communities. They are setting an example for all of us.

Pray for a teen(s) in your life. Encourage them to use their talents and gifts for God right now.

June 27

"I will be like the dew to Israel; he will blossom like a lily. Like a cedar of Lebanon he will send down his roots." Hosea 14:5 (NIV)

What a beautiful picture of God's blessings. First, we are refreshed by His daily "dew." If you walk out on your grass in the morning without shoes, your feet (or socks) will get wet. The imagery of dew indicates faithfulness. God is there every morning, ready to give us the nurturing moisture we need to start our day.

Second, it says we will blossom in His care. Lilies are a beautiful flower when in bloom. They come in a variety of colors and types. God is producing fruit in all of us in our uniqueness and variety. We are beautifully and wonderfully made.

Third, as we walk with Him, our roots grow deeper into His love. Cedar trees are known for their majestic presence and durability. The depth of cedar tree roots can vary, often extending anywhere from six to twelve feet deep. God allows us to send our roots deep into the soil of His goodness and love.

Allow God's morning dew strengthen you for the days ahead so that you can bloom and grow.

June 28

"...His splendor will be like an olive tree, his fragrance like a cedar of Lebanon." Hosea 14:6 (NIV)

Picking up from yesterday, Hosea 14:6 goes on to talk about the beauty of the olive tree. Olive trees have a unique beauty. The wood from the olive tree is a treasured commodity. Its oils are used in foods and medicines. Its fruit (the olives) are packaged and preserved.

Then he compares us to the fragrance of cedars. One of the websites I Googled described the fragrance of cedar this way: "a harmonious blend of earthy warmth, subtle sweetness, and woody richness. Cedarwood's aroma is a celebration of nature, offering a grounding and comforting olfactory experience." I believe God is saying that when we grow in Him, we are pleasant to be around and we are worth celebrating.

You are beautiful to God: unique, treasured, useful, and bearing fruit. His imagery in these verses once again paint such an amazing picture of His blessings when we repent and turn to Him (see Hosea 14:1-4).

Go out today being a strong aromatic treasure to be used by God!

June 29

> "...since you know that you will receive an inheritance from the Lord as a reward. It is the Lord Christ you are serving."
> Colossians 3:24 (NIV)

Throughout the years, I have worn many hats (as do we all):

- Wife
- Mom
- Teacher
- Sister
- Musician
- Athlete
- Sister
- Friend
- Leader

I have always loved the verse found in Colossians 3:24. It takes the pressure off of me to be a "people pleaser." One thing I have found is that it is impossible to please everyone all the time. Remembering that I am working for the Lord, not for people, frees me from getting stuck with the fear of rejection.

With the mindset of doing my best, as unto the Lord, I can focus on working with a positive and enthusiastic attitude. I can continue to hone my skills with God as my strength. I can truly work with a spirit of joy and purpose.

Of course, I don't always do this perfectly! I tend to go down the comparison rabbit hole. I dream about the grass that must be greener on the other side of the hill. And, darn it, I want people to like me!

The good news is that God sees our efforts and knows our heart. When we give Him our best, we can rest in His pleasure.

Do your best **for Him** this week.

June 30

> "So he left in Joseph's care everything he had; with Joseph in charge, he did not concern himself with anything except the food he ate..."
> Genesis 39:6 (NIV)

Joseph is such a great example to us of how to be a good employee. In Genesis 39:6 Potipher gave Joseph full responsibility over his household. The Bible tells us that Potipher didn't have to worry about a thing except what kind of food to eat.

Think about your boss. Can he/she fully trust you with everything you have been tasked to do? Are you reliable, trustworthy, and steady? Do you show up on time and leave on time? Do you keep your promises and fulfill your responsibilities?

My friend had a particularly tough boss in the last ten years before her retirement. There were many days she wanted to give her superior a piece of her mind, but she bit her tongue. When a personal crisis arose for her boss, my friend was there to help and pray for her. They didn't become best friends, but their working relationship changed because of how my friend responded (as opposed to reacted) with integrity.

Joseph faced some trouble, not of his own doing, but ended up promoted to a very high position. It is because he maintained his integrity. Think about ways you can ease the burden for your boss today. At the least, pray for the leadership in your life. Do your best at all times. Make your work place a better place!

July 1

"Then, because so many people were coming and going that they did not even have a chance to eat, he said to them, 'Come with me by yourselves to a quiet place and get some rest.'" Mark 6:31 (NIV)

My husband was part of the Worship Team one Sunday. When he went to the Thursday night practice, the Worship Leader had changed the song schedule completely. As it turned out, the drummer and one of the main guitarists were home because of family members testing positive for Covid. With a limited crew, they decided to do an unplugged worship set.

The grand piano was wheeled out on the stage and one acoustic guitar added to the accompaniment. It was a nice change. We could hear everyone's voices. There was a freedom in the service that inspired the pastor to call for a couple of spontaneous testimonies.

This week we will be taking our grandkids to the mountains. Our experience will once again be "unplugged" since there is limited cell service coverage where we'll be. I'm looking forward to using my phone just for tracking steps and for checking the time of day.

We spend so much time on our devices that it is a welcomed change of pace when we can go a few days without being tethered to technology.

We all need rest from time to time. Jesus even encouraged His disciples to take some time away from their busy schedules. Whether we need to take a break from our business or from our technology, here's a suggestion for this week: Plan a day, or part of a day each week, where you don't have access to your phone or computer. Spend time outdoors, taking walks, or playing board games with your kids.

July 2

"Do not be anxious about anything, but in everything, by prayer and petition, with thanksgiving, present your requests to God. And the peace of God, which transcends all understanding, will guard your hearts and your minds in Christ Jesus." Philippians 4:6-7 (NIV)

This is not the first time I have referenced this passage of scripture. Philippians is one of my favorite books, and these verses have played a big part in my life.

I loved reading and writing in school, but I have also always enjoyed math. So, the other day when I was reading God's Word from Philippians 4:6-7, I decided there should be an algebraic formula to help us remember not to worry.

When some people hear the word "algebra," they have an immediate feeling of panic. They either struggled with math in general, or they could never see the relevance a subject like algebra has to real life. Maybe this will change things for you.

P^3 = Peace

P to the power of three stands for pray, petition, and praise:

1) Pray constantly—be in a spirit of prayer throughout your entire day

2) Petition—be specific in your requests

3) Praise—Thank Him for His answers and His goodness

With those three powerful habits in our life, we will find true peace of mind and heart. Hopefully that is some algebra that you can get behind, even if it's not your favorite subject.

July 3

"for at one time you were darkness, but now you are light in the Lord. Walk as children of light." Ephesians 5:8 (ESV)

This verse gives us the command to "walk as children of light." How are we to do that?

As we look further in the passage, Ephesians 5:9-10 lists some of the fruit that is displayed when we are living in the light:

- Goodness
- Righteousness
- Truth
- Discernment (for what pleases the Lord)

Philippians 4:8 adds to this list of things we should be focused on:

- Whatever is noble
- Whatever is pure
- Whatever is lovely
- Whatever is admirable
- Anything that is excellent or praiseworthy

As we strive to be obedient to the Light, we can ask God to help us display His goodness, righteousness, and truth while guarding our minds with what is noble, pure, lovely, admirable and praiseworthy.
It's a start!

July 4

"Let us not become weary in doing good, for at the proper time we will reap a harvest if we do not give up." Galatians 6:9 (NIV)

Most of us will have today off from work. It's a national holiday that we all look forward to, but what about tomorrow? Are you dreading the work week? Do you feel tired before you even get started?

If so, you are not alone! Sometimes it feels like the days and weeks grind by. Nothing really changes except the date on the calendar. Your routine becomes a rut, and then you do it all over again.

Besides a caffeine fix to start each morning, this message from Paul has helped me as I face another week. Keep it up, don't give up; the harvest is coming.

The imagery is clear. While we wait for a seed to grow, we must continue the daily tasks of weeding, watering, and cultivating the soil. It is tedious and takes commitment, but the end result is a harvest.

What if you looked at your co-workers, your customers, your students, or your boss as the eventual harvest. The day-to-day tasks would take on new meaning. Don't grow weary of doing good—Not just because it will reap a paycheck in a couple of weeks, but because tomorrow, you just might see the beginnings of a sprout poking through the soil. Do not give up!

July 5

> "His master replied, 'Well done, good and faithful servant! You have been faithful with a few things; I will put you in charge of many things. Come and share your master's happiness!'"
> Matthew 25:23 (NIV)

I am coming to grips with the fact that I am a people pleaser. I like to follow rules, and I want people to like me. Are any of you with me?

It's not totally wrong to desire words of affirmation. For some, hearing words of affirmation is their main love language. However, when you are motivated solely by the approval of others, there is a problem. Let's look down some of the potential slippery slopes we approach with that type of ambition:

- Giving up your convictions to fit in
- Getting depressed when you receive criticism
- Losing your joy when your perceived "success" isn't obtained

In a conference I recently attended, I was reminded more than once that being a best-selling author or presenting on the "big" stage should not be my goal. My focus should be to bring glory to God, to serve those who are right in front of me, and to be obedient to the King of Kings and Lord of Lords who has called, saved, and redeemed me.

Let me encourage you today. You are doing a great job. You are blessing your family, your neighbors, and your colleagues. But my words and approval are NOTHING compared to when you hear the Lord say, "Well done, good and faithful servant" (Matthew 25:23).

July 6

"The Father of compassion and the God of all comfort, who comforts us in all our troubles, so that we can comfort those in any trouble with the comfort we ourselves receive from God."
2 Corinthians 1:3b-4 (NIV)

I have written before about our annual trip to Family Camp. A few years ago, my husband and I took four of our grandchildren, ages six to ten, by ourselves. As we started our journey, one of them began to second guess being away from mom and dad for five days, and she was struggling with actually getting in the car to head up the mountain. In spite of tears and anxiety, we (grandpa and grandma) provided encouragement and assurance that we were going to have a great time and that we would never put her in a situation that would make her miserable. We reminded them of the fun of years past. The nerves settled and we were on our way.

Upon picking up the six-year-old a few hours later, we were confronted with more tears. This grandson had never been to camp before. He had already spent a couple of weeks with some of his other cousins, and he really was missing his mom and dad. He stuck with his decision to come with us, but he quietly cried for the last thirty minutes of our journey.

I was amazed at how the other two in the car encouraged their cousin, giving him many of the same reasons we had just provided hours earlier, that he would have a great time. They shared about all of the fun things we would be doing, and assured him that the days would fly by.

Once we arrived and the fourth granddaughter joined us, all tears were forgotten. The week did fly by, and all four had a glorious time. There was not one tear, even at night, from any of them the rest of the week. They each caught a fish, rode in a canoe, explored in the creek, and met new friends.

The whole thing reminded me of how God uses the pain, fears, and anxieties we have experienced to allow us to help others who are going through something similar. He uses the comfort we received from Him to be an encouragement to others. Who is someone you might need to comfort today?

July 7

"Hear, O Israel: The Lord our God, the Lord is one. Love the Lord your God with all your heart and with all your soul and with all your strength. These commandments that I give you today are to be upon your hearts. Impress them on your children. Talk about them when you sit at home and when you walk along the road, when you lie down and when you get up. Tie them as symbols on your hands and bind them on your foreheads. Write them on the doorframes of your houses and on your gates." Deuteronomy 6:4-8 (NIV)

Many of my July journal posts are in regards to Family Camp since we are there every year during this season. Yesterday, I wrote about being there with four of our grandkids. Each morning, we had an opportunity to share in a family time of devotions before they went off to their kids' chapel. They always came back ready for lunch, and brimming with the stories, songs, and crafts that they had done.

Our evening services are outdoors. We take lawn chairs for the adults and spread a blanket in front of us for the kids. I always bring snacks, coloring tablets, and quiet activities for them to do to keep themselves busy. They are often intent on drawing or coloring, and it appears they are not paying attention.

Then, we get surprised by their spontaneous answer to the preacher's rhetorical question. We hear them humming the worship songs that were sung earlier, and see their heads look up toward the front in a most poignant moment.

I think that is part of what Moses was talking about in Deuteronomy 6 when he said to impress the commandments of God on our children. When we talk about them when we walk and sit and lie down throughout the day, they are getting it! What a blessing you will get when you see some of your efforts bearing a bit of fruit!

July 8

"This is the day that the Lord has made; let us rejoice and be glad in it."
Psalm 118:24 (ESV)

When our kids were young, they would often ask a question shortly after we started on a road trip, "Are we there yet?" I would try to patiently let them know how much longer we had, and we would do lots of things (pre-iPad days or even video players in the car) to try to entertain them in the moment. We would sing, read a chapter from a book, play games, and point out the scenery.

We are often impatient in our lives. We want to "be there." We want to accomplish our life goals and we strive so hard to get there, that we miss the present moments. God gives us grace for where we are right now, today! He wants our hearts. He wants us to be present with Him along the way.

On the island of Maui in Hawaii, there is a tourist must-do called the Road to Hana. It is a terribly windy and narrow road, and the guidebooks tell you to take it with caution. The thing about this day-trip is that it isn't necessarily about the destination. Hana is a lovely, small community, but if your only goal is to get there, you'll probably be disappointed. The joy is in the journey—making lots of stops to see things on the side of the road—things you would miss if you just rushed by to get to the end.

Setting goals is good, but rushing to get there or being disillusioned when we haven't "arrived" yet robs us of the joy of the journey. Take time to just be present with God today, right where you are. This is the day He has made for you, right now, and we should rejoice and be joyful in it! (see Psalm 118:24) He will keep molding you into the person He knows you can be, and some day, in Heaven, we will be able to truly rejoice in our final destination.

July 9

> "Trust in the Lord with all your heart, and do not lean on your own understanding; in all your ways acknowledge him, and he will make your paths straight." Proverbs 3:5-6 (NIV)

In my people-pleasing, perfection-striving life, I can get caught up in my own understanding. I think I am on the right path when people are responding to me positively and when my ideas are going as planned. And then, someone (or more than one) opposes me or the plan starts to fall apart.

I have learned that perfectionism can get in the way of faith. Perfectionism has a tendency to paralyze potential. often things can get a little messy before they become a reality. The fear of the messy can definitely create a faith stop.

My friend, Jen Hand, writes about putting your "yes" on the table, and turning faith-stops into faith steps. What that means is that we have to surrender our goals and dreams to Jesus, no matter what lies ahead. It means stepping into the unknown and the uncertain. That is really scary for the perfectionist types like me because I want to know what is ahead.

I'm not "perfect" at it yet, but I'm learning to let go of the reins so that God can direct my dreams. What dream has God been placing on your heart? I encourage you to put one foot in front of the other, and let Him lead you into life-changing miracles. Yes, it will be messy at times. You may even experience setbacks and problems along the way, but trust God with all of your heart. Don't lean on your own understanding. Acknowledge Him to lead you in His perfect way!

July 10

"Then Jesus told his disciples a parable to show them that they should always pray and not give up." Luke 18:1 (NIV)

Jesus taught an important truth in the parable of the persistent widow. In this word-picture, a widow keeps asking the judge for justice. Each time he puts her off, she just comes back again, asking for the same thing. Eventually, the judge gives in and grants her justice against her adversary.

If an evil judge brings about justice, Jesus went on to teach, how much more will God bring justice for his chosen ones who cry out to him (see Luke 18:7).

It's easy to give up when prayers don't seem to be answered the way we think they should. Just remember, there are cycles of cultivating, planting, and reaping. To get to the final product you have to go through your planting and growing stages. God is interested in developing your consistency and trust. He tells us to keep asking, seeking, and coming to the throne of God for help and wisdom.

Jesus tells us to "...always pray and never give up." As I see it, you have two choices:

Option 1: Pray continually

Option 2: Lose heart

Which one will you choose today?

July 11

"Examine yourselves to see whether you are in the faith; test yourselves. Do you not realize that Christ Jesus is in you—unless, of course, you fail the test?" 2 Corinthians 13:5 (NIV)

THIS IS A TEST!

Those are not necessarily words that we want to hear. But Paul's exhortation in 2 Corinthians 13:5 is to look inward. He was specifically asking them to pray for discernment, not to act out of their own whim or because of accusations by others. So, as I see it, this is a daily exam. Seeking God's wisdom is a Biblical principle that we must apply each day and with each decision or action we take. It doesn't come automatically with age (Shoot!), or I'd be golden.

This type of introspection should be performed with God's guidance. Our prayer must be in line with David's prayer-- "Search me, O God, and know my heart; test me and know my anxious thoughts. See if there is any offensive way in me, and lead me in the way everlasting." Psalm 139:23-24.

How is your heart today? Do you have any anxious thoughts? Are you living in a way that is offensive to God? Are you allowing Him to lead you in righteousness so that you can be used by Him?

You can relax! I'm not going to grade you on this test, but God will patiently teach you and me, and remediate where needed.

July 12

"She gave this name to the LORD who spoke to her: 'You are the God who sees me,' for she said, 'I have now seen the One who sees me.'"
Genesis 16:13 (NIV)

When we played with teams in my classroom, I always preselected the squads. It was usually pretty random, choosing students with a 1-2-1-2 count. Ones go here; twos go there. That way, you didn't have the playground pick where someone felt like they were being chosen last.

I think I had a heart for those kids who felt like they were never chosen or wanted because I remembered being picked last for things. I was never the popular kid, and I can remember walking into a crowded cafeteria and feeling invisible. Everyone was in conversations except me, and no one seemed to see me.

Maybe you can relate to feeling unseen. Well, here's some great news. We have a God who sees, "El Roi." He isn't just looking for "key players" or the ones with the right credentials. He sees the overlooked. He has a special place in His kingdom for you! You are uniquely fit into His body to serve in ways no one else can.

It is God's character to notice every heartache, every unspoken word, every sacrifice, and every longing of each individual. Then He weaves your story together with the stories and talents of other believers so that each part of the body helps the other parts grow.

Maybe you're the one who needs to "see" someone walk in the room and love on them. Pray that God uses you to be His eyes this week.

July 13

"Trust in the Lord and do good; dwell in the land and enjoy safe pasture." Psalm 37: 3 (NIV)

My college friend, now sister-in-law, Cathy, wrote a song in college based on Psalm 37. It never made it to the #1 charts, but it was a great tune and wonderful reminder that we need to trust, commit, delight, and rest in the Lord.

When we do these things, He promises the desires of our hearts. He declares that our righteous reward will shine like the dawn. He assures us of His presence and safety.

So, we commit, trust, and delight, but we don't always want to rest (also translated "be still," and "wait"). We tend to commit our worries, only to take them back as we try to fix the problem ourselves. We do an okay job of delighting until the problem seems to linger beyond our timeline. Our trust seems to only last as long as our patience. But waiting is the key. God has our good in mind, and He sees the big picture. He knows the perfect timing and will bring it to pass in His way and will.

Even when we don't understand the chapter our life is currently in, we can trust the author. God continues to write our stories and brings us to safe pasture.

July 14

"Then little children were brought to Jesus for him to place his hands on them and pray for them. But the disciples rebuked those who brought them. Jesus said, 'Let the children come to me, and do not hinder them, for the kingdom of heaven belongs to such as these.'"
Matthew 19:13-14 (ESV)

The evening air was cooling. The stars were beginning to twinkle above the treetops. We had watched our grandkids run up and sing the song they had learned in their morning class. Worshiping in the outdoors was amazing. The kids now sat on spread-out blankets in front of our lawn chairs, coloring and keeping quietly busy, while we listened to the evening message.

At the end of the Bible teaching, there was a call to the audience to come forward if you desired to be more like Jesus. Many walked toward the altars, and there was a final prayer for our deeper commitment to Christ. When the prayer ended, the pastor admonished us to look around and find someone to hug.

We were surprised to see my youngest son and our five-year-old grandson when we turned. Apparently, when people started to head to the front, he had asked his daddy why people were going forward. His dad told him, "They want to be more like Jesus."

He turned to his dad and said in a very matter of fact way, "I want to be more like Jesus." So, they joined the rest of the group up front.

It makes me smile to think how innocent kids' logic can be at moments like this. His tone indicated that it was the simplest decision in the world. Of course, he wanted to be like Jesus. We would do well to "turn and become like children" (See Matthew 18:3). The kingdom of heaven, after all, belongs to them (Matthew 19:14).

July 15

"'Where, O death, is your victory? Where, O death is your sting?' The sting of death is sin, and the power of sin is the law. But thanks be to God! He gives us victory through our Lord Jesus Christ."
1 Corinthians 15:55-57 (NIV)

I have a vivid and fun memory of the Kansas City Chiefs winning the Super Bowl in 1970. I lived in Kansas City at the time, and I was in my sophomore year of high school. It made an indelible impression on me. I became a football fan from that moment forward, and I've stayed true to the Chief's, even after moving to California, and even in their not-so-successful seasons.

As great as that victory was, with the entire city celebrating and congratulating each other as if we had done the work on the field, the title of Super Bowl champs wouldn't come again until 50 years later. The joys of that moment were temporary, at best.

It is different with Christ's victory. You see, He defeated death! He is Champion forever, from now until eternity. He is triumphantly present with me now until death brings me home, making me a winner as well.

1 Corinthian 15:55-57 says, "Where, O death, is your victory? Where, O death is your sting? The sting of death is sin, and the power of sin is the law. But thanks be to God! He gives us victory through our Lord Jesus Christ."

Give the Lord a shout out today! Thanks be to God! Celebrate your victory in Him!

July 16

"There is surely a future hope for you, and your hope will not be cut off."
Proverbs 23:18 (NIV)

David Busic states in *Way Truth Life, Discipleship as a Journey of Grace*: "The central problem of our age is not too much stress, but too little hope."

Our world is so full of uncertainty. Just listening to the news or trying to raise children can cause worry and stress. But here is what we know:

- God loves us.

- God will not turn His back on us.

- God will not abandon us.

- God will hold us up and strengthen us in our darkest hours.

- No matter what the future holds, we know Who holds the future.

This is the empowering hope of a Christian, grounded in the past, present, and future love of Jesus through His sacrificial death and resurrection.

With whom can you share this hope?

July 17

"I wait for the Lord, my soul waits, and in his word I put my hope."
Psalm 130:5 (NIV)

Today when we call someone who is already on the line, we will typically get a voice message saying they are unavailable. We usually are given a choice to leave a voice message or send them a text message. In the old days, we would get a busy signal. There would be a steady beep-beep-beep on the other end of the phone.

When God is trying to get through to you, does He get a busy signal?

Part of praying is listening. We can't do all the talking and expect God to answer. We have to let Him speak. Sometimes it is through His Word. Sometimes it is through a thought that is placed in our hearts by the Holy Spirit. We can't allow ourselves to be so busy, that God can't get through to us.

Take time each day to be still before God. Don't let him hear a "busy signal." Be expectantly waiting for his word of hope.

July 18

"...We do not know what to do, but our eyes are upon you."
2 Chronicles 20:12b (NIV)

Are your prayers a steering wheel or a spare tire?

When I first read this question, I ignored it. I didn't really grasp the meaning. Then, I read it again and began to ponder the analogies.

Does my prayer life steer me through life? Does prayer guide my every move and decision?

OR

Do I just pray when I have a problem? Do I treat prayer like a spare tire, keeping it in the "trunk" until there is an emergency?

Prayer is having conversation with God. We are to do it throughout the day, without ceasing. Jesus provided an example of going away to find a place to pray in the early morning hours. There are many models of excellent prayers throughout the Bible.

One of my favorites is King Jehoshaphat's prayer in 2 Chronicles 20:12 when a vast army was getting ready to attack them. He ends his prayer by saying, "We know not what to do, but our eyes are on you."

How might you deepen your prayer life? Do you need to set aside a time by yourself and God, perhaps in the early morning? Maybe you will start with repeating the Lord's prayer every day, pausing on each line to contemplate what it means (see Matthew 6:9-13). Another great way is to study King Jehosaphat's prayer and admit you need God's help, even in learning to pray!

July 19

"Consider it pure joy, my brothers and sisters, whenever you face trials of many kinds." James 1:2 (NIV)

Some of my most respected friends are those who suffer chronic disease and pain. The fact that they can live with joy amazes me.

One of those friends has daily pain with Lupis and its complications. She always has a smile on her face and explains that she chooses joy.

For my *Coffee Shop Chronicles,* I interviewed those with cancer, infertility, auto-immune diseases, heart issues, and grievous losses, who learned to count their trials as joy because of Christ in their lives. They are truly inspiring people.

Most of the time, my problems are miniscule compared to the suffering that these friends are going through. Their pain really puts my grumbling into perspective.

We can't control everything that happens in our lives, but we can choose our attitude toward the things that come our way. You see, life is 10% what you make it and 90% how you take it.

Choose joy. Choose gratitude. Choose God!

July 20

"Praise the Lord, O my soul, and forget not all his benefits—"
Psalm 103:2 (NIV)

The minute we experience a delay or a disappointment, we tend to forget what God has done in our past. Psalm 103 reminds us:

- He forgives all our sins

- He heals all our diseases

- He redeems our life from the pit

- He crowns us with love and compassion

- He satisfies our desires with good things

These are the tip of the iceberg. There are over 7000 promises in God's Word. He has a plan and a purpose for you. He never leaves us (even in the delays and disappointments).

As you reflect on the benefits of God, praise Him! Take time to remember today!

July 21

"Come and listen, all you who fear God; let me tell you what he has done for me." Psalm 66:16 (NIV)

At Grounds for Hope, I try to encourage you to "Stay Grounded, Keep Connected, One Cup, One Story, at a time." Today's verse reminds us that your story matters!

The Psalmist was calling people to come and listen to his story. He shared some of that story in the verses surrounding his invitation:

- He turned the sea into dry land (v. 6)

- He rules forever (v. 7)

- He has preserved our lives and kept our feet from slipping (v. 9)

- You brought us into a place of abundance (after testing us) (v. 12)

- I cried out and God surely listened to my prayer. (v. 19)

- God did not withhold his love from me! (v. 20)

Sharon Jaynes says, "Your willingness to place your story into God's holy hands will lead you to full redemption, where the pain loses its power to do you harm and gains the power to do others good. Your wounds can become the source of your greatest strengths."

Invite someone to coffee. Tell your story of God's goodness to you.

July 22

"Against all hope, Abraham in hope believed and so became the father of many nations, just as it had been said to him, 'So shall your offspring be.'" Romans 4:18 (NIV)

Do you see what happened here? Abraham relied on the Word of God. God promised Abraham that his offspring would become many nations. God delivered on that promise.

God delivers on His promises to us. We need to remember (I'm speaking to myself here) that He doesn't promise a care-free, painless life. He doesn't say He will give us every whim and wish that we utter.

Here is what He does promise:

- He is with us always.
- He is faithful
- He cares about us

We must rely, against all hope, on God's Word. When we read about what God can do our hope is revived. In hope, we can believe!

Trusting God is not always easy, but it is necessary if we are going to get through this life. Problems from our perspective are transformed when we depend on God's viewpoint.

July 23

"He guides the humble in what is right and teaches them his way."
Psalm 25:9 (NIV)

Our first-born son was such a strong-willed and stubborn child. We really worked throughout his toddler years shaping his will, trying not to break his spirit. He turned into a fine young man, husband, father, and teacher, so I guess we did something right. We couldn't be prouder of him!

I guess he came by it honestly, since I must say I have personally had many a willful streak throughout my years. Sometimes I learned humility through hard circumstances, having to discover some of the same lessons over and over again.

The humility in this verse is referring to a characteristic we should allow God to develop in us. This happens as we embrace the space where He has placed us, looking for opportunities to learn from Him. He promises to guide us and teach us along the journey. I surely would rather humble myself than to be humiliated because of unwise actions.

God is setting opportunities before you today to learn and grow. When you come humbly before him, He will teach you His way.

July 24

"You, Lord, are all I have, and you give me all I need; my future is in your hands." Psalm 16:5 (GNT)

I recently read an article comparing "Scarcity Theology" with an "Abundance Mindset." I'm really not smart enough to know what those are, but, in a nutshell, it was asking us to contemplate whether we live like there's not enough or as though there's plenty to go around. Do we act like we have just enough to get by or do we show gratitude for all we have?

Too often we go through each day wishing for something more, seeking the green grass on someone else's hill, or complaining about what we don't have. We even complain at times about what we do have. If it's not the biggest, newest, and best, it is not good enough.

But God wants us to live in the knowledge of His abundance. He offers us grace, unconditional love, power to live our lives, and peace beyond understanding. Instead of focusing on the house we hope to have or the job we are aiming to procure, we have enough to be thankful for each and every moment.

Sure, we should make and strive for goals, but our reliance should be on God. The glory belongs to Him alone for our achievements and our failures, because when I'm weak, He is strong.

Live with and work in the "Abundance Mindset" that God's Spirit is available to us all the time. He is more than enough. I am enough in Him! Thank Him today for all you have!

July 25

"I will exalt you, my God the King; I will praise your name for ever and ever. Every day I will praise you and extol your name for ever and ever."
Psalm 145:1-2 (NIV)

I can't imagine praising God forever. For ever and ever seems like a long time. My finite brain cannot really fathom it. So, I will just have to focus on the part that I can comprehend and take hold of: "Every day I will praise you…"

You see, forever starts today (and the next day, and the next day).

- When you wake up, praise God.
- When you drive to work, extol His name.
- When you are interacting with your colleagues, exalt God the King.
- As you are heading home, glorify Him.
- As you lay your head on your pillow, thank the Lord.

Start giving God forever glory by doing it today. Show it in what you say and how you live and work.

July 26

"They will still bear fruit in old age, they will stay fresh and green."
Psalm 92:14 (NIV)

I love retirement! Some of my friends who are close to my age and approaching their retirement years keep asking me about it. What's it like? How do you fill your time?

Here is one way to look at life, whether retiring or not. I borrowed this from Rick Warren, but what it said to me was that we never stop working for God. He can fulfill us at every stage and age along the way:

1) Grow—keep learning from God's Word and practice what you hear/read

2) Sow—Be generous—

    - with your time (in retirement you have a lot more time to volunteer for your passion projects)
    - with your finances (with good planning, you should have plenty to live on and plenty to share with others)
    - and with your talents (God can create new ministries in your life if you let Him).

3) Go—Obey God; look what Moses and Abraham accomplished in their "retirement" years.

I hope this encourages you as you work as unto the Lord this week.

July 27

"He is before all things, and in him all things hold together."
Colossians 1:17 (NIV)

A lot is said about our identity these days. We hear about:

- Gender identity
- Identity theft
- Career identity
- Personal identity

The world wants us to search within for our identity, but we won't find it there! We are encouraged to find purpose in our career, our accomplishments, relationships, or possessions. Those things will never satisfy our deep need for belonging and purpose. We will just drift from one thing to another, being completely controlled by them.

Our only hope to find purpose and identity is in a relationship with Jesus Christ, our Creator. In Him alone, all things are held together, including us!

Trust in Him. Talk to Him. Get to know Him, and you will discover your purpose!

July 28

"You make known to me the path of life; in your presence there is fullness of joy; at your right hand are pleasures forevermore."
Psalm 16:11 (ESV)

The other day we were driving along a 2-lane highway. We passed a sign that warned us of "Rough Road Ahead." Sure enough, within the next few hundred feet, the road got bumpy and gravelly. The sign helped us to prepare for the rough road, slowing down before we reached it. Just knowing it was coming added to our feeling of security—no surprises on this road!

Wouldn't it be nice to have that in our lives? A sign that warns us or a flagger to wave us to a stop before it's too late. Too often, we get surprised by the rocky and treacherous circumstances in our lives, and we spiral out of control.

But that's where faith comes in. No matter where our paths lead, God is with us. He cares. He helps us navigate the bumps and potholes. His Word is a constant reminder to keep our eyes focused on Him.

We may not have a warning sign for the specifics of what is ahead, but we do have God's promises and directions on how to navigate through the rough patches.

If you are on a rough road right now, be assured, God knows all about it and wants to help you through it. His presence will fill you with joy.

July 29

"Now, Lord, consider their threats and enable your servants to speak your word with great boldness." Acts 4:29 (NIV)

Peter and John had experienced transformation. They went from being fearful disciples to bold evangelists. They had just been before the Sanhedrin who questioned them under what authority they were speaking. After they gave their Spirit-filled response, they were released with threats of punishment if they did not remain quiet.

Peter and John had experienced a true remodeling of their hearts by God, allowing Him to demolish pride, adjust their priorities, and conform into the image of Christ. They returned to their people and prayed with them for God's further anointing and miracles through His Son, Jesus. They were granted God-confidence (not self-confidence) as they began to obediently bring the Gospel to the world.

We have this same opportunity. Our uncertainties can be an invitation for growth. When we are in the middle of a problem, we need to learn to change our question from, "When can I get out of this?" to "How can I grow through this?" We can pray for confidence from God as we face our day.

Do you need a boost of boldness? I encourage you to read all of Acts 4 sometime this week.

July 30

> "For in six days the Lord made the heavens and the earth, the sea, and all that is in them, but he rested on the seventh day..."
> Exodus 20:11a (NIV)

When our kids and grandkids were toddlers, they fought their naps and bed time. Once they gave in to this non-negotiable event, they were always so much better prepared to face the rest of their day. On those occasions where they didn't get as much sleep as they needed, everyone around them suffered. As parents/grandparents, we made sure this avoidable suffering happened far and few between. Why? Because we loved them and knew what was good for them (and probably for our own sanity as well).

Our Heavenly Father loves us and knows we need rest as well. He commanded it (Exodus 20:9-10) as an important moral dictate. Sometimes we fight this commandment. We act like life will fall apart if we don't keep working and doing. The opposite is actually true...life will fall apart if we don't take time to rest from our work. And those around us will suffer if we fail to comply.

When I write, I try to take five-minute breaks every twenty-five minutes. I walk around the house or empty the dishwasher. Many teachers give their kids a brain break. If recess is too far away and they can tell the kids are starting to fall asleep or get antsy, they stick an exercise video in to get them moving. Breaks, rests from our work, are important!

Take a break today. Maybe even take a nap. It might just be one of the most spiritual acts you can do.

July 31

"We are hard pressed on every side, but not crushed; perplexed, but not in despair, persecuted, but not abandoned; struck down, but not destroyed." 2 Corinthians 4:8-9 (NIV)

Do you have a sense of being hard pressed on every side? Maybe you are perplexed or persecuted or struck down. Perhaps you don't feel like that right now, but you have in the past or you will in the future.

Paul expressed some of these feelings as he wrote to the Corinthians about the frailty of humanity. But he also encouraged them with the fact that God is there with us and will not let us be crushed, abandoned, or destroyed (see 2 Corinthians 4:7-9).

God may not take you out of the pain, but He will give you faith-filled ability to get through it. Our faith grows in our waiting rooms, as we learn to rely on God to accomplish His purpose, even when we are in the middle of a storm.

Pray this prayer with me today:

Lord, give us Your resilience and perseverance to keep going and believing that You are working behind the scenes. We don't want to be wallowing in our self-pity and miss seeing what you can do. May we allow you to work on our character while we wait. We give You our lives! Amen.

August 1

"For we are God's fellow workers; you are God's field, God's building."
1 Corinthians 3:9 (NIV)

May I add God's manuscript—blank pages where He is writing your story. Because if I'm being honest, I was terrified when I started writing my first book six years ago. I knew that there were so many possibilities waiting for me outside of my comfort zone, so I went for it! I'm so glad I set a goal with God and kept after it to completion.

Our dreams can be exciting and scary at the same time. God is the God of possibilities and He wants you to realize the desires of your heart. It works best when you walk hand-in-hand with God, letting Him guide your specific steps—being a fellow worker with God. It's so satisfying when you get a confirmation that your obedience and steps of faith are being blessed.

One day, out of the blue, I got a text from Aleta. She was reading one of my books in the doctor's waiting room while waiting for her husband's PET scan. She texted, "I brought your book to keep my mind on heavenly things instead of the 'what ifs' that so easily want to creep into my thinking. I'm a little over halfway through the book and finding it very encouraging." She included a picture of Higher Ground in the message.

Her heartfelt words gave me such joy and affirmation of God's direction and love. It was a wonderful surprise that reminded me that the hard work of sitting at the computer, pouring over words and formats, was truly His work.

Friend, whatever you are striving toward today, let God lead. Give your dreams and your fears to Him. He wants you to succeed. Take delight in Him, and watch how He builds your building, cultivates your field, and fills your pages.

August 2

"How many are your works, O Lord! In wisdom you made them all; the earth is full of your creatures." Psalm 104:24 (NIV)

Have you ever thought about how a click of a camera button has the ability to capture a moment in time? Pretty amazing!

There are many once-in-a-lifetime memories that I love to reminisce about as I look through old photos, like special vacations with family and friends. Taking people to Larraine's for a shave ice and getting the tour of her Maui property is always high on the list. Larraine runs her business from her humble yet beautiful ocean-front property. It's totally off the beaten path, but she is always happy to show you around. Taking a picture in her "backyard" is breathtaking. I can't even begin to describe the shades of blue and green of the ocean contrasted against the lava rock cliffs. A picture can't do it justice.

There is a string of videos I enjoy pouring through of our grandkids learning to boogie board. We kept filming them, knowing that one of them would catch the perfect wave. Rewatching that textbook ride as the right wave brings them all the way into shore is definitely in the top ten memories.

But there are some day-to-day moments that make my heart happy, too, like viewing the majestic mountains that surround our city here in the Central Valley, being reminded that God, the Creator, is in control. I need to make an effort to take pictures of it so I can cherish the memory forever.

Take some time to look back and enjoy some of your photos, but also find something that you see everyday that brings you joy. Maybe you can take a picture of it, but whatever you do, give God thanks!

August 3

"[looking away from all that will distract us and] focusing our eye on Jesus who is the Author and Perfecter of faith [the first incentive for our belief and the One who brings our faith to maturity], who for the joy [of accomplishing the goal] set before Him endured the cross, disregarding the shame, and sat down at the right hand of the throne of God [revealing His deity, His authority, and the completion of his work]."
Hebrews 12:2 (AMP)

Is there anything you are a bit insecure about? For me, it's worrying that I'm not enough. Although I struggle with this, I am working every day to turn things around by going to God's Word and reminding myself Who called me and Who has qualified me for the tasks that are mine.

Hebrews 12:2 reminds me to fix my eyes on Jesus, the author and perfecter of my faith. He has made me enough. Yes, He continues to write my story, and He continues to write yours! He pioneered our salvation story, and He keeps showing up, building our character, honing our skills, and working all things for His good. Nothing surprises Him, and He is making the story perfect through His redeeming love.

Whatever you may be insecure about, know this, friend: you are enough! Keep your eye on the Author and Perfecter of your faith!

August 4

"My dear brothers and sisters, take note of this: Everyone should be quick to listen, slow to speak and slow to become angry."
James 1:19 (NIV)

I don't know about you, but I can get embarrassingly distracted when I am listening to someone. Instead of fully attending to their part of the conversation, I am thinking about what I might say next, or I am thinking about what I need to do next, or I'm, honestly, just zoning out.

I read a quote by Lynn Cowell the other day. She said, "Listen to learn."

I have failed to learn what some people are really saying because I have my own agenda. This is even true sometimes of my conversation with God. It is too often one-sided. I need to listen so I can learn from Him.

Lord, help me to be quick to listen and ready to learn how to build relationships Your way. Help me remember that I have two ears and one mouth for a reason. I need to do twice as much listening as talking. Thank you for desiring a relationship with me, one in which we both contribute to the conversation. Amen.

August 5

"Therefore, there is now no condemnation for those who are in Christ Jesus." Romans 8:1 (NIV)

Romans 8:1 is a victorious, encouraging truth that we can grab onto. We like to hear that there is no condemnation in Christ, but the verses that follow are just as important and exciting. You see, it's through Christ Jesus that I can be free of that condemnation. It is because He has given us His Spirit to help us live for Him.

- Jesus has set you free from sin and death (v. 2)
- The righteous requirement of the law is fully met (v. 4)
- When we are governed by the Spirit, there is life and peace (v. 6)
- The Spirit gives life (v. 10)
- We are children of God (v. 14)
- We are co-heirs with Christ (v. 17)

There are so many benefits from living according to the Spirit. The choice seems obvious—live in Christ Jesus and live free!

August 6

"I have told you these things, so that in me you may have peace. In this world you will have trouble. But take heart! I have overcome the world."
John 16:33 (NIV)

If anyone told you life would be easier once you turned your life over to Christ, they were wrong!

Jesus didn't mince words when He told us we would have trouble. Our troubles don't go away just because we have asked Christ into our lives. In fact, they might even increase because Satan is trying to discourage us.

But here's the hope you can cling onto today. "But take heart! I [Jesus] have overcome the world" (John 16:33).

Are you having overwhelming troubles today? Know that you are not alone.

I do not say this glibly or without having experienced victory through pain myself. The Overcomer brings peace to the overwhelmed, every time!

August 7

"For our struggle is not against flesh and blood, but against the rulers, against the authorities, against the powers of this dark world and against the spiritual forces of evil in the heavenly realms." Ephesians 6:12 (NIV)

Today's passage talks about what we struggle/wrestle with. It's NOT against flesh and blood (that person we think is our enemy), but it's against Satan and his minions.

The word wrestle in some of the translations of Ephesians 6:12 indicates a face-to-face battle. Satan wants to get into our face!

In the 1990's, a gesture was made popular via a sitcom. It was meant to be a sarcastic way of saying "I'm not listening." You might have seen someone put their hand up toward someone and say, "Talk to the hand." What they mean is, "Get out of my face. I'm not listening."

It wouldn't necessarily be a good idea to try this with another person. Especially when, as I mentioned on August 4 that I'm working on listening to learn. What this attitude and posture is definitely suited for is to let Satan know you are not listening to his lies!

What if, instead of putting up our hand, we put up the "the shield of faith," and told Satan, "Talk to the shield." Now that's using your armor! Don't let him get into a face-to-face battle with you. Extinguish all those fiery arrows of the enemy by knowing, by faith, that He who is in you is greater than he who is in the world.

August 8

"Each of you should use whatever gift you have received to serve others." 1 Peter 4:10 (NIV)

As I took my walk the other day, God and I had a conversation. I was feeling a bit discouraged. I had made a mistake earlier in the week. I was feeling like my influence wasn't making much of a difference. I was lacking direction for the next "thing" to work on. I expressed myself to God, then I tried to just listen.

What God was whispering to me at that moment was that I needed to stop trying to "make" something happen on my own. I couldn't compare myself to anyone else. I just needed to lay my desires, successes, and failures at His feet. God assured me that I was to bring the little that I had to Him, and He would use it for His glory. It didn't matter how big or small the results seemed to me, they would be the result of obedience, and that was enough.

Later in the day, I came across a quote by Lysa Terkeurst that I had written down in my journal. "There is an abundant need in this world for your contributions to the Kingdom—your thoughts, your words and artistic expressions—your exact brand of beautiful. Know it. Believe it."

Maybe you need this reminder today, as well. Your gifts and abilities are uniquely designed for unlimited possibilities. Rest in that truth this week. Keep on contributing to the Kingdom. Continue to hone your skills. Leave the results to God!

August 9

"As iron sharpens iron, so one man sharpens another.
Proverbs 27:17 (NIV)

Accountability is a great way to accomplish your goals for your life. Grabbing a friend makes it easier to:

- Stay consistent in an exercise regime
- Read God's Word every day
- Work toward a career path
- Break a bad habit

Whatever it may be, knowing someone will be checking in with you makes a big difference.

We were challenged at Family Camp this year to memorize a passage of scripture—1 Thessalonians 5:23-24. Each morning, people were invited to recite these verses. The brave ones who stood before the crowd weren't perfect. Some needed prompting. Some stumbled and hesitated over the words they were trying to recall, but they did it!

I wasn't brave enough to stand, but I did try to memorize it. I said it to my husband a couple of times, so that counts as my accountability. The sharing of the goal and bumbling through the early recall efforts reinforced what I was trying to do and made me stronger for the next time.

What is it you need some accountability for this week? Try sharing it with a trusted person in your life and see how it goes.

August 10

"Be wise in the way you act toward outsiders. Make the most of every opportunity. Let your conversation be always full of grace, seasoned with salt, so that you may know how to answer everyone."
Colossians 4:5-6 (NIV)

Most of us have heard the phrase "random acts of kindness," usually attributed to Anne Herbert. She was responding to a phrase she had heard (most likely on the news) that disturbed her: "random acts of violence..."

She decided to turn this negativity around. She wrote a book in 1993 highlighting true stories of spontaneous acts of kindness.

I actually love this idea, and I've tried to implement it into my life. There is actually something that works better for me. It is "intentional acts of opportunity." Using my words and actions to bless someone else comes from praying and reading God's Word, asking Him to show me the opportunities set before me.

Colossians 4:5-6 says, "Be wise in the way you act toward outsiders. Make the most of every opportunity. Let your conversation be always full of grace, seasoned with salt, so that you may know how to answer everyone."

I try to remember to pray in my car before entering any establishment, whether it is the grocery store, hair salon, school, church, etc. I ask God to show me who needs an encouraging word or random act of kindness. Sometimes it is just a smile. Sometimes I "pay it forward." Other times I ask the clerk or person in line how they are doing, and sometimes God uses that question to open up real Spirit-led conversation.

Let's be intentional each day. Who needs your kindness today, this moment?

August 11

"Then Peter came to Jesus and asked, 'Lord, how many times shall I forgive my brother when he sins against me? Up to seven times?' Jesus answered, 'I tell you, not seven times, but seventy-seven times.'"
Matthew 18:21-22 (NIV)

My husband and I are approaching our fiftieth wedding anniversary. Just typing that makes me feel old. We are often asked what the secret to our marriage has been. There are a few things that come to mind.

First and foremost, we have kept God in the center of our relationship. We haven't always gotten along perfectly. We have those real moments when we don't necessarily even like the other person, but our commitment to each other has been unwavering. It was a covenant we made with each other and with God. We have learned to forgive and ask for forgiveness. God has helped us when we have sought His wisdom.

Whether it is your work environment, your marriage, ministry, or friendship, here are some other keys to remaining fulfilled. Choose relationships over rules. Value people more than policy. Decide on love over law.

This is coming from a rule follower! And yes, we need to maintain discipline in our lives and in our society. However, when it comes to having life-long relationships, we need to build bridges, lead with kindness, show patience, forgive, and give the people in our lives a second, third, or seventy-seventh chance. That's what Jesus did for us!

August 12

> "For these commands are a lamp, this teaching is a light, and the corrections of discipline are the way to life." Proverbs 6:23 (NIV)

Have you ever given a child a flashlight? They immediately want to shine it all over the place—on the ceiling, in your eyes, in their mouth (ok, I'm pretty sure we've all done that one).

On one of our summer camping excursions, we put one of our grandsons in charge of lighting our path with his flashlight. We explained why it was important to light the path and not other things. We needed to see where we were going! He actually took his responsibility seriously, and we made it safely to our destination in the dark.

God provides a lamp for our feet and a light for our path ((See Psalm 119:105). That light is His Word, His commands, His teaching and correction. It gives us what we need for that next step. It guides us by illuminating just the few steps in front of us. His Word is the way to life (Proverbs 6:23).

It is encouraging to know that we aren't stumbling blindly through life. We know our eternal life in heaven is where we are going, but we have to walk in trust since we can't see the final destination yet. Trusting in God is a sure thing. He won't leave us alone to try to earn our way there.

God, through His marvelous Word, will light the way for you each step of the journey!

August 13

"A gentle answer turns away wrath, but a harsh word stirs up anger."
Proverbs 15:1 (NIV)

I immediately got defensive when my husband wanted to do further research (over and above what I had already done) on a purchase we were wanting to make. I got snitty, and said something like, "Fine, do it your way!" He later came to me and told me he ordered the one I had found, but immediately saw from our bank statement that it was not a legitimate company. We had to stop our credit card payment and go through a few other hassles. He was sweet, and didn't give me the "I told you so," attitude or tone.

When would I ever learn? It wasn't so much about the product as it was about my stubbornness and prideful response to someone I dearly love.

Proverbs 15:1 says, "A gentle answer turns away wrath, but a harsh word stirs up anger." (NIV) The Greek word for gentleness refers to a wild stallion that has been tamed. It is strength brought under control for the master's use. That's such a great picture. That's what I want to be! Strength brought under control for my Master's use.

I don't know if anyone else out there can relate to this. I hope I can learn my lesson this time around. If you have your heart and tongue under control, just smile and go on with your day. If you feel like you still have some things to learn in this area, pray this prayer with me.

Lord, take my wild, competitive, self-serving thoughts and words captive today. May I be open to your training, in the moment as well as long term. Forgive my brashness and turn my weakness into the strength of your gentleness. Amen.

August 14

"The fear of the Lord is the beginning of knowledge, but fools despise wisdom and instruction." Proverbs 1:7 (NIV)

Our pastor preached a summer series in Proverbs. Each week he compared the wise against the foolish person. We were challenged to seek wisdom through the fear of the Lord (see Proverbs 1:7).

We often make life much more complicated than it needs to be. If we seek God and ask Him for wisdom, He will be faithful to give it to us. We think we have to be some knowledgeable guru to have the term "wisdom" bestowed upon us. It is just the opposite.

We need to be humble and respectful before God, our Maker. We need to stop depending on our feelings, our self-sufficiency, or our own learning and understanding (see Proverbs 3:5-6), and begin depending on God's guidance. We need to ask Him to help us.

"If any of you lacks wisdom, he should ask God, who gives generously to all without finding fault, and it will be given to him" (James 1:5, NIV).

If you have something today that needs to be infused with godly wisdom, ask God to help you. Ask others to pray for you.

August 15

"For God, who said, 'Let light shine out of darkness,' made his light shine in our hearts to give us the light of the knowledge of God's glory displayed in the face of Christ." 2 Corinthians 4:6 (NIV)

My husband and I helped with Vacation Bible School this summer. The theme response each day was that no matter what is happening in your life, "Shine Jesus' Light." It was so cool to hear the students shout this truth about how to handle their good days, bad days, sad days, dark days, bright days, and everything in between.

On day one, they handed out a glow-in-the-dark wrist band that said "Watch for God." They called them our God watches. It was to remind us to recognize God in our day-to-day lives. We were all encouraged to share things we had seen from the previous day as we met each morning. Students saw God in nature, in people, in events, in acts of kindness, etc.

Sometimes when I get up in the middle of the night, I will see my "God watch" glowing on my counter. It reminds me each time that even in the middle of our darkest night, God's light shines. He shows up through His presence and comfort. He sends people to help us. He provides glimpses into His love and character that are overwhelming.

Where do you see God today? I'll start...I see God in my loving husband! Man, he gets to put up with a lot.

Your turn! List some things in your journal or just pray or sing a song of praise to the Lord.

August 16

> "If I speak in the tongues of men or of angels, but have not love, I am only a resounding gong or a clanging cymbal."
> 1 Corinthians 13:1 (NIV)

You've got to **love** 1 Corinthians 13. It's the "Love Chapter" of the Bible (if you aren't familiar with it, be sure you look it up). It is often quoted at weddings, and the descriptions of love in these verses will play out to be the crux of a successful marriage.

But we are called to love like this in every way and with everyone. In *The Way, Truth, Life* booklet our church went through this spring during Lent, it states, "Love is the heart of the matter. Anything less than love does not hit the high mark...of a holy life."

Of course, we will fail at times. When I think of our marriage, I can't even begin to tell you the number of times one or both of us has had to ask for forgiveness from each other and God for failing to be patient or kind, being self-seeking or easily angered. In the long-run, God's grace has seen us through those times. We are here, not because we have done things right, but because God has helped us to grow and mature in Him as a couple and as individuals.

Commit to reading this passage this week. You can read the whole thing every day, or just a short line or two each day. Whatever method you use, it will be a great reminder of how we are to live out our lives with one another.

August 17

"Like newborn babies, crave pure spiritual milk, so that by it you may grow up in your salvation." 1 Peter 2:2 (NIV)

I love junk food. Chips, cookies, chocolate, ice cream, chocolate chip cookie dough ice cream…sometimes I even crave it. If I eat to my "satisfaction," then I don't have an appetite when it comes to the main meals and true nourishment.

When I'm being really good, I get rid of the junk food. If it's not in my cupboards, it can't tempt me. Then, lo and behold, within a few days I'm craving the good stuff—give me an apple or a dallop of cottage cheese!

Our spiritual life is the same. We need to stop filling up on the junk food. To crave pure spiritual milk (see 1 Peter 2:2), we have to be intentional about limiting the things that will thwart our desire for God. Things like:

- Phone Time (Facebook, games, scrolling for whatever…)

- TV (Netflix, Binge watching a series, sports, news)

You get the idea. None of those things are bad in and of themselves, but they can tend to push out the time and desire we have for reading the Bible, going to church, or taking time to pray.

Here's your challenge for today: Work at removing one junk food item from your pantry/fridge. Limit one screen distraction this week.

In place of those things, spend some time with Jesus! Your cravings for spiritual milk will lead to craving the solid food of God's teachings (Hebrews 5:14).

August 18

"Now faith is being sure of what we hope for and certain of what we do not see." Hebrews 11:1 (NIV)

Hebrews 11 is sometimes called the "Hall of Faith." The verses in this chapter highlight men and women of faith throughout the Bible who lived by faith and not sight. The only way they could do that was to look to God and His promises and believe them, even when they didn't see the results right away.

We can all add our names and stories to Hebrews 11. I actually have written in my Bible the addition of verse 41 that starts, "By faith Jerry and Jan..." We are continuing to learn to keep our eyes on Jesus, the Author and Finisher of our faith. (Hebrews 12:2).

Rick Warren has a way with words. In his April 23, 2023, Daily Hope with Rick Warren devotional, he reminded us to fix our eyes on the eternal, not the temporary (2 Corinthians 4:18). In his wordsmith fashion, he penned these thoughts:

> "If you look at the world, you'll be distressed. If you look within, you'll be depressed. If you look to Jesus, you'll be at rest."

There is something about the rhythm and rhyme of these Biblical truths that resonate with me. As we divert our attention away from our problems to the One who solves the problems, we have renewed hope for the day.

Pray these words as you go about your day:

Today, by faith, I will look to Jesus!

August 19

"The Lord is good to those who wait for him, to the soul who seeks him."
Lamentations 3:25 (ESV)

Scriptures that tell me to wait make me cringe a little. I'm not too patient. I like things to happen now (if not yesterday). I don't want to wait in line at the store, for the red light to turn green, for my prayers to be answered.

When we visit Hawaii, I get a sense of what God is trying to say to me. No one in Hawaii seems to be in a hurry. They call it "Aloha Time." For the most part, they live a relaxed, easy-going lifestyle. It is easy to slip into that mode, especially when we are already on vacation.

Psalm 27:14 says "Wait for the Lord: be strong, and let your heart take courage; wait for the Lord!" (ESV)

Isaiah 40:31 states: "But they who wait for the Lord shall renew their strength; they shall mount up with wings like eagles; they shall run and not be weary; they shall walk and not faint." (ESV)

Lamentations 3:25 promises: "The Lord is good to those who wait for him, to the soul who seeks him." (ESV)

These are just a few of the many verses about waiting on the Lord. We learn that waiting on Him takes courage, renews our strength, and blesses our lives. Maybe we can dub our waiting lifestyle "Alleluia Time."

August 20

"Each of you should look not only to your own interests, but also to the interests of others." Philippians 2:4 (NIV)

If you have ever wondered what a good definition for humility is, this wins the gold star:

"True humility is not thinking less of yourself; it is thinking of yourself less." (C.S. Lewis)

God's Word says something similar in Philippians 2:4 as Paul is talking about being humble: "Each of you should look not only to your own interests, but also to the interests of others." (NIV)

He goes on to cite Christ as an example of this kind of humility: "Who being in very nature God, did not consider equality with God something to be grasped, but made himself nothing, taking the very nature of a servant, being made in human likeness." Philippians 2:6-7 (NIV)

The thought of the very God of Heaven leaving His throne to enter my world is overwhelming. He did this for me, out of His love! Humility that is motivated by love puts others first.

Pay attention to people around you today. Think of their interests. Listen intently to what they are saying. Love them. Extend grace. You will be doing what the Lord requires of you.

August 21

"Let everything that has breath praise the Lord. Praise the Lord."
Psalm 150:6 (NIV)

We could not live without oxygen. It is vital to all living organisms. We wouldn't even think of starting our day without it. Actually, it is one of those things we don't think about too often because it is readily available as we inhale and exhale.

My online exercise regimen has added breathwork videos. I don't often do them, but I do understand the benefit of filling your body with fresh oxygen.

We need spiritual oxygen as well. Sometimes we need to just stop and breathe in the mercy and grace, peace and joy, that is available to us through our loving God. God's love fuels your hope, and "...hope is the oxygen for your soul." (Bonnie Gray) We shouldn't even think of starting our day without it!

Let's practice some Biblical breathwork:

Breathe in...God's love
Breathe out...the negative statements about you that Satan tries to get you to believe

Breathe in...the goodness of God
Breathe out...the divisive, negative "news of the day"

Breathe in...God's hope
Breathe out...despair and frustration

Now that you get the idea, you can use other Bible-based breathwork patterns that speak to you. And because you have breath, be sure to praise the Lord.

August 22

"The Lord your God is with you, he is mighty to save. He will take great delight in you, he will quiet you with his love, he will rejoice over you with singing." Zephaniah 3:17 (NIV)

When each of our sons had their first child, one of the gifts we offered to them was a rocking chair. I had such great memories of rocking our boys as babies and toddlers, singing over them, and rejoicing in their beautiful lives. It was important to us that our boys and their wives had the same opportunity with their kids.

Our oldest son and his wife lived with us for a year during a job and relocation transition. They had just had their first baby girl. In the middle of the night, she would sometimes get a little colicky and cry. My son would be bouncing and rocking her, singing softly and comforting her in the best way he could. It is a precious image that will remain with me forever.

God gives us a picture in Zephaniah 3:17 of how He does this same thing with us. "The Lord your God is with you, he is mighty to save. He will take great delight in you, he will quiet you with his love, he will rejoice over you with singing." (NIV)

There are some days when I just need to feel God's love and protection over me in this way. I can imagine Him holding me, rocking me, singing to me, and shushing me. He assures me that it's going to be ok, and that He is with me, delighting in the creation He made me to be.

If you are in a season where you need this assurance, take a minute to picture yourself in God's arms. Let Him fill you with His joy and delight. Rest in His presence.

August 23

"The Lord is my strength and my shield; my heart trusts in him, and I am helped. My heart leaps for joy and I will give thanks to him in song.
Psalm 28:7 (NIV)

The imagery of the shield over us is powerful. The shield stands between us and our adversary, and must be lifted in faith over our minds, hearts, and bodies. God comes to battle for us and provides strength and a shield that is impenetrable.

We are filled with joy and thanks to God in song. I began a list of ways God shows His strength, things that bring me great joy:

- He is a strong tower (Proverbs 18:10)
- He never sleeps nor slumbers (Psalm 121:4)
- He is my refuge (Psalm 46:1)
- He is my redeemer (Job 19:25)
- He is my Shepherd (Psalm 23:1)
- He delivers me (Psalm 18:2)
- He defends me (Psalm 31:1-2)

Think of ways God has shown you His strength. Give thanks to Him in song.

August 24

"Finally, brothers, whatever is true, whatever is noble, whatever is right, whatever is pure, whatever is lovely, whatever is admirable—if anything is excellent or praiseworthy—think about such things."
Philippians 4:8 (NIV)

For the next 4 days, we will be focusing on this passage in Philippians. We are going to take two of the words at a time and break them down into practical terms. As we fight to remove intrusive thoughts from our minds, we can bring those thoughts captive before God. We also must fill our minds with good things so that the tentacles of destructive thoughts cannot take root.

Here are some questions to consider for our first two attributes:

"Whatever is true"—Is it actually true? Are there facts to back it up? Does it line up with God's Word? God's Word—what He says about me and His love for me—will never change.

"Whatever is noble"—Does it hold to a high moral standard? What Christ has done for me is the most noble, self-sacrificing thing I know to dwell upon. Are my thoughts in line with Christ's example and servant-heart?

Do your thoughts focus on what is true and noble?

August 25

"Finally, brothers, whatever is true, whatever is noble, whatever is right, whatever is pure, whatever is lovely, whatever is admirable—if anything is excellent or praiseworthy—think about such things."
Philippians 4:8 (NIV)

This is the second day we are focusing on this passage in Philippians. Our two words today are right and pure.

Here are some questions to consider about these two attributes:

"Whatever is right"—Is it righteous? Is it in accordance with God's law? Doing right when no one is looking is integrity. I can think about what is right even when it goes against cultural norms.

"Whatever is pure"—Does it lead to purity—seeking a life of a redeemed child of God and casting out sin? I think of the purity and innocence of babies. God's creation is pure and beautiful.

When our minds dwell on what is right and pure, we live as unto the Lord. Jesus is our perfect example of being righteous. He turned the norms of the world upside down. His love for little ones was because He realized they had an innocent and pure faith that rivaled the belief system of the scholarly priests of that time.

We, too, can think and love what is right and pure. It will help keep evil and impure thoughts from infiltrating our minds.

August 26

"Finally, brothers, whatever is true, whatever is noble, whatever is right, whatever is pure, whatever is lovely, whatever is admirable—if anything is excellent or praiseworthy—think about such things."
Philippians 4:8 (NIV)

This is day three of focusing on this passage in Philippians. Our next two words are lovely and admirable. If our thoughts dwelt on things that are lovely and admirable, we would be living victoriously.

Here are some questions to consider about these two attributes:

"Whatever is lovely"—Is it a beautiful or pleasing thought? I think of someone's smile, the people who serve us daily, a new flower bud popping forth. People who have changed lives, living for Jesus, are always lovely!

"Whatever is admirable"—Does it deserve respect and attention? Are you looking for the good in others? Can you try to put yourself in their shoes? Do you take time to know their story?

I hope you are answering the questions for yourself and adding to the lists I have proposed.

August 27

"Finally, brothers, whatever is true, whatever is noble, whatever is right, whatever is pure, whatever is lovely, whatever is admirable—if anything is excellent or praiseworthy—think about such things."
Philippians 4:8 (NIV)

This is our last day to focus on this passage in Philippians. Our last two words are excellent and praiseworthy.

Our last two attributes are similar in meaning and are placed together:

"Anything that is excellent or praiseworthy"—Does it deserve to be praised? God is worthy of our praise. We can pray through the Psalms and give Him glory for who He is and the things He has done. We can be aware of God's goodness and excellence as we look for Him in our daily lives, giving Him thanks.

My husband testifies that this verse helped him get out of a cycle of negative thinking and talking during his college years. It turned his life around. That is excellent and praiseworthy in itself.

List in your journal ways that God shows His excellence in your life.

August 28

"Therefore I will boast all the more gladly about my weaknesses, so that Christ's power may rest on me." 2 Corinthians 12:9b (NIV)

I fought the tears as the teacher handed back my spelling test. I had missed one! I couldn't bear not having a perfect score. Yes, I was only eight, but this was a pattern in life that I would have to fight even into adulthood.

Many of my classmates would have been jumping for joy to only miss one spelling word. I knew I could do better, and my mistake was careless and unnecessary.

You see, perfectionism can be paralyzing. We should always strive to do our best, but nobody is perfect. Holding ourselves to that standard can be debilitating.

Try this change of thinking. Admit your weaknesses/failures to God and seek His help. Work steadily. Get started on the project. When you get stuck or have to start over, try boasting about your weakness. That's when God's power can take over and reside in you (2 Corinthians 12:9).

Our key verse has changed my life. I can now be okay with failure and imperfection. I can rest in Christ so that His power can rest on me. It is freeing and exhilarating.

Boasting in our weakness may seem counterintuitive, but the alternative is a joy stealer. Work with the joy of the Lord this week!

August 29

"He who goes out weeping, carrying seed to sow, will return with songs of joy, carrying sheaves with him." Psalm 126:6 (NIV)

In order to reap a harvest, we have to do the grueling work of planting, watering, weeding, and pruning. All that work in the heat of the summer can get one down. Then the insects come and try to destroy what has been tended and cared for. We may get discouraged and want to quit, but we must keep tending the crop even when we're—

- Tired

- Distracted

- Stressed out

- Deep in grief

God's Word gives us permission to let the tears flow while we are carrying the seeds, sowing and tending the garden of life. If we plant with faith, we will reap a harvest. Our tears will turn to songs of joy. We will be able to live a life of abundance.

I'm comforted by the fact that our tears are put in a bottle (Psalm 56:8). God sees each one and keeps track of them. If our bottled tears are accompanied by prayers, those prayers are placed in a bowl of incense that keeps lifting sweet aromas to the Father in Heaven (Revelations 5:8).

Cry. Sow. Reap.

August 30

"Therefore encourage one another and build one another up, just as you are doing." 1 Thessalonians 5:11 (ESV)

It was our son's birthday (May 7), but he wasn't here to call and wish a happy day. He wasn't around to share with in celebration. It was another reminder and trigger of the grief we have experienced over the past years.

Since one of his favorite treats was root beer floats, I posted something that day about how we were going to remember him over this fizzy ice cream treat. We were out of town, but we went to the store and bought the needed ingredients.

Later that evening, our care group sent us a video. Even though we weren't with them, they had recognized our pain. As they met that night, they picked up their own ice cream and root beer. They were having floats in his honor and as a token of their support for us.

Though it brought tears to our eyes, it also brought a smile to our faces. God was letting us know we were not alone. He had sent our friends and their message to us as a comfort in our sorrow.

It's the little things that matter. Who do you know who needs a word of encouragement, an invitation to coffee, or a reminder that they are not going through this life alone?

August 31

"Then he continued, 'Do not be afraid, Daniel. Since the first day that you set your mind to gain understanding and to humble yourself before your God, your words were heard, and I have come in response to them. But the prince of the Persian kingdom resisted me twenty-one days...'"
Daniel 10: 12-13a (NIV)

Are you waiting for a prayer to be answered, a solution to your problem, relief from your pain? Waiting can be so hard, especially when God seems to be silent or uninterested.

Believe me when I say, I have been there, wondering if God even hears my pleas. That's why Daniel 10:12-13 is a comfort to me. Daniel had been waiting for an answer to his cry. Finally, an angel came to deliver the message that from the first day God had heard Daniel's words. The answer was delayed for twenty-one days because of a battle in the heavenly realms. Even the archangel Michael had to step into intervene.

There are two things from this story that encourage me:

1) From the very first utterance God hears our cry.

2) He is working, even if it seems to us He is silent.

Friend, do not give up praying and crying out to God. A delay is not a denial. It means God is fighting for you!

September 1

"A sluggard's appetite is never filled, but the desires of the diligent are fully satisfied." Proverbs 13:4 (NIV)

On the first Monday of this month, we will be celebrating Labor Day. I hope you can have the day off, enjoying a bar-be-que with family--a day of little or no working!

Work is worth celebrating. I know we get tired of going into our jobs every day, and vacations are great, but if we had nothing to do, no way to bring in a little income and some purpose to our day, life would become empty and meaningless. Without working, we most likely would not be able to take those desired vacations. Lack of work breeds idleness, and idleness is the root of trouble!

Without keeping our mind and body productive, it's easy to fall into vices such as laziness, lasciviousness, or poor health habits. Not working may have negative effects on your mental health, your familial relationships, and society in general. Laziness and lack of initiative will always leave us lacking, while diligent and hardworking individuals will experience full satisfaction in their endeavors.

It is also important to have a good work/rest balance. That's another lesson for another day. But for now, whether you are retired or working full-time; whether you are volunteering or working part-time; whether you are working from home or working in the home (and that is WORK); be grateful for your job and work as unto the Lord (Colossians 3:23).

Celebrate all that you and those around you do to make your life spin efficiently on all cylinders. If you receive a service or product this month, make sure you thank the employee who is "laboring" on your behalf.

September 2

"Your basket and your kneading trough will be blessed."
Deuteronomy 28:5 (NIV)

I LOVE being in the kitchen. Creating new delights for the family has always been in my wheelhouse of favorite hobbies/pastimes. I have not always been fond of cleaning up my kitchen messes, but it definitely comes with the territory. I'm trying to learn to clean up as I go, but inevitably I will have several projects going at once and the dishes and mess pile up quickly in the sink.

Whether fixing, cleaning, or enjoying the created treat, it's all part of the package deal when you work in the kitchen. I'm trying to look at the messy piles of evidence as part of God's blessing. Having a sink full of dishes means I have a kitchen to work in, with working appliances and modern amenities. Seeing the splatters on the stove means that we have the capability to buy and prepare food. The messy counters remind me I have loved ones to share my messy life with. I may not have a basket and a kneading trough, but my pantry and my Kitchen Aid mixer are definitely blessed (see the key verse).

I ran across this poem the other day, and thought I'd share it with you. I hope it brings a smile to your face as it did mine.

THANK GOD FOR DIRTY DISHES

Thank God for dirty dishes
They have a tale to tell
While others may go hungry
We're eating pretty well
With home, health, and happiness,
I shouldn't want to fuss
By the stack of evidence
God has been good to us.

By Tracy Minjeras

September 3

"A time to weep and a time to laugh, a time to mourn and a time to dance." Ecclesiastes 3:4 (NIV)

While I'm on a cooking theme (see September 2), I thought I'd share this story I found in my archives:

The other day we were going through some of my mother-in-law's pictures and recipes. She is now staying in a skilled nursing facility, so we (her kids) are starting to sort through some of her things. It's nostalgic and certainly a little sad as we reminisce about all the wonderful meals and treats she prepared for us through the years, but is no longer able.

Among her things I found this "recipe." It literally made me laugh out loud. I hope it brings you a little slice of joy today. (Please do not try this at home!)

ELEPHANT STEW

1 Elephant
Seasoned Brown Gravy
2 Rabbits (optional)

Cut elephant into bite-sized pieces. This should take about 2 months. Cover with brown gravy and cook over kerosene fire for about 4 weeks at 465°. This will serve 3,800 people. If more are expected, add 2 rabbits. Do this only if necessary, as most people do not like to find hare in their stew.

She certainly had a great sense of humor. She knew there was a time to laugh and dance. They didn't always have a lot when it came to worldly goods, but their home was full of joy. Enjoy a dose of her cheer today!

September 4

"Every good and perfect gift is from above, coming down from the Father of the heavenly lights, who does not change like shifting shadows." James 1:17 (NIV)

Today is our anniversary. We were married in 1976, the year of the Bicentennial birthday of our nation. My dad "threatened" to only pay for the wedding if we decorated in red, white, and blue. We were able to talk him down from that one.

It has been hard to always plan a get-away on our anniversary date. There are often other plans for the Labor Day weekend that we can't get out of, so we often carve out some time on another day close by. We love a delightful adventure exploring some new places. We enjoy eating out, usually a steak dinner since that is not our normal fare. One year we were together with family and we got a bit pampered by our kids and grandkids.

It doesn't really matter how or when you celebrate. What matters is that you do celebrate—life, love, hope, joy and peace. Our Heavenly Father has given us so many good things.

I hope you find something you can celebrate today, a good and perfect gift from above.

September 5

> "Each one must give as he has decided in his heart, not reluctantly or under compulsion, for God loves a cheerful giver."
> 2 Corinthians 9:7 (ESV)

The church gets a bad rap for "always asking for money." I know the last thing any of us wants to hear at church is a request for funds.

Here's the deal though--If we were just all obedient to the Lord, there would never be a need to ask for money from the pulpit. Here's a three-part challenge when it comes to what we tend to hold on to so closely:

#1 Don't let the mention of money (tithes/offerings) be a deal breaker at your church. Just talk to God about what He wants for you to give. It's His anyway. Then give with a joyful heart.

#2 Live generously. Once you have given your tithe, find other ways to bless others and spread a little joy.

#3 Challenge: Find someone at church today or someone you run into this week (not pastoral staff. They get a month of appreciation next month). Slip them a $20 bill or a note of gratitude or encouragement. It will make your day as well as theirs.

Jesus was the ultimate example of giving. He gave Himself, willingly and counted it joy (Hebrews 12:2). Let's be generous as well, and stop getting caught up in the offering plate that goes by at church.

September 6

> "Do not be afraid or discouraged because of this vast army. The battle is not yours, but God's." 2 Chronicles 20:15b (NIV)

If you are a do-er, like me, you want to be in the middle of the fray, taking action and making things happen. You are a problem-solver and you want to find a solution fast. I believe God gives us action steps in our lives and helps us to fulfill them, but what happens when He is telling you to rest, stay put, or be still?

I have always been enthralled with the story of King Jehoshaphat's battle in 2 Chronicles 20. There was an ominous army coming against God's people. As the king went before God in prayer, God's answer was clear. "Do not be afraid or discouraged because of this vast army. The battle is not yours, but God's" (2 Chronicles 20:15b).

The instructions went on: Take up your positions; stand firm; see the deliverance the Lord will give you (see 2 Chronicles 20:17). In this particular battle, God's army was to stand still and let God do His thing!

God never changes, but that doesn't mean he is stagnant. He moves and communicates according to each situation so that we will listen to Him and learn to trust. The constant in His instructions is the "do not be afraid" part. The flexibility comes in the action verbs.

In Exodus, the Israelites, through Moses' leadership, were told to wait, go, gather, don't gather (on the Sabbath), turn back, stand firm, be still. Other places in Scripture we are directed to take up our armor, stand our ground, flee (from Satan), go (to spread the Gospel), run, walk.

Over the next few days, we are going to explore some of these commands. Hopefully you will get a better understanding of what God is asking you to do in the various circumstances of your life.

For today, embrace God's promise that He is with you in the battle. You do not need to be discouraged or afraid. Whether you are to advance headlong into the struggle or turn and run, God will give you your marching orders. Trust that He is constantly fighting on your behalf.

September 7

"Be on your guard; stand firm in the faith; be courageous; be strong."
1 Corinthians 16:13 (NIV)

Of the many action commands that God gives, the first one we are going to study is "STAND."

"Action?" you may say? Isn't standing a passive way of approaching a problem?

In several verses, standing comes with a preparation, deep resolve, and trust. Ephesians 6:13 says "...and after you have done everything...stand." You must get ready, daily, with the armor of God.

I Corinthians 16:13 says to "be on your guard." We must be watchful as we stand firm, not just twiddling our thumbs, waiting around.

Philippians 4:1 says, "that is how you should stand firm in the Lord, dear friends!" He is referring to keeping our mind on heavenly things, awaiting our final transformation with hope. There is nothing passive about that. It takes work to keep our minds on our heavenly citizenship rather than our earthly one.

God is calling all of us to stand—stand firm—stand prepared and watchful. I don't know what you are facing today? I just want to encourage you to put on your armor, be wise and watchful, and focus on your hope in Christ.

September 8

"I run in the path of your commands, for you have set my heart free."
Psalm 119:32 (NIV)

Some of my friends run marathons. I am always so impressed by their dedication and stamina. I also think they are a bit crazy. As they stay on the race's marked path, they inevitably "hit their wall" as they approach mile 13 (or 17 or 20). It is only with perseverance, determination, and the people on the sidelines cheering them on that they keep on going. There is always joy at the finish line!

In Psalm 119:32, the psalmist declares that he runs in the path of God's commands. Are you running in the path of God's commands today? It will set your heart free!

Hebrews 12:1 (one of my all-time favorites) tells us to "...run with perseverance the race marked out for us." Are you struggling with keeping on? Do you feel like dropping out of the race? Stick with it! It is so worth it! And remember what Christ did for you, so that you will not grow weary and lose heart (see Hebrews 12:3).

The Christian life is a long-distance race, not just a sprint. We WILL face trials (hit our walls), but the Author and Perfecter of our faith is beside us the entire way! You are NOT running alone.

How is your race going today? Are you leaping in joy or are you discouraged and bogged down? Either way, you will only go forward one step at a time. Grab a friend and go to coffee, or take a walk or a run together. Encourage each other along the way!

September 9

"If we walk in the light, as he is in the light, we have fellowship with one another, and the blood of Jesus, his Son, purifies us from all sin."
1 John 1:7 (NIV)

Today's action command is "walk." We are reminded throughout the Old and New Testament that we are to walk:

- By faith, not by sight (2 Corinthians 5:7)

- Humbly with our God (Micah 6:8)

- In good works that God has created for us to do (Ephesians 2:10)

- By the Spirit, not the flesh (Galatians 5:16)

- In God's ways (Zechariah 3:7)

- In newness of life (Romans 6:4)

That is a lot of walking for a lot of life. Oh, how these verses remind us that we need to stay grounded in God's Word. How can we be humble, know what God has prepared for us to do, remain in the Spirit, live by faith, and walk in the light if we are not immersing ourselves in God's Words for us.

What a gift He has given you to help you through this life! A personal letter from Him to you.

Claim His promises! Apply His truths! Obey His commands! Live according to His Word (Psalm 119:9).

September 10

"Now then, stand still and see this great thing the Lord is about to do before your eyes!" 1 Samuel 12:16 (NIV)

As we wrap up our study on God's marching orders to us, we are going to end with something that may be a little surprising—the command to "stand still."

As with the command to "stand," "stand still" is not passive, as it may seem at first glance. In Psalm 46:10, we read, "Be still, and know that I am God." This verse isn't written in the middle of a field of flowers with a sky filled with spotty clouds. It's not about being quiet when there is peace and stillness around us. This verse comes in the context of verses talking about war; it's about the uproar among nations and kingdoms and God's power and might.

We all go through daily battles of various kinds. It is good to slow down...stop...and contemplate our God. He is powerful, just, gracious, loving, sovereign, and kind. He is our refuge and strength, even when the mountains fall into the sea (see Psalm 46:1). He is our Peace in the middle of our storm, even when waves are raging around us.

Maybe being still for you means you are practicing patience. Psalm 37:7 says, "Be still before the Lord and wait patiently for Him." Waiting and being patient are probably my worst virtues. Yet, stewing and fretting over things out of my control doesn't get me anywhere. Resting patiently in the Lord focuses my energy in the right way.

Take a moment to be still before God today. Trust and believe in faith that He has your back and that He is God. Say a prayer of thanks that you don't have to be the one in charge! Exalt Him among the nations and in the earth! Watch what He is about to do!

September 11

"Oh, the depth of the riches of the wisdom and knowledge of God! How unsearchable his judgments, and his paths beyond tracing out."
Romans 11:33 (NIV)

God is the source of all knowledge and wisdom. A look at the narrative of love that consistently and powerfully runs from Genesis to Revelation is just one proof of His Divine Wisdom.

Then came Jesus, who is Wisdom Incarnate. He came from above and is "pure, peace-loving, considerate, submissive, full of mercy and good fruit, impartial and sincere" (James 3:17). We can learn wisdom from Him, have a relationship with Him, and strive to be more like Christ every day.

With all of that in mind, it is mind-boggling that, "If any of you lacks wisdom, you should ask God who gives generously to all without finding fault, and it will be given to you" (James 1:5). He has made His wisdom available to us. If we just ask, He will give generously. That's a request I pray every day.

God's incredible plan of salvation, His blueprint for Creation, and His wisdom and knowledge are so vast. He is the source, the Person, and the Giver of wisdom. What else can we do but fall on our face before Him, and ask for His wisdom to fill our minds? What an incredible gift!

September 12

"God is not unjust; he will not forget your work and the love you have shown him as you have helped his people and continue to help them."
Hebrews 6:10 (NIV)

We were on our way to church for the 3rd or 4th time that week. Sometimes we went to help out in a specific ministry. Other times we were going to support the ministry with our presence. Sometimes it was preparation for something to come—worship team rehearsal, set-up for an event, or a planning meeting. It seemed a bit much! I wanted to turn around and go home for a nap.

Do you sometimes feel like you're going through the motions...that nobody really cares or sees what you are doing? Whether at work, at home, in the community, or in your church, it can be difficult to keep on keeping on, especially when it feels like it's in vain.

Here's what God says on the subject: "God is not unjust; he will not forget your work and the love you have shown him as you have helped his people and continue to help them" Hebrews 6:10.

He sees; He takes note; He does not forget what you are doing. And whether or not anyone else takes notice, we are a blessing to God when we help others. We are His, and we are showing Him love when we help His people.

Of course we need boundaries. We need to learn to say "no" to some things so we can be more effective in others. But I hope that this is motivation for today for you to keep serving and working...for God!

September 13

"But the wisdom that comes from heaven is first of all pure; then peace-loving, considerate, submissive, full of mercy and good fruit, impartial and sincere." James 3:17 (NIV)

A couple of days ago (September 11), we looked at James 1:5 which encourages us to ask God for wisdom because He is so rich in it (Romans 11:33) and will give it to us generously.

Today we will look at wisdom from the perspective of James 3:17: "But the wisdom that comes from heaven is first of all pure; then peace-loving, considerate, submissive, full of mercy and good fruit, impartial and sincere." (NIV)

This list reminds me of the fruit of the spirit (Galatians 5:22-23). It makes me realize that wisdom is not about what we know but about what we sow.

So, here's this week's wisdom test. If you are seeking God's wisdom in the decision you are making or the problem you are facing, you should be at peace. You should be treating others involved with mercy, impartiality, consideration, and humility.

God wants to build your integrity, not just your intellect. How'd you do? Are you passing the wisdom test? God will help you!

September 14

"But we have this treasure in jars of clay..." 2 Corinthians 4:7a (NIV)

We live in jars of clay (2 Corinthians 4:7), and as someone once said, "I'm just a cracked pot."

Life is hard. We suffer physical, emotional, and spiritual hardships because we live in a fallen, broken world.

All this fragility seems hopeless. But God said, "My grace is sufficient for you, for my power is made perfect in weakness." (2 Corinthians 12:9)

Our pastor posed this question a few Sundays ago: Are you going to choose to be a victim or choose to receive sufficient grace?

We can go around blaming everyone and everything else for our problems, and listen to Satan's voice about how futile life is. OR

We can let God complete what He wants to do in our lives, focusing on our dependence on Him, even if all the flaws are not removed.

God's grace and mercy is new every morning (Lamentations 3:22-23) and is proportionate to our need. God knows what we need, and He extends His grace to us. The caveat is that we have to be willing to receive it. Just as the children of Israel had to gather their manna each morning (Exodus 16:4), we must do the work of gathering the goodness that God has made available to us.

Friend, His grace is sufficient for YOU today. Let Him take your weakness and show you His strength! Let His light shine through the cracks in your jars of clay.

September 15

"For we are God's masterpiece. He has created us anew in Christ Jesus, so we can do the things he planned for us long ago."
Ephesians 2:10 (NLT)

Yesterday, I talked about how we are cracked pots, jars of clay, that God wants to use for His glory. He becomes our perfect strength in the midst of our weakness.

To further illustrate this point, there is a Japanese art called Kintsugi. In this art, they repair broken pottery with lacquer, dusted with gold, silver, or platinum. Something beautiful results out of the broken pieces.

You are God's masterpiece (Ephesians 2:10), His Kintsugi. He takes your past, your present, your brokenness, and your failures. He covers you with His blood mingled with His love, grace, and peace. Your broken pot becomes a true work of art, ready for usefulness in His kingdom.

No matter what you have been through, you can count on the Living Creative God to heal and mend your hurts. Go and live out His purpose for you!

September 16

"Why are you downcast, O my soul? Why so disturbed within me? Put your hope in God, for I will yet praise him, my Savior and my God."
Psalm 42:11 (NIV)

There was a particular year in teaching that I will never forget. I had a really rough class. It took everything within me just to show up. I would drive to work feeling downcast and discouraged. My only hope was in God, so I praised Him all the way to school. I would crank up worship music and declare Scripture over my day.

Some days it feels like God is silent. Our souls cry out for God and we ask Him why we have this turmoil within us (Psalm 42:11). The Psalmist knew this type of desperation, but instead of drawing away, He drew near to God. He told Him how he was feeling. He longed for God as the deer pants for water (Psalm 42:1). He remembered God's goodness in the past—His salvation, His love, His steadfastness (Psalm 42:4). This brought him to a place of hope once again.

We may not understand the times of seeming silence and despair, but we can trust in God's character. We can cry out to Him, seek Him, and remember His goodness. We can put our hope in God and praise Him. He is the lifter of our heads, our Rock and our Salvation.

September 17

"But to you who are listening I say: Love your enemies, do good to those who hate you." Luke 6:27 (NIV)

I love how God's Word complements itself. The other day, I read two seemingly unrelated, separate scriptures:

"Rejoice with those who rejoice; mourn with those who mourn" Romans 12:15.

"...Love your enemies! Do good to those who hate you" Luke 6:27.

They both reminded me that we are not meant to do life solo. We are to share each other's burdens, joys, and hurts. We are to respond to mistreatment or differing viewpoints with a blessing.

Both of these verses spurred me to some action steps. I wrote some cards to some of my Bible study ladies to encourage them in the Lord. I wrote a couple of texts to some people in my life who are not believers but who I needed to bless.

I don't always do things right, but this particular day, the directive was pretty clear.

Who do you need to encourage or bless today? Get out some notecards or your phone, and let God speak to and through you!

September 18

"So in everything, do to others what you would have them do to you, for this sums up the Law and the Prophets." Matthew 7:12 (NIV)

How do you react when someone cuts you off, says something horrible about you or to you, or does something that is just plain mean? I know my first response is always to defend myself or get back in some way.

A few years ago, I heard this quote that helped me deal with conflict: "Hurt people hurt people."

Instead of lashing back at them, maybe we could be like Christ and pay attention to their hurts, needs, and interests. I don't think we need to let people walk all over us, but we can certainly begin to turn the tide when we tune in and listen, showing them we care. If it is impossible to have a civil conversation with them, we can certainly pray for them, asking God to heal their hurt.

The converse of that statement is also true: "Healed people heal people." You see, when the love of God has cleansed you and changed you into a new creation, you are poised to be a blessing and help others who are in pain.

Let these thoughts help you in your daily interactions and prayer life. Be in the business of healing, not hurting.

September 19

"...because you know that the testing of your faith produces perseverance." James 1:3 (NIV)

Some people are workout junkies. They live to go to the gym. They are constantly thinking about their physical health. They take good care of their muscles by stretching them, pushing them to certain limits, and pounding them out through muscle massage. They understand what it means to build muscles.

Whether you are a workout junky or not, this makes spiritual sense: "...What God does with our faith must be something like workouts. He sees to it that our faith gets pushed and pulled, stretched, and pounded, taken to its limits so its limits can expand." If you have ever wondered why God tests your faith, it's so that it can strengthen and grow.

If you feel like you are being stretched and pulled in your faith right now, take courage! God is expanding your spiritual faith muscles. He wants you to learn perseverance and trust. He wants you to learn to consider it joy when you face trials.

Do a faith work out today. Thank God for His faithfulness as you face your current trial. Let Him know that you are grateful that He is your Heavenly Trainer, as you are joyfully strengthened in your faith over the next few weeks, months, or years.

September 20

"Do all things without grumbling or disputing, that you may be blameless and innocent children of God without blemish in the midst of a crooked and twisted generation, among whom you shine as lights in the world."
Philippians 2:14-15 (ESV)

What an inconvenience! A delayed flight was announced as we arrived at our airport check-in. What were we going to do now?

I love how this author and philosopher put it: "An adventure is only an inconvenience rightly considered. An inconvenience is only an adventure wrongly considered" (G. K. Chesterton).

Life is filled with choices and perspectives. When things aren't going the way we planned, we can grumble and complain, or we can roll with the punches and see where our circumstance leads us. Who is being put in our path that wouldn't otherwise be there? What lesson is God teaching us?

Our adventure that day was that I got to meet someone who was in line with us trying to figure out her schedule. She was much more stressed because she needed to be at the destination for a business meeting. As we talked, I silently prayed for her.

Thinking we'd never see each other again, what a surprise to find her in the seat right next to me on the return flight home ten days later. We had a chance to share our "adventures" and we ended up praying together before the flight landed. (There's much more to this story in *Solid Ground,* Chapter 6.)

So how will you think of your next snafu in plans: An inconvenience or an adventure? A frustration or an opportunity? A chance to grumble or a chance to shine?

September 21

"Love is patient, love is kind. It does not envy, it does not boast, it is not proud." 1 Corinthians 13:4 (NIV)

There was a commercial for Alka Seltzer in the early 1970's that claimed, "Try it. You'll like it!" The advertisers were promoting their product as a relief for all your stomach acid woes. The result of not using the "plop, plop, fizz, fizz" product was portrayed as something akin to misery.

We often encounter people who have a view of Christianity that keeps them from wanting anything to do with Jesus or the church? Unfortunately, they are missing out on so much, and we can see their ultimate misery. If they would only try it, we lament, they would like it! Even more, they would receive the grace, love, peace, and joy that only our Savior can give!

G. K. Chesterton, an English writer and Christian apologist said it this way, "The Christian ideal has not been tried and found wanting. It has been found difficult and left untried."

May we live in such a way that the "Christian ideal" is so attractive to others that they want to know the reason for our hope (1 Peter 3:15). Doing everything packaged in love (1 Corinthians 13) will at the least, get them curious. When we have the opportunity to live out and share what Christ has done for them, it will open the doors for them to accept what Christ has done for them. Oh, what a relief it will be!

September 22

"This, then is how you should pray: 'Our Father in heaven, hallowed be your name..." Matthew 6:9 (NIV)

I hate to admit it, but I feel like my prayer life is lacking. I start praying and get distracted. I have no problem reading God's Word and meditating on it through journaling, but I usually stop there. I realize that communicating with God in this way is a type of prayer, but I want to be a better intercessor for others' needs. I want to be able to place my day and my future in God's hands in a much more intentional way.

So, I'm working on it. This past year, we had a sermon series on prayer. At the same time, I was going through a Bible study about praying through the Psalms. It is something I guess I will continue to work on throughout my earthly existence.

I've known people who set a chair next to them and speak to it as though Christ were sitting there. I've done that in the car when I'm driving somewhere by myself. I will imagine Jesus is sitting in the car with me, and we have a conversation.

Why is prayer so important? Here is what Oswald Chambers says: "...Prayer doesn't fit us for the greater work, prayer is the greater work."

In those times when I feel in tune with the Spirit as I walk and talk with God, I believe God is doing His great work within me. My soul rests and my focus remains on the One who matters most. Prayer is working smarter, not harder.

How is your prayer life? God even welcomes our questions about how we should pray? He wants us to commune with Him!

September 23

"I have hidden your word in my heart that I might not sin against you."
Psalm 119:11 (NIV)

The amplified version of this verse says, I have "treasured and stored" God's Word.

When we hide something in our hearts we are storing and treasuring it so that at just the right moment, we can draw on its truth. In this case, there is a cache of Biblical ammo ready for us to use to fight sin when temptation comes.

One of my temptations is to show myself disrespect as God's creation by being defeated, allowing others' words to crush me or letting my failures define me. The treasures stored for this purpose remind me of my identity in Christ.

Do you hide God's word in your heart? Do you truly treasure it and store it in that deep inner place where it can spring to life when you need it? It takes intentionality. Here are a few ways I have attempted to stay connected to God's Word:

- Memorization
- Sticky note with a verse written on it and taped to my mirror, dashboard, or kitchen counter (sometimes all three)
- Worship music, especially songs with Scripture embedded
- Daily quiet time with God

Whatever you do, however you do it, treasure God's Word each day!

September 24

"How can a young person stay on the path of purity? By living according to your word" Psalm 119:9 (NIV)

Does it sometimes seem like an impossibility for a young person to stay on the right path in our culture? I can get very anxious as I pray for my grandkids, knowing some of the philosophies and ungodly ideals that are thrown at them as though they are normal and right.

The writer of Psalm 119 had some of these very same thoughts. He penned this question/answer couplet: "How can a young person stay on the path of purity? By living according to your word" Psalm 119:9 (NIV).

I know this to be true in my own life. I have to stay in God's word to know what He approves of and thinks. Without connecting to God every day, I have no spiritual power, no way to stay on the right path.

Pray this prayer with me today for the young people in your life?

Lord, it is tough to stay pure and keep on Your path. We know it is impossible to do without staying connected to You and Your Word. We pray today for those young people who are in our lives who face so many conflicting messages about what is right and wrong. Lord, make your Word come alive for them. Help them to care more about Your approval than the approval of people. Give them spiritual strength for each day, and help me to pray without ceasing for them. Amen.

September 25

"I am still confident of this: I will see the goodness of the Lord in the land of the living" Psalm 27:13 (NIV).

Psalm 27 is an amazing Psalm of David. He declares the Lord as his light and salvation, knowing and believing that God will protect him from his enemies. He rehearses the goodness of God—his beauty, His sheltering, His foundational dwelling place, His help, and His faithfulness, to name a few. (Let me encourage you to read the entire Psalm on your own.)

All this time, He is in the middle of the fray, not knowing or seeing how God is going to fix things. Then David inserts this statement: "I am still confident in this: I will see the goodness of the Lord in the land of the living" Psalm 27:13 (NIV).

We can have that kind of faith in our desperate circumstances as well. Even when we can't see how God is working for our good, we can choose to see and rejoice in His present goodness while we are waiting.

What can you thank God for right now, even if you are in the middle of waiting for His answer? Pen it into your journal, or make up a song and sing it to God. Look for His goodness!

September 26

"But from everlasting to everlasting the Lord's love is with those who fear him, and his righteousness with their children's children—with those who keep his covenant and remember to obey his precepts."
Psalm 103:17-18 (NIV).

We are called to share God's love and righteousness with the generations that come after us. Remembering and obeying are two specific ways we can leave a lasting legacy. David shares a couple of practical points with us in the key verse for today.

When we obey God's laws, we are modeling for our kids and grandkids how to live a righteous life. They watch and listen more than we realize—

- How we react to the other drivers on the road
- What we do when we have been given too much change back from the clerk at the store
- How we treat our spouse
- What we do when faced with a problem

We can "remember" out loud all the things God has done and is doing. When we are together as a family, build conversations around—

- God's answers to prayer
- The beauty and awe of His creation
- Their unique identity in Christ
- How God helped you through a trial or temptation

We all want the Lord's love and righteousness to be with us and with our children's children. Pray this Psalm over yourself and your loved ones each day, and commit to obeying and remembering God's teachings.

September 27

"In God, whose word I praise, in God I trust; I will not be afraid. What can mortal man to do me?" Psalm 56:4 (NIV)

We can praise God's word because it is ageless, enduring, and relevant to all languages and cultures. It is stable, constant, and forever loving.

We can trust in God because of His Word. Even if we feel attacked, we know that our God is greater than any mortal man. He has defeated death and Satan through the resurrection of His Son, Jesus.

We live in a society plagued by fear. They worry about what might happen if their family falls apart, if they experience financial failure, if the nation goes to war, or if a natural disaster occurs. We do not need to be consumed with these thoughts. God has comforted us with His words over and over again: Do not be afraid. I am with you! (Isaiah 41:10; Deuteronomy 3:22; Joshua 1:9; Isaiah 43:5; Jeremiah 30:10-11).

Walk in this truth today: God is with you! You do not need to be afraid. You can live a life of victory!

Praise God. Praise His Word. Trust His faithful deliverance.

September 28

"The discerning heart seeks knowledge, but the mouth of a fool feeds on folly." Proverbs 15:14 (NIV)

Martin Luther once stated, "You can't keep the birds from flying over your head, but you can keep them from building a nest in your house."

Proverbs 15:14 says it this way, "The discerning heart seeks knowledge, but the mouth of a fool feeds on folly." (NIV)

Another translation says, "A wise person is hungry for knowledge, while the fool feeds on trash." (NLT)

Rick Warren commented that we can't control what thoughts come into our heads, but we can control what we do with them. In regards to what we watch he asks, "Are you hungry for more knowledge of God, or are you content to keep a steady diet of entertainment that breaks his heart?"

It's not always easy, but we need to guard our hearts and minds from the constant barrage of foolishness that is thrown at us every day. The best way to do that is to fill our minds with the Truth of God's Word.

September 29

"He replied, 'Because you have so little faith, I tell you the truth, if you have faith as small as a mustard seed, you can say to this mountain, 'Move from here to there,' and it will move. Nothing will be impossible for you.'" Matthew 17:20 (NIV)

Do you know how big a mustard seed is? They are the tiniest of seeds. They measure about 1 ½ to 2 mm (approximately 0.05 inches) in diameter.

Jesus prefaced this statement with "Because you have so little faith, Truly I tell you…" He concluded by saying "Nothing will be impossible for you."

He recognized the puniness of our faith, especially in lieu of the power that is available to us. In essence He was saying, "It's not the size of your faith that matters but where you put your faith that makes the difference."

I met a beautiful lady at a retreat one weekend. She shared with me how God had taken her into some hills a short distance from her home. She had always thought of those hills as mountains. Looking from a distance they appeared much larger than they were. When she traveled to them, they were hardly even hills. She kept saying, "Where is the mountain? There is no mountain!"

God spoke that same message to her heart regarding her "mountain" of meth. He whispered to her, "There is no mountain! Meth is not a mountain for Me and My power!" She was freed from her addiction! Praise to the Lord.

Do you have mustard seed faith for something in your life right now? Ask God. He can move mountains! Nothing is impossible with God!

September 30

"A fool gives full vent to his anger, but a wise man keeps himself under control." Proverbs 29:11 (NIV)

It's not a sin to be angry, but we can become angry in our sin (Ephesians 4:26). Even Jesus was righteously angry at the misuse of God's temple (Mark 11:15-17). It's what we do with our anger that makes a difference. We especially need to be careful and keep under control the words we say. They cannot be taken back once they have spewed forth.

One author put it this way, "Put your mind in gear before you put your mouth in motion."

Oh, how I need to remember this!

The last fruit of the Spirit listed in Galatians 5:22-23 is self-control. A Bible teacher that I loved and respected often said that she thought self-control should have come first. If we maintained self-control, all the other fruit would fall into place.

I want to be wise. I want to show self-control with my mouth, my anger, my frustrations. It can only happen with the help of the Holy Spirit as I surrender my emotions to Him!

October 1

> "Being confident of this, that he who began a good work in you will carry it on to completion, until the day of Christ Jesus."
> Philippians 1:6 (NIV)

Have you ever started a big project, only to put off finishing it? It's always so satisfying when we finally come back to it and complete the job we started.

We never have to worry about God putting us aside to finish later. He is working on us all the time, transforming, refining, and molding us into His perfect purpose.

We might try to get our motivation for changing or improving ourselves from books or seminars. We might have lots of trainings at our job or be pursuing higher education to better ourselves. However, our true motivation for "becoming" is found in God's Word. He promises us so many wonderful things!

Today, focus on the fact that you are a work in progress. Do not get discouraged if you don't feel like you have made it yet, whether that means work, or tasks, or character development. Keep hoping in the Lord for your guidance and strength and power to move forward.

Remember (and be confident in this): He who began a good work in you will carry it on to completion until the day of Christ Jesus (Philippians 1:6).

October 2

"There is a time for everything, and a season for every activity under heaven;" Ecclesiastes 3:1 (NIV)

It's already October! Fall has begun, and we are starting to actually get some cooler weather. In some parts of the country the leaves are turning into beautiful yellows, reds, and oranges.

I am so thankful for the change of seasons. It is always a reminder to me of the work that God does in our own lives.

Fall represents that time of year when we are ready for harvest. We have done the hard work of planting and maintaining the soil. The seeds have sprouted, ripened to maturity, and we can reap bountiful fruit.

Maybe it's coincidental, but I published my first two books in the fall. It seemed fitting that I was reaping the "harvest" of all those hours of interviews, writing, and editing.

Our lives do not necessarily follow the timing of the natural seasons. You might be in a summer or winter season right now. Just know the harvest is coming! Winter might look like weeping and mourning. Summer may be the time to heal and build. Your spring most likely is a time of planting seeds for your future.

Lean into whatever season you are in at this time in your life. God has a purpose for each one.

October 3

> "And this is my prayer: that your love may abound more and more in knowledge and depth of insight, so that you may be able to discern what is best and may be pure and blameless until the day of Christ, filled with the fruit of righteousness that comes through Jesus Christ—to the glory and praise of God." Philippians 1:9-11 (NIV)

I do not know who you are. I'm not sure why you decided to pick up this book and read this devotional today. I do know this—God loves you and I am praying Philippians 1:9-11 with you in mind.

I have prayed this prayer over my children and grandchildren many times. I may be the only one standing in the gap for them (Ezekiel 22:30). You may need someone to stand in the gap for you as well.

Receive this today. I thank God for you. Though I may not be able to call you by name, I will pray for you, Beloved Reader. I pray that you will have a knowledge of God's love that will reach to your very heart and soul. I pray that as you gain insight into God's Word and the sacrifice Christ made for you on the cross, that you would also gain discernment.

My prayer continues that you would know with certainty that you are saved, pure and blameless because of the blood of Christ that covered your sins. As you persist to live a life of righteousness, I pray that your work and ministry would be fruitful and successful. I pray that your relationships with friends and family would also bear the fruit of your steadfastness and faithfulness to the Savior.

I thank God for you!

October 4

"For we do not have a high priest who is unable to sympathize with our weaknesses, but we have one who has been tempted in every way, just as we are—yet was without sin." Hebrews 4:15 (NIV)

I have read the gospels many times, but for the first time last week, a phrase stood out to me that I hadn't seen before. After Jesus fasted for forty days in the desert, the devil came and tempted Him. I always just thought, Jesus was a victor, He stood up to the devil, the end. One and done!

In Luke's account, however, it says that "When the devil had finished all this tempting, he left him until an opportune time" (Luke 4:13).

Even though it wasn't recorded for our eyes to read, this verse indicates that Satan continued to find moments when Jesus was tired or frustrated or hungry to try to thwart His ministry.

This new insight gave me a new hope and understanding of the passage in Hebrews 4:15. Jesus knew what it was like to be tempted as a human. He did not sin, but He completely understands what we are going through. He understands how hard it is to resist temptation. He empathized so much with us that He made a way out (1 Corinthians 10:13).

Satan's temptation tactics don't change up much. He preys on our weaknesses and tries to cater his sales pitch to our particular situation, but God is faithful and will help by providing a way out. I hope this brings you encouragement and hope as today.

October 5

"Do not be anxious about anything, but in everything, by prayer and petition, with thanksgiving, present your requests to God. And the peace of God, which transcends all understanding, will guard your hearts and your minds in Christ Jesus." Philippians 4:6-7 (NIV)

To be anxious about nothing is a tall order, but it is what we are admonished to do. The great thing is, we are given the way to make that happen.

When the writer of Philippians, inspired by God, told us to not be anxious about anything, it can be assumed he knew we would all feel anxiety. So when we start to spiral into that worry whirlwind, we are to bring everything, by prayer and petition, with thanksgiving, to God.

Prayer—Communicate with God—repent of your worry; let Him know how you are feeling; seek His wisdom and His will

Petition—Request for God to hear and answer your specific need. Remember to pray for His will. He will align your will with His over the course of time.

Thanksgiving—Give praise to God. Let Him know how much you love Him. Thank Him for working in your life. Thank Him for the answer in advance.

Anxiety and prayer are two opposing forces. When you add in a dose of thanksgiving, you have the antidote to worry. Tell Him everything and let His peace fill your heart. It works! Try it! Write out or say a prayer, giving your current anxieties to God.

October 6

"This is the day the Lord has made; let us rejoice and be glad in it."
Psalm 118:24 (NIV)

There is a special holiday for just about every day of the year. I'm not sure who declares these special days, but I'm usually the last to know. I missed son and daughter day last month. (Sorry boys!)

My coffee app let me know when it was National Coffee Day, and I had the opportunity for a few free cups.

I looked today's date up, just for fun. Here are a few of the crazy ones. Today is:

- Change A Light Day
- Mad Hatter Day
- National Badger Day
- National Coaches Day
- National Noodle Day
- National Transfer Money to Your Daughter Day
- World Cerebral Palsy Day

I think it's fun to celebrate. If none of these resonates with you, go ahead and make it National You Day. Do something nice for yourself. Better yet, do something nice for someone else. Believe it or not, we get more fulfillment in giving than receiving.

Maybe you can change a light for someone else, or do something special for a coach in your life. Whatever you decide to do today, remember that the Lord made this day, and we have many reasons to rejoice and celebrate.

October 7

"Jesus called them together and said, 'You know that the rulers of the Gentiles lord it over them, and their high officials exercise authority over them. Not so with you. Instead, whoever wants to become great among you must be your servant, and whoever wants to be first must be your slave—just as the Son of Man did not come to be served, but to serve, and to give his life as a ransom for many.'" Matthew 20:25-28 (NIV)

A few decades ago, our church choir performed a musical called *The Witness*. It was the story of Jesus' life and ministry leading up to the crucifixion and resurrection.

I played the mother of the sons of Zebedee who went to Jesus to request that her sons would be seated at the right and left of the throne in His Kingdom. The song I sang was called "My Boys," and the character was pleading the case for her sons.

In one of the performances, the character playing James sat back on the block. I can't remember if the wooden prop splintered and broke or if he just lost his balance and fell backwards, but it was an impromptu moment in the play. We all laughed and went on with the script.

We chuckle at this Biblical scenario, but we are not all that different. We want to receive accolades and rewards for our service and good works, whether we admit it out loud or not.

Jesus' words are as true today as they were back then. We are here to serve, not to be served. If we can just get a handle on that, our "witness" in this world will be powerful.

Who can you serve today? Your family, your neighbors, someone in need? Pray for God to show you His heart.

October 8

"'What do you want me to do for you?' Jesus asked him. The blind man said, 'Rabbi, I want to see.'" Mark 10:51 (NIV)

Toward the end of his ministry, Jesus was walking on the road to Jericho. A blind man heard that Jesus was coming, and he began to call out, "Jesus, Son of David, have mercy on me!"

He would not be silenced by the crowd. He just called out louder. Soon Jesus called for him to come near. It seems obvious, but Jesus asked the **blind** man what he wanted Him to do for him.

He said, "I want to see!" and Jesus healed him. It was immediate and miraculous. After living the life of a beggar for so long, perhaps Bartimaeus didn't know what else to do, but the Bible tells us he received his sight and followed Jesus along the road.

It should be obvious what we want as well. We should want to be able to see, not just physically, but spiritually. Paul understood this and prayed for all of us:

"I pray that the eyes of your heart may be enlightened in order that you may know the hope to which he has called you, the riches of his glorious inheritance in his holy people." Ephesians 1:18 (NIV)

That is my prayer today for you and for myself. "Lord, help us to see, and be so grateful for the hope that you give us that we follow you, fully and completely."

October 9

> "Ask the Lord of the harvest, therefore, to send out workers into his harvest field." Matthew 9:38 (NIV)

I have mentioned it before, but it bears repeating. I love baptism Sundays. A couple of years ago we had a young girl (around 10), an older gentleman, and a young adult man give their testimonies and get baptized. It was a lifter of my faith to hear of new commitments to a life with Jesus and watch them solidify their commitment with the ritual of baptism.

Later that day we got to attend the induction of a pastor into his first church. This man had been at our church for many years and was now answering a call to preach. We get to send him and his family out to continue God's work.

At a more recent baptism service, we were on vacation, so we watched it on line. I later heard that there were fifteen new commitments to faith in Christ from that service. Not coincidentally, there were fifteen baptism candidates.

God continues to seek and call new believers and send workers into the world to spread the gospel. Are you as excited as I am? He is not finished with us yet! And He invites us to be participants in His harvest as co-workers with Him (1 Corinthians 3:9).

October 10

> "I remember the days of long ago; I meditate on all your works and consider what your hands have done." Psalm 143:5 (NIV)

I was talking to a friend the other day. We were talking about the importance of looking back on our lives to remember the good things God has done.

It's not that we dwell in the past, but when we forget what He's done in the past, we tend to doubt or forget that He is just as capable in the present.

My friend talked about how the Israelites had a history of looking back on the stories of the past from generation to generation in order to move forward. He called it, "Backing into the future."

Another way to think about it is that remembering the past helps us trust in the present and have hope for the future.

As you move forward today, what can you look back on in your life that you are thankful for?

I'll start: I'm am grateful for God leading us and guiding us to live in Bakersfield. Who would have guessed this would be my home for so many years? Even though Bakersfield often gets a bad rap because of its extreme heat and unique culture, God knew where we needed to call home, and it has been His perfect place for us to work, minister, and raise our family.

Your turn—journal your thanksgiving as you reflect on God's faithfulness in the past.

October 11

> "Humble yourselves, therefore, under God's mighty hand, that he may lift you up in due time. Cast all your anxiety on him because he cares for you." 1 Peter 5:6-7 (NIV)

Did you know that our problems and pain are really blessings in disguise? If you didn't feel any pain, you would not realize you needed to see a doctor. You might never get diagnosed or find out a problem that can be fixed with modern medicine. Our problems are often caused by something that has a deeper root, and only when complications arise do we dig around to find the source.

The other day, we were watching TV. My husband detected a high-pitched sound that I couldn't hear. Upon investigating, we discovered that a filter in the rear of our refrigerator had split and water was spewing everywhere. It was already leaving a puddle, but we were able to turn off the valve and clean up the excess liquid. Later that evening, we held hands and prayed a prayer of Thanksgiving. What if we had gone to bed without noticing it? We would have had quite a different problem on our hands! The sound and the puddle of water were warning signs to help us take care of something that could have been so much bigger.

My friend, Chris, who has his story in *Higher Ground,* realized that being hospitalized for Covid-19 was what allowed the doctor to discover that he had multiple myeloma. The detection allowed him to begin receiving treatments that would have otherwise been very delayed.

God cares about the minute details of our lives. Instead of complaining when something seems to be going wrong, we need to ask what God is trying to reveal to us. What could this be an indicator of? Small or big, He is showing you that He cares about the intricacies of your life.

October 12

"After that, we who are still alive and are left will be caught up together with them in the clouds to meet the Lord in the air. And so we will be with the Lord forever. Therefore encourage each other with these words." 1 Thessalonians 4:17-18 (NIV)

I was supposed to go to Kansas to celebrate a friend's 60th birthday**. Unfortunately, life got in the way and I had to cancel my trip. My friend had cancer, and it appeared that her days were numbered without divine intervention and healing. I was so excited to be observing her milestone year.

The party went on without me. I enjoyed it through photos and a Happy Birthday call.

We have to miss things some times. I think often of all the celebrations that were postponed, altered, or completely canceled during 2020 and the pandemic restrictions—weddings, graduations, proms, camps, retreats...

You know what the good news is? We will have eternity to celebrate together. Believers in Jesus get to look forward to an eternal party and feast. Are you ready? The hope and grace of Jesus is for all who accept Him as their Savior. I so want to see you there some day.

**My friend was able to visit us before Christmas that year. It was amazing to spend time with her. She has passed since then, making that time together even more precious. It also is one more person I can't wait to see again in Heaven!

October 13

"There is no fear in love. But perfect love drives out fear, because fear has to do with punishment. The one who fears is not made perfect in love." 1 John 4:18 (NIV)

Love is a great motivator. I recently attended my husband's 50th high school reunion. I wasn't looking forward to sitting around a group of people I didn't know. The day before the reunion, I read Ephesians 1:4 that said God chose us before the world was even created. I was reminded that my identity didn't depend on what my husband's former classmates thought of me. My identity is who I am in Christ. (It's rather embarrassing to admit that I'm still concerned about what people think of me at my age!)

The bottom line is that I went with a different attitude than I had originally pondered. I actually had a good time and looked for other people who were not talking to anyone, engaging them in conversation. It was very freeing!

First John 4:18 tells us that there is no fear in love. Love casts out fear! Is there something you are fearing or dreading? Remember who you are in Christ. He will get you through the experience without fear or timidity. Don't look to the world to define you. Look to the Word!

October 14

"Then he said to them, 'The Sabbath was made for man, not man for the Sabbath.'" Mark 2:27 (NIV)

The other day some of our relatives drove down the state of California from the San Francisco airport. It was mid-day, but they still ran into a lot of traffic. Much of the way it was stop-and-go. It took them about 6 hours, and that was after a 4-hour flight. By the time they reached us, they were spent physically and mentally. We had dinner, and then they went to bed.

On the way back to the airport a week later, they decided to take a scenic highway. They took in the beauty of the California coast. Their car kept moving even though it was a little slower paced. The trip took just under 5 hours, but they were much more relaxed when they arrived in plenty of time at the airport.

Our life journeys are a little like that. Sometimes we are in hectic stop-and-go traffic. We just can't seem to get traction in our jobs, our families, or in our ministries. We feel exhausted and discouraged. God wants us to slow down and take the scenic route. He wants us to slow life down. When we do that, we recognize the beauty along the path, and we enjoy a sense of refreshment. We can spend time with Jesus, praising Him for the beauty surrounding us.

I'm sure that is part of the reason God established the Sabbath. By Jesus' time on earth, the Jews had put so many requirements and restrictions for keeping the Sabbath that the burden of keeping the Sabbath had lost its effectiveness. We can take Sabbath rest throughout the day, not just at the end of the week. Take a few moments here and there to stop and smell the coffee, or the roses, or whatever aroma speaks to your heart. Slow down your pace and appreciate the people and privileges in your life. Sabbath was made for you!

October 15

"The Lord is close to the brokenhearted and saves those who are crushed in spirit." Psalm 34:18 (NIV)

God's Word is alive and active! Something you read one day can speak to you in a completely different way another day. Sometimes the message hits because of a distinct time or circumstance you are going through at the moment.

During our fresh time of grief, several people shared this verse with my husband and me. Psalm 34:18 says, "The Lord is close to the brokenhearted and saves those who are crushed in spirit."

When you are grieving, these two words, "brokenhearted" and "crushed," are perfect descriptors. As we waded through our new reality with our son being gone, the weight of this truth was suppressing. We were brokenhearted. We felt crushed by the circumstances.

The promise here is that the Lord is close! He never left our sides. He comforted and continues to comfort us, showing up in little and big ways. Sometimes it was through His people, sometimes through His Word, sometimes through a gift or quote; many times it was through the beauty of nature.

Whatever sorrow you are facing, have faced, or will face, God is there! He will draw close to you. We are so grateful for His presence. You can be comforted by His closeness as well.

October 16

> "I lift up my eyes to the hills—where does my help come from? My help comes from the Lord, the Maker of heaven and earth."
> Psalm 121:1-2 (NIV)

During the summer of 2022, we were surprised to see the mountains around our town. When we would walk in the morning or drive out to visit my mother-in-law in her skilled nursing facility, it just seemed like the hills were extra vibrant. A typical summer around Bakersfield is hazy and hot. The smog from all the northern California cities settles around the base of the three mountain ranges that border us on the south, east, and west. We can almost never see the mountains. The blazing heat seems to make it worse.

But here we were, in the middle of July, and even into August. I remember making the comment about how grateful I was to be able to look to the hills and actually see their beauty. And then, our world was turned upside down.

Almost immediately, when we got word that our son was in ICU in San Diego, I thought of those hills and the verse from Psalm 121:1-2. "I lift up my eyes to the hills—where does my help come from? My help comes from the Lord, the Maker of heaven and earth."

We immediately went to the Lord. We petitioned for Him to save our son's life. We cried out to the Maker of heaven and earth, the Creator of our human bodies and souls. We don't know why God chose to not heal him on this Earth. We do know that He is completely free of any chains, bondage, illness, disease—fully healed in Heaven.

We continue to seek the Lord. We thank Him for the years we had with our boy. We seek His face to help us and his little family to get through this somehow. We know God will do it. He is faithful. He is where our help comes from!

October 17

"My grace is sufficient for you, for my power is made perfect in weakness." 2 Corinthians 12:9a

One of the ways my weaknesses are manifested is when I get a migraine. They used to come much more often. I take a preventative medicine once a month, but I still get an occasional one. When I have one of those headaches, I really feel limited, incapacitated, and inadequate.

There have been a few times when I have had to power through the pain because we had company or an event I couldn't get out of. God is always there to help me through those challenges. He wants me to experience Him in a new and complete way.

As I have learned to rely on Christ, I have come to see that weakness is not a sign of God's cruelty but a reminder of His kindness. He wants to be with me as I admit my weakness and glory in the fact that He is God. It's at my weakest points, I become more aware of God's limitless and infinite resources, abilities, and energy.

My friends, we live in a broken world. None of us are perfect. None of us are God (thank goodness!). When we can grasp the fact that our weaknesses are the perfect place to experience God's power, we will be quicker to accept His help and sufficient grace!

Come to Him in holy humility today. His power will be made perfect in your weakness!

October 18

"God, whom I serve with my whole heart in preaching the gospel of his Son, is my witness how constantly I remember you in my prayers at all times; and I pray that now at last by God's will the way may be opened for me to come to you." Romans 1:9-10 (NIV)

The apostle Paul was always praying for the churches he helped establish. In Romans 1:9-10 he says, "I remember you in my prayers at all times." His desire was to be able to come back to visit them again, see them face-to-face, if it was God's will.

We have been the recipients of this kind of prayer. When we were going through our son's life-and-death ordeal, over and over again, my husband or I would receive texts from literally hundreds of our friends letting us know they were in constant prayer. Some would pray through the night. Others would wake up praying, or they would think of us throughout the day. Many said they wished they could do something for us. They would say something like, "All I know to do is pray." My response was always, "If you are praying, you ARE doing the greatest thing you can possibly do."

Even after our son was gone, people continued (and still continue) to lift us in prayer. I was pretty sure my women's group had orchestrated a schedule in which I would get an encouraging note and prayer each day for several weeks in September. They denied that it was a planned schedule, but God knew that I needed their love and prayers and support. He organized the chain of texts through the prodding of His Holy Spirit in the lives of my dear sisters in Christ!

Remember to pray! If God puts a person or circumstance on your heart, lift it to Him. Let those involved know you are praying. It will be a great encouragement to them!

October 19

"In your anger do not sin." Ephesians 4:26a (NIV)

It would be great if we never got angry—no matter what the boss said, regardless of how our teenagers behave, even if the umpire makes a bad call. The good news is that anger is an emotion we were created with—in and of itself, anger is not sin.

How we respond to anger may lead us into sin. Repressing it can lead to depression. Bottled up anger will eventually lead to an explosion. Expressing it inappropriately can make us moody, sarcastic, or manipulative.

The only way to handle it is to confess it. Give the anger, and its cause, to God. Talk to Him about it and ask for wisdom as to how to handle it. You may need to cool down before having an honest conversation with your boss. You can let your teenager know you are angry and why, but affirm your unconditional love for him/her.

It takes practice and self-control. The Holy Spirit wants to help you, and He will if you take your anger to Him.

October 20

"For my yoke is easy and my burden is light." Matthew 11:30 (NIV)

One of my favorite parts of Disney's "Snow White and the Seven Dwarf's" rendition is when Snow White's new little friends go off to work singing and whistling. They seem to enjoy what they are doing and make it even better by making music while they are doing it.

Rick Warren says: "If you are stressed, carrying an overwhelming load, it's not from Jesus. His burden is light (see Matthew 11:28-30). God wouldn't give you a list of things to do and not give you the time to do them. If you are stressed over time, you are either too busy, or you are not using your time wisely."

These statements were all a bit convicting. I pride myself with being able to multitask and check my to-do lists off each day. It's okay to be organized, but I need to work on the stress part. I get worked up when I can't get to the end of the list for the day. I get headaches from pushing too hard. I get cranky when others don't meet my time-line expectations.

Here's how I want to change. I want to enjoy my work. I want to work, imagining Jesus working right alongside me, whistling a praise tune and lightening my burden. I want those around me to be captured by my joy, love, and grace.

I hope you will join me in these challenges.

October 21

"Now when Daniel learned that the decree had been published, he went home to his upstairs room where the windows opened toward Jerusalem. Three times a day he got down on his knees and prayed, giving thanks to his God, just as he had done before."
Daniel 6:10 (NIV)

I have always had a problem with the term "self-esteem" or "self-confidence." I understand the need to have a humble and realistic positive attitude about our abilities. But the greater faith I have in "me" the less satisfied I will be. When I do fail, what happens to my self-esteem or confidence then?

Daniel didn't act on self-confidence when he knelt by his window to pray. Knowing the consequence of his actions based on the king's edict, Daniel could only have been acting on God-confidence. He knew and had experienced God (remember his buddies in the fiery furnace), and that gave him the confidence he needed to pray in spite of the decree.

As you get to know God better through His Word and through experience witnessing miracles (think about the last time you saw a baby born or watched a flower bloom), your confidence will grow. We can do all things, but not because we have a positive self-view. We can do all things because of Christ who gives us strength (see Philippians 4:13).

Do you need some confidence today? One of my Facebook followers told me she had heard the term "God-fidence" used for this. Christ will build you and embolden you.

October 22

> "Teach me your way, Lord, that I may rely on your faithfulness; give me an undivided heart, that I may fear your name."
> Psalm 86:11 (NIV)

The amplified version of this verse replaces "that I may rely on your faithfulness" with "I will walk and live in your truth." When I walk and live in God's truth, I can only do it when I am relying on His faithfulness. As I learn more of the Scriptures and their promises, they accompany me on my life's journey.

Let's break the rest of the verse down. "Teach me your way, Lord." We must be willing to learn from Him. It's one thing to read the Bible every day, but we must be intent on applying it. I think about my students when I was in the classroom. I could teach all day, but the goal wasn't to teach. It was for the students to learn.

"Give me an undivided heart" means that as I walk and live in the Truth I am surrendered completely to God. Nothing else can come in the way or take first place in our lives. Jesus must be our Number One. When we keep Him first, we live with an attitude of gratitude and praise of Him. We are in awe of His goodness at all times—the good and the bad.

Make this your prayer today: *Lord, help me to walk and live in Your truth today and every day. Amen.*

October 23

"Restore to me the joy of your salvation." Psalm 51:12a (NIV)

I read a story once about a Christian woman who lived an embittered life. She was caustic in the way she treated others, and complained just about everything. In a late season of her life, she had a heart-changing moment with Jesus. He showed her the damaging effects that her attitude was having on those around her. He revealed how her bitterness was resulting in personal pain and sorrow.

She miraculously made a turn-around. She asked God to forgive her for all the years she had wasted and made a point to live out the rest of her life with joy.

The Bible has a lot to say about joy:

"The **joy** of the Lord is your strength." Nehemiah 8:10b

"Restore to me the **joy** of your salvation." Psalm 51:12a

"But the fruit of the spirit is love, **joy**, peace, forbearance, kindness, goodness, faithfulness, gentleness and self-control." Galatians 5:22-23a

"May the God of hope fill you with all **joy** and peace as you trust in him," Romans 15:13a

And these are just a few examples. Are you displaying the joy of the Lord in your life? If not, if you are a cranky Christian, you are making God look bad. Our joy is part of our witness to the world. If you have lost it, ask God to restore your joy. He is faithful, and He will do it!

October 24

"**Rejoice always**, pray continually, give thanks in all circumstances; for this is God's will for you in Christ Jesus."
1 Thessalonians 5:16-18 (NIV) (emphasis mine)

Someone recently reminded me of the importance of being grateful, especially for the things we so easily take for granted. So, I have decided to take a daily inventory for the next few days of some of these privileges and things I don't normally give a lot of thought to, and make it a point to be thankful for them.

Today, I am rejoicing in my legs. Even as old as they are, my knees still work, my hips are functioning, and my ankles and feet are healthy. They allow me to walk, hike, climb stairs, pedal a bike, and get down on the floor to play with my grandkids. Getting up is a little more tricky, but I rejoice that I can still do it!

My friend had a fall in late August. She broke both heels, and had to have surgery to repair multiple fractured bones. As part of her recovery, she had to stay off of her feet completely for three months! Sometimes it's when we don't have something that we realize how much we really appreciate it. Her accident has provided opportunities for us to be her hands and feet—taking meals, running errands, walking her dogs, going into visit with her since she can't easily get out and about.

We have talked about her eventual rehab. She will have to relearn to walk. She will probably do some therapy in a pool to ease into weight bearing activities. She is looking forward to those days ahead when she can hop in her car on her own and drive to the store or to work.

I am grateful for my legs! I hope you are as well. Rejoice in them today!

October 25

"Let everything that has breath praise the Lord. Praise the Lord."
Psalm 150:6 (NIV)

Day two: I am thankful for the air we breathe, and the breath we can take to fill our lungs with life-giving oxygen. I usually don't think too much about the act of breathing, I just do it, over and over again, about 20,000 times a day. What a miracle of God—we have been fearfully and wonderfully made! (Psalm 139:14)

At the time I wrote this, we had just been at the coast for a little vacation. The ocean breezes and refreshing clear air was invigorating. Toward the end of the time there, we were getting some residual smoke from a couple of wildfires in Northern California drifting down to the Central Coast. Then, an overnight rain cleaned the air, and the skies were filled with spotty clouds and beautiful blue heavens.

When we came home and prepared to sing a worship set for the following Sunday's service, one of the songs we were learning was called "Praise!" At the beginning of the song, to the rhythmic clapping of the congregation and the beating of the drums, we all shouted, "Let everything that has breath praise the Lord!" (Psalm 150:6)

Once again God affirmed His goodness and I am so thankful that I have breath to praise Him.

If you have breath...you know what to do...Praise the Lord!

October 26

"Open my eyes that I may see wonderful things in your law."
Psalm 119: 18 (NIV)

My eye wouldn't stop watering! It wasn't the normal allergic reaction I sometimes have for an hour or so in the mornings. This went on throughout the day. I went to urgent care, and sure enough, I was treated for an eye infection.

The drops I was given cleared things up pretty quickly, and I was forever grateful for good health care and ways to take care of our eyes. I don't typically take my sight for granted since I wear corrective lenses. Without them, things can be pretty blurry!

I could make an extensive list of all the beautiful things I see and praise God for each day, but I'm going to let you take over today.

What are some reasons you are thankful for your eyes? What have you seen most recently that thrilled your soul (physically or spiritually)? Put your thoughts in your journal.

October 27

"Whoever believes in me, as the Scripture has said, streams of living water will flow from within him.'" John 7:38 (NIV)

Have you ever thought about water? Californians certainly have since we just finished a seven-year drought. We were asked to limit the watering of our lawns. We were encouraged to be conservative in the use of household water for showers, dishes, and washing of clothes. Laws were passed regulating the amount of water flow rates in our toilets.

Yet, even in the middle of all that, I could go to the tap and turn on the water. I could get a drink when I needed it and keep my pool filled throughout the summer. You can imagine how excited we all were when we had a couple of really wet years. For those who get consistent rainfall, you might be rolling your eyes, but we were doing the dance of joy every time the precipitation started. Record snowfalls ensured the water tables and rivers would remain at normal levels and above.

We have a team of marathoners at our church who run to raise money for countries that don't have access to clean water. Just seeing pictures of the young women carrying heavy jugs of water on their heads for miles and miles motivates me to want to help in the efforts of bringing safe water to their communities.

I am thankful for water! Jesus said he is the Living Water (John 4:13-14). With Him we will never again thirst (spiritually). Dig deep into that well of life today. And don't forget to conserve our H_2O as well.

October 28

"Always give thanks to God the Father for everything, in the name of our Lord Jesus Christ." Ephesians 5:20 (NIV)

Today I am going to be a very practical. With Thanksgiving coming next month, I want to praise God for some of our modern conveniences. I usually don't give a second thought to:

- Turning on a light switch
- Letting the dishwasher wash my dishes
- Drawing ice and cold water from my refrigerator and knowing my foods are being kept at the right temperature
- Turning on my stove or oven to fix a meal, bake, or even self-clean

I don't know how most of this stuff works, but I do not take lightly that I have at my finger tips:

- A blender
- A mixer
- A crockpot
- A microwave
- A curling iron
- A cell phone
- A bazillion other electronic wonders

I am grateful for those who invented these things. I am grateful for those who can repair them when broken. I am forever grateful for God who has given mankind the ability to invent and create and make life's daily tasks easier.

Thank God today for your favorite appliance or modern convenience.

October 29

"I always thank God for you because of his grace given you in Christ Jesus." 1 Corinthians 1:4 (NIV)

As part of the days of remembering to be grateful, of course we want to remember to be thankful for our families. I have two amazing families. One is blood related. They are all very precious to me!

My other family is my church family. We have gone to the same church for forty plus years. Many of the people there are like brothers and sisters. I know they would be there for me in time of need (they have proved it over and over). I know we would drop anything to help them if they needed it.

I do not take either of these family groups for granted. I don't know what people do without the Lord and without the body of Christ. I am beyond grateful that most of my blood relatives are also part of the family of God. It's a double blessing, for sure!

Let someone special to you know this week how much you love them!

October 30

> "On that day Holy to the Lord will be inscribed on the bells of the horses, and the cooking pots in the Lord's house will be like the sacred bowls in front of the altar." Zechariah 14:20 (NIV)

There are certain daily chores that I don't really enjoy. Cleaning bathrooms and ironing reign pretty close to the top of unfavorite tasks.

Other things don't feel like work to me. I like to cook. Being in the kitchen brings me joy. Vacuuming feels good—it's a little bit of exercise (sometimes dancing) combined with cleaning—and it's done toward the end of my cleaning routine. It marks that I am almost done.

Whether I like the jobs or not (and not just housework), if I do them as unto the Lord (Colossians 3:23), the menial becomes purposeful. Zechariah describes our worship at the coming reign of the Lord. He says that "Holy to the Lord" will be inscribed on the horses' bells and the cooking pots (Zechariah 14:20-21).

What if we thought of it this way: "Every common thing becomes holy when used for God's purpose and service." Now the bathroom sink and the iron are holy vessels for the kingdom of God when I think about the little hands that will be washed and the clothes that will be clean and ready for the day. My computer becomes holy ground as I type words of encouragement to others. Going into work every day is an act of holy service as I touch the lives of those with whom I work with the love of Jesus.

What is one of the things you are least fond of doing? How does it change your attitude when you think of it being inscribed with "Holy to the Lord?"

October 31

"Therefore each of you must put off falsehood and speak truthfully to
his neighbor, for we are all members of one body."
Ephesians 4:25 (NIV)

Happy Halloween! I'm looking forward to seeing all the littles come to the door tonight dressed in their costumes. One of my grandkids is going to be Elsa. Another is going to be a velociraptor. I'll look forward to pictures of all 9 of them before the evening is up.

We might not be dressing up for Halloween, but sometimes we wear masks. We don't want people to see who we really are. We hope our costumes cover our weaknesses, our faults, or our pasts. We think that those things will give people the wrong impression of us.

Just the opposite is true. When we admit we need help or talk about how we are overcoming our pasts, it shows our true strength. People are drawn to the honesty, and they realize that they are not alone. We live in a world where we are all broken in some form or another.

As the kids are all getting suited up in their cute costumes for the night, let's work at taking our masks off. Be real. Be understanding of others. Live a life of honesty.

November 1

"Therefore, since we are surrounded by such a great cloud of witnesses, let us throw off everything that hinders and the sin that so easily entangles, and let us run with perseverance the race marked out for us."
Hebrews 12:1 (NIV)

Yesterday we celebrated Halloween. It's not my favorite holiday. I am way more into the cutesy costumes than all the horror and gore! So, let's focus on today's celebration. It is All Saint's Day. Think about all the saints who have gone before us, and be thankful for their influence in your faith.

Of course, there are those saints like Paul of the New Testament who has left his lasting letters and admonitions for us to read and learn. There are also those in your life who have kept the faith, fought the good fight, and probably many who have prayed for you through the years.

Today, I choose to honor my dad. Thanks, dad, for modeling the life of Christ in our home in a real and tangible way! Was he perfect? Of course, not, but he was loving to us and showed his love for the Lord throughout our lives. I miss him, and wish I could call him and tell him how much I love him. The best thing I know to do, instead, is to live out the life he taught me, with perseverance.

Write the name of one Saint (past or present) in your journal who has meant something to you. Thank God for them, and maybe send them a text or note if they are still living.

November 2

"I the Lord do not change. So you, O descendants of Jacob, are not destroyed." Malachi 3:6 (NIV)

We have an OLD digital clock we have kept by our bed. I only look at it if I get up in the middle of the night. It has an antiquated system where it changes the daylight savings time automatically on the last Sunday of October and April. Since we don't do it that way anymore, you are getting a clearer picture of how long we have had this particular clock.

Last Saturday I woke up. The clock said 5 AM. I couldn't go back to sleep, but I made myself wait until 6:00 to actually get up. When I came out to the living room, I realized it was really 7:00. The old clock had already set itself back an hour. We weren't scheduled to have Daylight Savings Time until the following week.

The mornings will eventually begin to be lighter and the evenings darker as fall and winter progress. I am usually a little more motivated to wake up to the light, but I'm equally motivated to snuggle under the covers at an earlier bedtime.

One thing I am so grateful for—God does not change like the time. He is constant, and He is the same yesterday, today, and forever. We don't have to worry about His "system" being old and irrelevant. What worked in Bible times, works today. What He said about Himself from the beginning of time still rings true today. His promises never change or fail. His truth cannot be manipulated or philosophized into something more modern or popular.

When we have this constant and absolute guide for our lives, we have a plumb line with which to center our lives and decisions. God's faithfulness will see us through life so that we are not consumed or destroyed. Let your heart be reassured through this promise of consistency and dependability.

November 3

Perfume and incense bring joy to the heart, and the pleasantness of one's friend springs from his earnest counsel." Proverbs 27:9 (NIV)

My mom loves road trips. My sister, cousin and I took my then 88-year-old mom on one of these trips down memory lane, visiting many of the spots where she had grown up.

While on the trip, she dropped her phone in the water of a white porcelain bowl (if you get my meaning), rendering it useless. We even went to a store called U Break I Fix. They couldn't help us.

She felt a little bit lost without her phone contacts, but she had brought along her iPad as well. She still had access to emails, Facebook, and text messages...UNTIL she accidentally left the iPad behind at one of our relative's homes.

Yikes! How frustrating it can feel when we are not able to stay connected. Maybe we are too attached to our devices, but I do know it is important to stay connected to people. Learning what they are doing through Facebook is not the same as spending time with them in conversation, especially if it can be done in person.

The reason this is important is because God created us to be in community. Our time together with my mom in the car and over meals and coffee was priceless. She did end up recovering her iPad and replaced her phone, but we didn't really need them to enjoy the pleasantness of our conversations.

Take time this week to get with someone you haven't talked to in a while. You will both reap great spiritual and personal benefits—and you won't even need your phones while you are at it!

November 4

"The eye cannot say to the hand, 'I don't need you!' And the head cannot say to the feet, 'I don't need you!' On the contrary, those parts of the body that seem to be weaker are indispensable."
1 Corinthians 12:21-22 (NIV)

I should have listened to my inner urging. "Put the backpack away so you don't run into it in the night." I had just returned from a trip and I was too tired to finish replacing this small item to its storage spot. I rationalized that I would remember that it was there, it was tucked up close to the desk, and I certainly wouldn't feel it if I did kick it.

WRONG! My left foot didn't quite clear it as I got up in the dark. It should have felt soft and pliable, but there must have been a book or something else hard that I had tucked inside for the return plane trip. By the end of the next day my second toe was black and blue. It was difficult to get a shoe on, and I was trying my best to stay off of my feet because of it.

I usually don't give my second toe a second thought, but when it was hurting, I KNEW it was there.

The body of Christ is the same way. We are joined by one Spirit. We are critical to the carrying out of God's kingdom. No one is considered more special or important than the other. Often those who are doing the behind-the-scenes work are more critical than the ones up front.

We need to honor each other. Rejoice when your sister or brother rejoices and weep when they weep (Romans 12:15). Don't wait to appreciate each other. Send a note of thanks. Let someone know how much they are loved and how crucial they are to the body of Christ.

November 5

> "The people living in darkness have seen a great light; on those living in the land of the shadow of death a light has dawned."
> Matthew 4:16 (NIV)

As we start into November, our thoughts turn to Thanksgiving. It's more than just a holiday. It is a way of life that brings us meaning and purpose.

I read this quote by Billy Graham recently, "Grief's darkness fades in the sunlight of thanksgiving."

He is not saying that our grief will just go away or that we will not continue to feel sorrow. He is saying that when we focus on what we have, when we are thankful for the good things in our lives, when we are grateful for the amazing gifts from God that cannot be taken away from us, then grief begins to lessen in strength.

We need to open the eyes of our heart to what God is doing all around us. We need to lift up our eyes and recognize the God of heaven and earth (Psalm 121:1-2), and let His light shine down upon us.

November 6

> "Then I heard the voice of the Lord saying, 'Whom shall I send? And who will go for us?' And I said, "Here am I. Send me!'"
> Isaiah 6:8 (NIV)

I received a surprise phone call the other day. I was enjoying a little quiet time when my cell phone started buzzing. I looked at the name that popped up, and I knew it was a call I needed to take.

I had reached out to this person a few weeks before through a text. Their silence didn't really surprise me, but this phone call did. I thought they might text back at some point, but to hear their voice was a sweet surprise. Our conversation had been prayed for before it happened. I was so pleased to be able to speak love and hope into this person's life.

I want to encourage you to be obedient to God's nudging. Send that note or text without any expectations of return or acknowledgement. Pray over the words you send, and pray for the person you are sending it to. Let God surprise you as He is quietly working behind the scenes.

I have often heard our key text (Isaiah 6:8) preached when spurring people to answer a greater calling like becoming a pastor or missionary. But I believe it is appropriate for the smaller tasks God wants for us to do as well. If you don't do it, who will? God is calling you!

Do you have someone in mind today that needs to hear from you? Obey the still small voice in your spirit and reach out to them.

November 7

> "But I have stilled and quieted my soul; like a weaned child with its mother, like a weaned child is my soul within me."
> Psalm 131:2 (NIV)

We were sitting on the mountain cabin deck, taking in the beautiful sky and the grand trees surrounding us. My friend was next to me, sipping her morning tea, wrapped in a couple of blankets. Suddenly she whispered, "Don't move."

I stilled my beating heart in time to look to where she was pointing. There was a family of four deer passing us on the left. They paused, looked us straight in the eyes, determined we were not a threat, and then moved on. We saw them again later on our walk. What a blessing!

We tend to miss blessings in our lives because we don't get quiet enough to notice them. We recently had to get our brakes fixed. My husband noticed they weren't sounding right only because he had rolled down the car windows on a pleasant afternoon. The timely discovery came right before we were taking a trip to see our grandkids. The mechanic said that we would have surely had severe damage if we had made the trip before the repairs were made. Of course, we had to fork out some unexpected cash. It was an inconvenience on the day before we were getting ready to leave on our trip, but we saw it as a blessing from God!

Whether you are sighting a deer or discovering a potential hazard before it happens, there are so many ways God shows up in your day. Try looking for these special moments; still yourself long enough to reflect and actually see what is going on around you.

November 8

"Then Jesus said, 'He who has ears to hear, let him hear.'"
Mark 4:9 (NIV)

The other day I proofread one of my GFH posts the day before it was to appear. I caught a typo in the verse I was getting ready to send out to readers. Instead of saying "Dear friends..." it read "Deaf friends..."

I quickly changed it and breathed a sigh of relief that I had seen it in time. As I contemplated the mistake, I realized that there are times when the scriptures might correctly read, "Deaf friends." We hear and read God's Word, but we don' really listen and comprehend. It's as if our spiritual ears are deaf.

Jesus knew we needed to listen with our spiritual ears. He often admonished the crowds he spoke to when he said, "He who has ears, let him hear" (Matthew 11:15). He wasn't just telling good stories. He was illustrating and teaching about the very heart of God. He wanted us to hear with our hearts and work to understand what He was sharing with them.

My prayer today is that my spiritual eyes and ears are opened every morning to the fresh things that God is wanting to say to me.

November 9

"So then, just as you received Christ Jesus as Lord, continue to live in him, rooted and built up in him, strengthened in the faith as you were taught, and overflowing with thankfulness."
Colossians 2:6-7 (NIV)

Gratitude can be a great motivator, but it's not always easy. How do I overflow with thanksgiving (see Colossians 2:7) when times are tough, things don't make sense, or my prayers seem to be unanswered?

Here is one piece of advice that I read recently in a Rick Warren devotional. "Don't look at what's lost, look at what's left." No matter how dire our situation is, there is always someone who has it worse. There are always things "left" in our lives that we can rejoice over.

Jesus is bigger than our problems. In faith, we can leave our suffering and pain to Him, knowing He is in control. Remember the part about it not always being easy? Isaiah 43:2 reminds us that **when** we pass through the water, and the river, and the fire, we will not be overwhelmed or consumed. James 1:2 tells us to consider it pure joy **when** we face trials. You see, my friend, **it's when**, not **if**. That's why we must practice and grow, choosing to be grateful.

I pray that you (and I) can live in a spirit of thanksgiving in spite of any hardships today.

November 10

"Don't let any unwholesome talk come out of your mouths, but only what is helpful for building others up according to their needs, that it may benefit those who listen." Ephesians 4:29 (NIV)

My father-in-law was a man of few words, especially when it came to compliments. He wasn't critical by any means, but when he did give you a verbal or written (in birthday cards...) appreciation, you knew he was sincere.

My husband's main love language is words of affirmation. Since that is not one of my primary languages, I have to work to remember to affirm him. I would be so sad if I felt like he didn't know that I appreciate and love him.

When something is appreciated, it means it is raised in value. We can minister to others with heartfelt appreciation. It doesn't have to be far and few between, but it must be genuine, specific, and true. Build them up. Encourage them. Pray for them!

Who in your life needs to be appreciated this week? How might you go about raising their value?

November 11

"And the peace of God, which transcends all understanding, will guard your hearts and your minds in Christ Jesus."
Philippians 4:7 (NIV)

On the morning of our son's Celebration of Life service, I read Philippians 4:4 "Rejoice in the Lord always. I say it again: Rejoice!" (NIV)

I was a little miffed at God for bringing that before me on this particular morning. I stewed for a while about this seemingly unfair expectation at this very moment. As I thought about it more, however, I realized that being obedient in this way brought about what my husband and I had been experiencing throughout the ordeal. God's peace had exceeded anything we could comprehend (Philippians 4:7).

It doesn't say to rejoice for your problems. It says rejoice in the Lord. He wants to carry our burdens. He wants us to worry less and rest more. This quote stuck out to me: "Worry is just stewing about doing."

Most of the time there isn't much we can do. If we are to take action of any kind, God will give us the wisdom and strength we need for the task. Worrying about it is just stewing about doing.

Are you stewing today? Change tactics and rejoice instead. Praise the God who is the healer of broken hearts and who sets the captives free!

November 12

"They all joined together constantly in prayer..." Acts 1:14 (NIV)

I recently read that if we prayed as much as we worried, we'd have a lot less to worry about. It made me chuckle until I realized how seriously true it is!

We are to pray without ceasing. I tend to worry for a bit, then I think it is probably worthy of prayer. What if I prayed first? An earnest prayer would leave the issue in the hands of almighty God, and worrying about it afterward would be like reneging on my trust.

When we deposit money into our bank account, we don't turn around immediately and withdraw the entire amount thinking that we can do a better job of securing it under our pillow or wherever we might think to put it. When we deposit our worries into the trust of God, we need to leave it there!

What do you do first—Worry or Pray? Let's turn the tide of worry into a flood of prayer. Better yet, bring some others together for some united prayer.

November 13

"But Ruth replied, 'Don't urge me to leave you or to turn back from you. Where you go I will go, and where you stay I will stay. Your people will be my people and your God my God." Ruth 1:16 (NIV)

I recently read a devotional by Holley Girth in which she looked at Naomi and Ruth. She shared how Naomi was wrapped in despair and felt like life had ended for her. She was bitter and could not see a future. Ruth chose to follow her mother-in-law, help her, be her encourager.

We find ourselves in both of these women at different times. Sometimes we are the one speaking words of life into someone else. Sometimes we need a friend who will come beside us and share life-giving truth, even when we don't understand what God is doing at the moment.

Either way, "Anxiety tells us, 'It's all over.' But faith and the Ruth's in our lives remind us, 'God isn't finished with your story yet.'"

Here is my Ruth Truth for you today: Your story isn't over! It is just beginning. Watch and see what God is going to do!

November 14

"Dear children, let us not love with words or tongue but with actions and in truth." 1 John 3:18 (NIV)

Have you ever seen someone offer thanks for something, but their body language or their actions say something completely different? The teenager who says, "Thanks a lot!" while rolling her eyes. The employer who tells you thanks for doing your job, but grumbles and complains over all the little things that don't go his/her way.

John F. Kennedy once said, "As we express our gratitude, we must never forget the highest appreciation is not to utter words but to live by them."

I believe that words of appreciation are important, but let's also live a life of gratitude. Stop the grumbling (I speak to myself!), and share the love and joy that God has bestowed upon you. Match your words and your actions. Definitely tell someone you appreciate them. Then follow up with showing your appreciation by doing something for them. It can be as simple as a smile or a hug. It can be a present of some kind, or even better the gift of your time.

November 15

"The Lord is my shepherd, I shall not be in want." Psalm 23:1 (NIV)

I woke up around 2:00 AM and couldn't go back to sleep. I hate it when that happens. Then I started to pray. I have some of my best communion with God during those wee hours of the morning.

This particular time I was drawn to pray Psalm 23 over some people who need Jesus in their lives. We can all relate to this Psalm. In the next few days, I am going to highlight some of the specific verses.

In verse 1, the Psalmist declares the Lord as his Shepherd. If Jesus is our Shepherd, that means we are like sheep. Oh, how true that is! We, like sheep, have gone astray and turn to our own way (see Isaiah 53:6). The Shepherd means for us to not be in want. I'm not sure why we fight Him and insist on trying it our way first.

As you pray for those in your circle who need Jesus, pray that they would recognize their need for the Good Shepherd. Pray that they would see their strivings in this life as futile and useless without God. Pray that they would be drawn to the Savior who provides everything we need.

November 16

"He makes me lie down in green pastures, he leads me beside quiet waters, he restores my soul, he guides me in paths of righteousness for his name's sake." Psalm 23:2-3 (NIV)

When our kids were little, they often made naps or bedtime a fight. We, as parents, knew they needed to be "made" to lie down and be still. If they didn't get their rest, they would be cranky and agitated later.

Though I love my naps now, I still fight resting in the Lord. It's not intentional, but I allow myself to get all worked up about life—my problems, my schedules, the news, the culture. Jesus knows I need rest. Sometimes He has to "make" me lie down. Sometimes He does that through a verse reminding me to come and bring my burden to Him so He can lighten the load (see Matthew 11:28-29). Other times He brings life to a halt through a time of illness or trial, when I can do nothing but depend on Him.

Psalm 23:2-3 talks about how the Shepherd makes me lie down in green pastures and leads me beside quiet waters. He restores me and guides me in the right paths. My desire is that I will get to a place where I don't fight the rest. I want to give into the goodness and blessings He has in store for me.

Are you fighting His rest today? Lean into Him and let Him restore your soul!

November 17

"Even though I walk through the valley of the shadow of death, I will fear no evil, for you are with me; your rod and staff,--they comfort me."
Psalm 23:4 (NIV)

Psalm 23:4 is often quoted at funerals. "Even though I walk through the valley of the shadow of death..." I think too many of us stop at this phrase and realize that grieving is like walking through this dark valley.

I have come to realize that not only do we walk this valley when someone passes away, we are walking in and through it daily. Our world is full of sin and the destruction that it leaves in its wake. It is like the picture I took near a friend's cabin where a mountain fire took out acres of trees and left only charred remains.

The good news is in the rest of the verse! As believers in Christ, we don't have to fear the evil we are walking through. We know that God is with us and will comfort us through whatever we are facing. We have an eternal view as we walk through this life. We see beyond the destruction to our eternal home. There is hope.

Just like in the picture that I took, there are green mountains and blue sky beyond the burnt ground. That is the comfort we can live with.

Our friends who don't know Jesus need that kind of hope and comfort. Can you imagine going through this world without having the assurance that God is by your side? If you are praying for someone to come to a saving knowledge of Jesus, breathe a prayer right now. Say their name, and pray for them to come under the authority of the Shepherd's rod which He uses to guide, rescue and protect us. Pray that they will come under the support of the Shepherd's staff and be comforted knowing that He has their best in mind.

November 18

"You prepare a table before me in the presence of my enemies. You anoint my head with oil; my cup overflows." Psalm 23:5 (NIV)

As we will be preparing our tables for Thanksgiving very shortly, we are putting out the best dishes, setting each place for the guests, and planning a very special menu. We are excited about the gathering of family and friends who will share memories and gratitude, who will have to leave the table with their belt loosened a bit. It will be a time full of love and goodness as we rest and relax and sit around the house together.

This is just a small picture of what it will be like in Heaven. Jesus is preparing a table for us. He plans to honor us and fill our cup and plate to overflowing. Goodness and love will follow us as we dwell with Him forever. Our holiday meals pale in comparison.

Enjoy your friends and family this season! Give God thanks for all the goodness and abundance He has bestowed upon you.

November 19

"Surely goodness and love will follow me all the days of my life, and I will dwell in the house of the Lord forever." Psalm 23:6 (NIV)

We occasionally dog sit our grand dog. She is as cute as a button, but she gets underfoot at times. She tends to follow me all over the house, like she's afraid she will miss out on a treat or a belly rub or something else of importance.

This pursuit is sweet. Another pursuit I can think of is when my husband was courting me. He made sure I knew he loved me. When we were apart, he would write me letters every day. When we were together, he made sure we did things to enjoy each other's presence. When he asked me to marry him, he had picked out the right ring and had just the right words to make me leap for joy as I cried, "YES!"

God's pursuit is in a category of its own. He follows us AND leads us (Psalm 139:5). His pursuit is called goodness and love, and it is forever! He never will leave us nor forsake us (Deuteronomy 31:6), and someday I will be with Him in heaven forever.

If you are not feeling his love and goodness right now, invite him into your presence. He is a prayer away. It may just be that you need to turn around and recognize that He has been there all along.

November 20

"God is love. Whoever lives in love lives in God, and God in him."
1 John 4:16 (NIV)

One of the first Sunday School verses I memorized was a portion of 1 John 4:16, "...God is love." It was a simple three-word statement that a pre-school child or kindergartener could learn.

I have spent the rest of my life getting to know this God of love. 1 Corinthians 13 is full of descriptors of God's loving character. He doesn't just have love, He is love. I want to live under His banner of love (Song of Solomon 2:4).

When a flag flies over you, it identifies you as a loyal follower. The banner carried above you indicates two things: 1) You are a protected asset under the person or thing the flag represents; 2) You are showing your allegiance by walking under it.

Under God's banner of love, we bow down in surrender to Him. We know the Jesus of love and can ask anything of Him. Under His banner is freedom, love, hope, healing, joy, and friendship.

"God is love!" A simple, yet profound truth. Have you received Him and His love? If not, you can ask Him into your heart right now. If you have been following Jesus for a while, bow in worship as you declare your gratitude for His love today.

November 21

"Then he said to them, 'My soul is overwhelmed with sorrow to the point of death. Stay here and keep watch with me.'"
Matthew 26:38 (NIV)

Our three-month old was having surgery for an inguinal hernia—a fairly routine and simple surgery, the doctor had told us. But as his parents, there was nothing ordinary about our first-born's surgery. We were in the waiting room, anxious for what was happening in the operating room of the hospital.

To our surprise, our pastor's wife showed up. She was there to pray with us, but she also waited with us. It wasn't a long surgery, and soon we received word that our boy was doing great and we were allowed to go see him. He healed quickly over the next few days, and, except for a small scar, you would never know he had ever had any medical issues.

I'll never forget, however, the presence of our pastor's wife and friend. She didn't have to stay. She could have prayed and been on her way. But there was something so comforting knowing that she was just there, sitting with us, waiting.

God understands the waiting room. His Son, Jesus, knew what was coming, and was "overwhelmed with sorrow to the point of death" (Matthew 26:38). He asked for some of His disciples to keep watch with him. Jesus knew the end result, but it didn't make the waiting any easier. We have to live in a place of trust in the perfect timing of God and the deliverance that is to come. Carole Holiday describes it like this: "Sandwiched between sorrow and the solution is the in between, the redemptive waiting room."

The great news is that Jesus is with us. He is ever-present as we wait for Him to redeem our stories. He gets our pain and grief. He understands our dreams and our difficulties, and how there seem to be nothing but dead ends.

And He waits with us. His presence comforts us, and He longs to let us know He has our problem under His complete sovereignty and control.

November 22

"But seek first his kingdom and his righteousness, and all these things will be given to you as well." Matthew 6:33 (NIV)

When Christ is at the center of our lives, we have a truly balanced existence. I once learned that when you are trying to figure out your priorities, you shouldn't make a numbered list. Instead, if you think of your life as a wheel, with Jesus as the hub, the other priorities of your life will fall into place.

Since a wheel turns, there will be different spokes on the top, depending on the season of your life, the time of the day, or the urgency of a situation. For example, when I am at work, my job is at the top for those eight hours. If I get an emergency call from my kids' school, the job spoke moves down, and my kids are placed at the top. The other priority spokes don't go away, they just get adjusted, and with God at the center, He helps me navigate the position of the wheel.

This way of looking at priorities has helped me through life. I hope it makes sense to you as well.

November 23

"The heavens declare the glory of God; the skies proclaim the work of his hands." Psalm 19:1 (NIV)

When my husband and I sing on our church's worship team, it requires us to be on stage for warm-ups, rehearsal, and fine-tuning our song set by 7:00 AM. I won't lie to you...getting up and getting ready by that early hour on a weekend day is TOUGH!

One particular Sunday in October, we were just arriving at the church parking lot. I was still a little in that dream state, finishing my first cup of coffee. As we were pulling in, a song came on the radio called "Jesus Does," by We the Kingdom. Here were the words being sung:

> *Who tells the sun to rise every morning*
> *Colors the sky with the shades of His glory*
> *Wakes us with mercy and love?*
> *Jesus does.*

We had no sooner heard those words when we looked up to see the most gorgeous sunrise. We were struck by the beauty of God's creation and the affirmation that He was with us. As we were preparing to worship Him in His sanctuary, He built a sanctuary in the sky for us to enjoy.

My husband, king of the sunset and sunrise pictures, captured the moment in a photo. We shared it with some of the other members of our team. I'm so glad we were awake that morning to see God's splendor.

Take a few minutes today or tomorrow to watch a sunrise or sunset. If it is not a particularly spectacular one, just gaze at the sky that God has made and give Him glory and honor and praise.

November 24

"Accept one another, then, just as Christ accepted you, in order to bring praise to God." Romans 15:7 (NIV)

At Grounds for Hope (my FB page and website), I like to remind us to "Stay Grounded, Keep Connected, One Cup, One Story at a Time." Our walk with God and life with Jesus as our Lord is definitely about being grounded in our beliefs and the truths of His Word. It is also about being connected and belonging.

You see, church isn't a place we go; it's a group of people we belong to.

Maybe you feel totally accepted when you go to church. GREAT! Who can you invite to lunch today who needs to feel seen and loved?

Maybe you feel alone when you walk through the church doors. I truly am sorry, but the same question is for you. Who can you invite to lunch or coffee this week so that you can begin to connect and feel a sense of community? I know at our church, there are always opportunities and invitations to join small groups and Bible studies. It's not the end-all, be-all answer, but it's a start. Believe me, you will soon find that those who may seem like "perfect" people are the same as you. We all have "stories" that help us to relate to each other and point to God's goodness and glory.

Take a step toward church, toward God, and toward others.

November 25

"And I heard every creature in heaven and on earth and under the earth and in the sea, and all that is in them, saying, 'To him who sits on the throne and to the Lamb be blessing and honor and glory and might forever and ever!'" Revelations 5:13 (ESV)

I know you are probably very busy this week getting ready to host company or getting ready to travel and eat! I hope that you will make (or have made if Thanksgiving has passed) great memories with family and friends.

I just want to leave you with a Billy Graham quote: "A spirit of thankfulness is one of the most distinctive marks of a Christian whose heart is attuned to the Lord."

Before our meal, we make it a point to go around the family circle and share things we are grateful for. One year I challenged everyone to think of a person(s), an activity, and an object that they were thankful for this year. It made the conversation a little more organic and fun, and gave the younger ones specific things to focus on.

After we share our gratitude, we pray for the meal and sing the Doxology.

> *Praise God from whom all blessings flow.*
> *Praise Him, all creatures here below.*
> *Praise Him above, ye heavenly hosts.*
> *Praise Father, Son, and Holy Ghost.*
> *Amen*

I tend to tear up as the harmonies are sung through the house.

Raise your voices with us and with all of God's creatures: Praise Father, Son, and Holy Ghost.

November 26

"How great is your goodness, which you have stored up for those who fear you, which you bestow in the sight of men on those who take refuge in you." Psalm 31:19 (NIV)

I was having my quiet time with God. I read a devotional by Jasmine Williams that struck me. She was talking about learning to live by the truths we know about God, even when it seems hard. She listed several: He is good (Psalm 31:19), He is faithful and trustworthy (Psalm 57:10); He loves us beyond measure (John 3:16).

I continued her list with one of my own:

- He is a strong tower (Proverbs 18:10)
- He never sleeps nor slumbers (Psalm 121:4)
- He is my refuge (Psalm 46:1)
- He is my redeemer (Job 19:25)
- He is my Shepherd (Psalm 23:1)
- He delivers me (Psalm 18:2)
- He defends me (Psalm 31:1-2)

Then Jasmine said this: "The view from our circumstances doesn't determine His greatness, but His greatness can empower how we view our circumstances."

Friend, we must trust God to help us. When we love and adore Him and remember the truths about His character, our circumstances are brought into perspective. He is great! He can help us see our life through His eyes and help us along the way.

November 27

"Your kingdom come, your will be done, on earth as it is in heaven."
Matthew 6:10 (NIV)

As our pastor preached through the summer series on Praying Dangerous Prayers, one Sunday he quoted Robert Law, "Prayer is a mighty instrument, not for getting man's will done in heaven, but for getting God's will done on earth."

In a novel series I read throughout the summer, a pastor and his wife were always praying "the prayer that never fails," which is "Not my will, but Your will be done, Lord." (Luke 22:42)

May our prayers reaching to heaven be more than a list of needs and wants. May they be tuned to the heart of our Father in such a way that in whatever way He answers, His name will be glorified. May our prayers usher in His kingdom on earth.

November 28

"Whether you turn to the right or to the left, your ears will hear a voice behind you saying, 'This is the way; walk in it.'"
Isaiah 30:21 (NIV)

It was an excruciating decision. We were happy in the location we lived and had no desire to move. My husband's job situation had been a bit precarious for several months, but he had just landed a decent position. It wasn't a career changing choice, but it would pay the bills.

Then we got an invitation to come to Bakersfield for a job that had room to grow. It was one of those times when it might have been fine to go either direction. There was nothing inherently wrong with either choice, so we chose to stay where we were. That lasted about thirty minutes. We had been praying over God's will for our lives, and neither one of us felt a peace about our decision. As soon as my husband called the Bakersfield company back and accepted, there was an immediate affirmation in our spirits.

We didn't hear an audible voice, but our spiritual ears were in tune with God. We knew we had to obey His leading.

How do we keep in tune with His voice? Reading His Word and praying, gathering others around us who can pray for God's guidance, and responding to the nudges to go one direction or another.

He is faithful to give us the next steps! Listen and follow Him!

November 29

> "Because of the Lord's great love, we are not consumed, for his compassions never fail. They are new every morning; great is your faithfulness." Lamentations 3:22-23 (NIV)

In a recent devotional by Kristin Miller, she stated that our understanding of our circumstances or future is not a prerequisite to trust.

I chewed on that thought for a couple of days, and here are a few of my thoughts:

- We can trust the Trustworthy. Even if I don't understand something, I can claim His promises because He is true to His Word.

- Put your faith in the Faithful. This is not too different than the above statement, but I can place my faith in Jesus willingly, believing He is faithful to deliver me.

- Peace in my path is a result of taking my hands off the steering wheel and letting Jesus guide me.

His compassions never fail and are new every morning. It doesn't matter what else is happening in our lives, we have every reason to trust the Almighty.

November 30

"But the fruit of the Spirit is love, joy, peace, patience , kindness, goodness, faithfulness, gentleness and self-control. Against such things there is no law." Galatians 5:22-23 (NIV)

It had been several years since we had a garden, and we were really enjoying our harvest. It never ceases to amaze me that many of the huge plants that are now visible in our garden boxes started as tiny little seeds.

Our spiritual fruit also start as seeds planted in our hearts at salvation. As we grow in our relationship with Christ, He is the One who helps our fruit to grow. He has chosen us to bear fruit that will last. If He has called you, you can trust that He is with you.

Galatians 5:22-23 provides a list of some of the fruit of the Spirit that is growing within us. Do you sense God working in your life? He is cultivating and maturing the seed(s) He planted.

December 1

> "Know therefore that the Lord your God is God; he is the faithful God, keeping his covenant of love to a thousand generations of those who love him and keep his commands."
> Deuteronomy 7:9 (NIV)

It's beginning to look a lot like Christmas. I can hear the carol playing in my mind right now. Even though the decorations and music and shopping might be coming into full swing, the spirit of Christmas should last all year—the spirit of giving and joy and anticipation. As you were gathered last week celebrating Thanksgiving and offering gratitude, you were actually practicing for December!

David Jeremiah put it this way: "In God's sight, it's beginning to look a lot like Christmas whenever we rediscover the simplicity of His love and bow down in thankfulness and worship, where we are and whatever our circumstances."

God's everlasting love and righteousness extends from generation to generation. What He gives to us elicits a posture of praise and a heart of giving. The thought of His love and faithfulness brings joy every morning.

May we bask in the simplicity of His love and continue with thankful hearts for all that Christ has done and is doing in our lives. Start by practicing worship and thankfulness right now.

December 2

> "Those who heard this asked, 'Who then can be saved?' Jesus replied, 'What is impossible with men is possible with God.'"
> Luke 18:26-27 (NIV)

Can you imagine it? A young teenager is listening to an angel tell her the Holy Spirit is going to come upon her, and she is going to bear the Son of God. She is also hearing for the first time that her relative, Elizabeth, is going to have a child in her old age, even though she had been considered barren. As Mary took all of this in, in wide-eyed wonder, the angel affirmed, "For nothing is impossible with God" Luke 1:37.

Later in Luke, Jesus has just told an eager rich ruler that he must sell everything and give it to the poor. He invites this man to follow Him, but the man becomes sad because he has much wealth. The disciples wonder at how anyone can possibly be saved...Jesus has just said it is easier for a camel to go through the eye of a needle!

"Jesus replied, 'What is impossible with men is possible with God'" Luke 18:27.

In the first scenario, God is bringing "impossible" physical life to two women. In the second situation, Christ is declaring "impossible" spiritual life transformation to anyone who believes.

God is the giver of life! Can you imagine it? Offer your impossible situations to God.

December 3

"You are the light of the world. A city on a hill cannot be hidden…in the same way let your light shine before men, that they may see your good deeds and praise your Father in heaven."
Matthew 5:14, 16 (NIV)

I never tire of looking at Christmas lights. Maybe if they were out all year, they wouldn't seem so special. But throughout the month of December houses around the city begin lighting up.

We try to take at least one evening to drive through some of the more elaborately decorated neighborhoods. It brings such delight. Even my 97-year-old mother-in-law used to "ooh" and "aah" over the sights. That's a lot of years to still be enchanted by something.

We are to be light in this world, shining around those who feel trapped in darkness. It can be as simple as taking cookies to a neighbor, smiling at the person who is walking by, yelling a thank you to the guy/gal who just delivered your package to your door.

Who needs you to be a light in their world today? Make sure your battery is charged and get out there and shine!

December 4

"In him was life, and that life was the light of men." John 1:3 (NIV)

Have you ever been to a light show? The lights pulsate off and on perfectly to the beat of the music playing in the background. It is a technological wonder.

I imagine the shepherds on that first Christmas night were awed by the light show. A multitude of the heavenly host appearing and praising God regarding the announcement of the Savior's birth, to the perfect beat of the heart of the Father. It wasn't a technological wonder. It was a supernatural spectacle. It was the opening number to the peace on earth that had been anticipated for centuries.

Jesus' light brought love and peace and joy. He is still the answer to our world's problems. Martin Luther King, Jr. is quoted as saying, "Darkness cannot drive out darkness; only light can do that. Hate cannot drive out hate; only love can do that."

Simple, but so profound! Love brings light and darkness cannot overcome it! There is no better way than to proclaim the truth of Jesus than to love those around us, even if they don't agree with us.

December 5

"For God so loved the world that he gave his one and only Son, that whoever believes in him shall not perish but have eternal life."
John 3:16 (NIV)

God is the perfect model of generosity. When you are generous with others because of God's generosity to you, it points others to God.

God's sending His Son to earth as a gift for us was an example of the first Christmas gift. The Magi brought valuable gifts to lay at the feet of the baby. Gifts are an integral part of the Christmas story.

Our gift giving traditions have gotten a little out of control. The materialistic advertisements and pressures of our culture have a tendency to get our focus on the wrong motives for giving. We should give at Christmas, and throughout the year, because God gave us SOOO much.

As you are planning your spending and the items that will land under the tree this year, consider God's extravagant love, His genuine peace, His fulfilling hope and joy. When you give, think of pointing others to Christ.

December 6

"Now faith is the assurance (title deed, confirmation) of things hoped for (divinely guaranteed), and the evidence of things not seen [the conviction of their reality—faith comprehends as fact what cannot be experienced by the physical senses]."
Hebrews 11:1 (AMP)

Our senses are bombarded during the month of December. We see decorations, lights, and trees. We smell pine, sugar cookies, and hot cocoa. We hear Christmas carols, the laughter of children, and the crackling of fires in the fireplace. We taste peppermint candies, cakes, cookies, and pies. We feel warmth in our hearts in spite of the cold temperatures. We sense the love and joy of those around us.

When it comes to faith, however, we can't always see, hear, taste, smell, or feel the things we hope for. But we can know, comprehend, and understand God's promises as fact. If we could see it all, we wouldn't need faith. It is a divine mystery that continues to grow the more we flex our trust muscles.

What are you hoping for today? By faith, know that God is working on your behalf!

December 7

> "And you, my child, will be called a prophet of the Most High; for you will go on before the Lord to prepare the way for him, to give his people the knowledge of salvation through the forgiveness of their sins, because of the tender mercy of our God, by which the rising sun will come to us from heaven to shine on those living in darkness and in the shadow of death, to guide our feet into the path of peace."
> Luke 1:76-79 (NIV)

There is a Christmas verse that I had never noticed before this year. It is right before Jesus was born. At the birth of John the Baptist, his father is finally able to speak (he had lost his voice because of his doubt). He actually sang a song. Maybe because it is at the end of the long first chapter of Luke that I have never noticed it before. I probably have just wanted to get to the next part of the story, "The birth of Jesus." But Zechariah's words are prophetic as toward the end he sings,

"because of the tender mercy of our God, by which the rising sun will come to us from heaven to shine on those living in darkness and in the shadow of death, to guide our feet into the path of peace" (Luke 1:78-79 NIV).

He was speaking of Jesus' coming. Here again we have the symbolism of light in the sunrise, shining in the darkness, guiding our path. We also see the theme of peace. The light is leading us to peace with God. It was His plan all along for us to have relationship with Him. Because of His tender mercies, He made a way for us to meet with Him, in spite of our sins.

What a Christmas story. We may never see the heavens light up with a multitude of angels, but we see the sun rise every morning, if we are watching for it. How can you watch for the Son rise (Jesus working in your everyday life)?

December 8

"Therefore, my dear brothers, stand firm. Let nothing move you. Always give yourselves fully to the work of the Lord, because you know that your labor in the Lord is not in vain."
1 Corinthians 15:58 (NIV)

This is one of the busiest times of the year. Sometimes I get a little weary of doing—cleaning, cooking, supervising, practicing, preparing...

Maybe Paul had these thoughts at times as well, because he encourages us in 1 Corinthians 15:58, "...Stand firm. Let nothing move you. Always give yourselves fully to the work of the Lord, because you know that your labor in the Lord is not in vain."

NOTHING done for the Lord is useless. Maybe it's not about the doing but the motivation behind the doing. Do as unto the Lord. It has a way of making the sheets I'm changing or the laundry I'm washing look a little different. When I think about the fact that I'm preparing this lesson or cooking that meal for the Lord, I don't get quite as tired. It doesn't even matter if the meal is not appreciated or the kids come tracking mud in on the freshly mopped floor. If it's for Him, it is not in vain.

What is making you weary today? I know there are lots of things going on in this busy season. Think about who you are really working for. Be encouraged! Don't let the little things get you down! Work for Jesus! He appreciates you, and He doesn't mind if you put your feet up for a few seconds and just chat with Him.

December 9

"Woe to those who call evil good and good evil, who put darkness for light and light for darkness, who put bitter for sweet and sweet for bitter." Isaiah 5:20 (NIV)

I was sitting around a table with people I knew and a few I didn't know. The ages ranged from one in his 20's to those in their 80's. We were there to celebrate a friend's 80th birthday party.

Over our delicious lunch the conversation meandered to one of the older members of our table. She was sharing how an indicator light kept coming on in her car. She didn't know what it was "indicating," so she had been ignoring it. Whoa! Woe to those who call their indicator light a nuisance and go on disregarding it!

We do that spiritually some times. We get a warning from our spirit, from a verse, or a message we hear. Instead of heeding it, we ignore it. We twist the truth, trying to let our indiscretion seem innocent and sweet instead of bitter. Discounting God's divine counsel leads to trouble. God's Word is designed to help us and keep us from going down a path of destruction.

For fun, think about how you would answer this question. Do you tend to:
- A. Take care of the warning light in your car right away
- B. Ignore it until absolutely necessary
- C. Look it up in the manual and try to figure it out on your own
- D. Other

Whether you have a warning light in your car or a cautionary "light" in your life, take care of it! As we enjoyed our pieces of birthday cake, we encouraged our elderly friend to get her car checked out!

I encourage you today to pay attention to the cautionary lights in your life.

December 10

"He who answers before listening—that is his folly and shame."
Proverbs 18:13 (NIV)

I listened to a podcast the other day. The guest speaker was sharing her philosophy of spending time around the dinner table, eating delicious farm-to-table foods. She made a statement that stuck with me.

As we sit with others over coffee or a meal, it allows us to stop and really listen. We can hear each other's stories and go to the next level of friendship. Her statement was that we need to "slow to the speed of listening."

Our lives move at a frantic pace most of the time. Even during the Christmas season with all the shopping, baking, social events, and family gatherings, we need to slow ourselves down so that we can truly listen.

As you allow yourself to "slow to the speed of listening" this week, pay attention to the difference it makes. Even now, stop and listen to the sounds around you. May it be practice for listening to the person(s) in your realm of influence that just wants to feel like someone cares.

December 11

"They disciplined us for a little while as they thought best; but God disciplines us for our good, in order that we may share in his holiness."
Hebrews 12:10 (NIV)

My husband and I have opposite ways of "fixing" something. I tend to do a quick patch job. It looks okay and does the job for the moment. He tends to research the solution, take his time, and make a more permanent fix.

I suppose there is a time and place for both ways. Sometimes you just need to have a quick repair until you can get to the more complete result. But in the long run, you want something that will last.

We tend to want God to fix things fast! We like immediate results, and we even rush in and try to do a patch job ourselves. The problem with this type of solution is that it isn't lasting.

God is always working on our character. He often lets us learn what it is like to fully depend on Him before we see our prayer get answered. He is not punishing us or putting us on hold as we might feel. He is giving us opportunities to grow, and He's in it for the long-lasting solution.

As parents, we do our best to help our children see the benefits of patience and trust in the process. How much more should we trust in our Heavenly Father to work for our good so that we may share in His holiness.

December 12

> "Each of you should use whatever gift you have received to serve others, as faithful stewards of God's grace in its various forms."
> 1 Peter 4:10 (NIV)

I grabbed a bookmark from my pile for the new book I was going to read. The front of the bookmark I chose had orange and pink flowers and leaves. Superimposed on these flowers in gold cursive lettering were these words: Love, Compassion, Comfort, Kindness, Grace, and Beauty.

A few days later, I happened to notice some penciled writing on the back of the bookmark. In shaky scrawl, I recognized this writing as my own. They were directions to the facility where we were headed in San Diego the morning we heard of our son's hospitalization.

Seeing those words triggered the anxiety and concern we had that morning and into the week. Rather than dwell there, I went to the front of the bookmark. I was reminded that during our week of saying goodbye to our middle boy, God and His people extended love and compassion, comfort and kindness, grace and beauty to us, over and over again!

We are still receiving those gifts. Yes, random things still trigger all the emotions of grief, when it is least expected. But God, who is rich in mercy, continues to reveal His love for us.

If you are in need of receiving love and compassion, allow others to serve you. If you are in a place where you can extend comfort and kindness to someone else, be God's faithful steward.

December 13

"I will say of the Lord, 'He is my refuge and my fortress, my God, in whom I trust.'" Psalm 91:2 (NIV)

The rain came down in a sudden downpour. Surprised by the unexpected deluge, we darted under a store front awning for some shelter. Later that afternoon, we were snuggled up with a hot drink in front of our fireplace, enjoying the security of our home's walls and roof.

Psalm 91 says the Lord is our refuge and fortress. A refuge can reference a quick place to duck and find shelter, like the storefront awning. A fortress indicates a more permanent place, intentionally built for exceptional security, like the inside of your home. We can trust God because He is there for us, no matter which type of shelter we need in the moment.

My mother-in-law, who just passed, was always quoting and praying all of Psalm 91 over us and our kids. We actually printed Psalm 91:2 on her graveside service program. It is a verse I refer to often.

Whether you need a quick shelter from the storm or a more lasting fortress that is inaccessible to the enemy, you can rest in the Most High's shelter. He will never let you down!

December 14

"Praise the Lord, my soul; all my inmost being, praise his holy name...who satisfies your desires with good things so that your youth is renewed like the eagles." Psalm 103:1, 5 (NIV)

In about a week, our living room will be transformed from a place of Christmas beauty, with a lit tree and decorations, into a heap of paper and boxes in about 60 seconds. I say this with complete joy, because watching the faces of the grandkids as they open their presents is so satisfying. It amazes me how quickly the conversion is made, but I hope you have as much fun watching the instantaneous unwrapping of all the gifts as you spent wrapping them.

Today's verse reminds us that we can have Christmas every day! We can open the Bible, communicate freely with our Father in Heaven, and enjoy His presence. He fills our lives with good gifts and renews our strength for each trial we might face.

Spend some time opening God's gifts today with wild abandonment. It will bring you joy, and it will bring joy to the Lord as well! He gave us gifts that they should be opened!

December 15

"You've kept track of my every toss and turn through the sleepless nights, each tear entered into your ledger, each ache written in your book." Psalm 56:8 (MSG)

While the world around you seems to be caught up in the bright lights and festive music, you may be feeling out of place and alone. Worry, grief, or pain are just a few of the emotions that can have you tossing and turning at night. Tears may flood unsolicited onto your pillow.

God's response to you is tender and caring. He is aware of your suffering and records each tear. He knows about your heartache and has plans to redeem your suffering (Romans 8:28).

You are not alone! Let the tears flow and your cries resound to the Lord, who loves you more than you will ever know!

December 16

"I have received full payment and even more; I am amply supplied, now that I have received from Epaphroditus the gifts you sent. They are a fragrant offering, an acceptable sacrifice, pleasing to God. And my God will meet all your needs according to his glorious riches in Christ Jesus."
Philippians 4:18-19 (NIV)

In our culture we are encouraged to look out for ourselves. And where does that get us? Dissatisfied and disconnected with others. We were created for a special purpose, but that does not mean that the world revolves around us.

In fact, when we focus on others, our own needs are met. Epaphroditus sent gifts to Paul. This sacrifice meant so much to Paul, but it also prompted him to say to the Philippians that God would meet all their needs according to the riches of his glory in Christ Jesus (Phil. 4:19).

Think about it. When we give to others—our time, our resources, our encouragement—we are the ones who get blessed.

December is a perfect time for you to bless others with your time and effort. If you are willing to sacrifice extra resources, watch out! Your needs will be fulfilled as well!

December 17

"Be patient, then brothers and sisters, until the Lord's coming. See how the farmer waits for the land to yield its valuable crop, patiently waiting for the autumn and spring rains." James 5:7 (NIV)

We are approaching the last day of fall. Soon we will be experiencing the beginning of the winter solstice. It is when we will have the least amount of daylight of any time of the year.

Do you think this worries the farmers? Are they fretting about next year's crops because the winter is upon them? James tells us that they are patient as they wait for the land to yield its valuable crops. They are resting as they wait for the proper time to plant their seeds, water their plants, and reap their harvest.

Maybe the winters of our lives are just times to prepare and learn to live in a place of patient expectancy on the Lord. He is in control. He is working behind the scenes. He wants us to trust Him.

At the time this devotional book was written, I had been facing a winter season. I had not written any new books, nor had I felt particularly inspired to move forward with any of the projects on the back burner. I had simply been waiting expectantly, and I believed that God would let me know in His timing when and what I needed to do.

His preparation period with me included some planting and tending the crops. I am currently in a season where things are starting to blossom and others are coming to full harvest. It was worth the wait!

What are you waiting expectantly for? God has a purpose for every season. Rest while you wait.

December 18

"Now it is God who makes both us and you stand firm in Christ. He anointed us, set his seal of ownership on us, and put his Sprit in our hearts as a deposit, guaranteeing what is to come."
2 Corinthians 1:21-22 (NIV)

It was a Wednesday night, and my husband and I were asked to share with a group of 9th and 10th grade girls. They had a set of prepared questions which we tackled, but we enjoyed the interactions along the way, making it as conversational as possible.

I hope they had some take-aways from our time together. If nothing else, I hope the message came across that life will be tough, but God is good! It is always too soon to quit, because He will work through our tough times to help us become the person He created us to be.

When we reflected on our lives, our marriage, our walk with God, we weren't perfect...AT ALL. We didn't always do things right or have a life free of fault. What we did do was keep our eye on Jesus. He always was able to help us get back on track.

I loved connecting with the younger generation. They need our prayers as they navigate through life. They are constantly being pulled to stop doing good and just give into their desires. If you have a young person(s) in your life, join me in praying for them to stand firm in Christ. They have their own calling and anointing, and Jesus wants to show them what is to come.

December 19

"May the God of hope fill you with all joy and peace as you trust in him, so that you may overflow with hope by the power of the Holy Spirit."
Romans 15:13 (NIV)

I was standing on the beach quoting this verse when the **as** stuck out to me. Such a small word, but so powerful in the light of the rest of the verse. "As" we trust in God suggests that we are in the process of waiting for something. We are to trust in God in the middle of that waiting, not after the circumstance has been resolved.

In Hebrew the word waiting implied patient expectation. The expectation that God will act is what fills us with hope, joy and peace.

What is God wanting to do in your life? How will His glory be revealed? Those are the questions we can focus on when we are in that waiting period of our lives. Just approaching life's difficulties in this way already elevates the problem from wondering if He will work to believing that the answers are coming. HOPE!

At Grounds for Hope I bank on that verse for you and for me! It is my theme verse, and that's why you have seen it several times throughout this devotional book (January 22, February 4). I can testify to the fact that I have been filled with joy and peace and hope during some of the hardest times in my life. You can claim the same blessings in your life! TRUST!

December 20

> "In the same way, the Spirit helps us in our weakness. We do not know what we ought to pray for, but the Spirit himself intercedes for us through wordless groans. And he who searches our hearts knows the mind of the Spriit, because the Spirit intercedes for God's people in accordance with the will of God." Romans 8:26-27 (NIV)

The kids are getting ramped up. The Christmas break from school is close if not already here. Their excitement about Christmas Day is becoming more and more climactic. They seem out of control. You are losing your mind. There is still too much to do. The constant activity and noise from the littles' high-pitched celebration is going to drive you to drink (coffee, of course).

If you are like me, you can feel discouraged at times about your parenting (grandparenting) skills, especially on those occasions when the children do not seem to be using any common sense or self-control. It's easy to think of all the things you could have done differently or better.

Maybe our own frantic pace is part of what is causing our kids to climb the walls. Here's the thing—we are all human. We are not going to be perfect or do things perfectly every time. That's why this sentence struck me: **It's more important to be praying parents than to be perfect parents.**

I'm not even a perfect pray-er, but I do know who to go to for wisdom and guidance! God is the giver of wisdom and He will help us to know when to slow down, when to take a moment to just cuddle with our kids, and when to speak about and model the real reason for the season.

Let's be praying parents and grandparents! When we even "mess up" our prayers, the Holy Spirit will intercede for us (Romans 8:27)!

December 21

> "But you, God, see the trouble of the afflicted; you consider their grief and take it in hand." Psalm 10:14a (NIV)

As I have studied the Psalms of lament, I have discovered several commonalities.

1) Crying out to God--Bringing our questions and concerns to the One who can shoulder them and do something about them.

2) Repeating the truths about God as revealed in His Word.

3) Praising God for His continued faithfulness

If all we do is cry out to God, we are missing out. The reminders of what God has done in the past, the repetition of God's good character, and focusing on His promises raise the ante. When we go on to step #2, we come to the place where feelings don't drive the train, truth does!

This is what repeating truths about God does for us: "Repetition produces revelation." And that revelation brings us to our knees in awe and wonder and praise (#3).

No, the problem doesn't magically go away, but we gain perspective on the sovereignty of God.

There are so many possibilities of the truths you can repeat. Our key verse today is one of them. He sees our trouble and takes our grief in His hands. Repeat the verse a couple of times. Meditate on its meaning. Praise God for being faithful to you during your times of trouble.

December 22

"Come to me, all you who are weary and burdened, and I will give you rest." Matthew 11:28 (NIV)

Some people are really good at trading or bartering. They can get the seller to keep lowering his price until they get the greatest value for their money. I love watching those people, especially since I'm not one of them. They will actually walk away if they don't get the vendor down to the right price, only to be called back and given their asked for deal. The seller does not want to miss out on an opportunity to trade his wares.

Matthew 11:28 reveals the best trade ever (for us). If we come to Jesus with our burdens, we get His rest in exchange. We don't even have to barter. He has set the deal on the table. All we have to do is accept it. If we walk away, God will not come after us begging to lighten our load. We have a responsibility to come and lay our burdens down so that He can take them from us and give us rest in exchange.

One author put it this way: "In His presence, we can trade the load that weighs us down for the love that holds us up."

If we conceal our concerns and hidden hurts, it can deplete our strength and joy. Draw near to Jesus, unload that burden, and rest in His love!

December 23

"After leaving them, he went up on a mountainside to pray."
Mark 6:46 (NIV)

Do you wonder why taking time to be with God is so important?

Jesus modeled it. He went up into the mountains to pray to His Father. He studied and knew the Scriptures as was evidenced in the way He could speak in the temple and combat Satan's temptations. He took time in the garden to wrestle through His struggle before facing the cross.

If Jesus needed these sacred pauses, how much more do we need to develop our holy habit of solitude.

I will always encourage you to stay grounded! Besides reading this devotional, look up the verses. Read what is before and after the key verse. Let God speak to your heart in the unique way the Holy Spirit individualizes the Word just for you. Here are a few ideas for your quiet time with God:

1) Read God's Word and pray in the morning—1st thing, before anything else, even before your feet hit the floor
2) Read God's Word and pray before going to bed
3) Take time in the middle of your day, during a break at work or school
4) Put Scriptures on noticeable places in your car, room, office, etc.
5) Listen to Christian music/radio
6) Find time to "be still" (Psalm 46:10), hopefully outdoors or somewhere in nature, and let God speak to you

Develop your holy habit of solitude.

December 24

"Because Joseph [Mary's] husband was faithful to the law, and yet did not want to expose her to pubic disgrace, he had in mind to divorce her quietly." Matthew 1:19 (NIV)

I can't imagine what was going through Joseph's mind and heart when he found out that Mary was pregnant. I'm sure he felt betrayed, deceived, and brokenhearted. Before the angel came to set him straight on things, he wanted to do the honorable and godly thing by divorcing her quietly. I'm sure he hoped it would all just go away without a big fuss, and he had to wonder where God was in all of this.

Charles Spurgeon says, "When we cannot trace His hand, we must trust His heart." Though this quote is true, it is also hard! Even after the visit from the angel, Joseph wanted to believe what God was doing, but he knew it would not be immediately evident to those around Nazareth that Mary held the Messiah in her womb. He had to relinquish his desire to want grab the reins and try to create the solution on his own. His trust meant full surrender of his life to his Savior.

For us, like with Joseph, it boils down to who I want to be my Savior. We will not find peace in trying to control our lives by being king of our own life. By surrendering to God, we are letting Him be Lord and we are building our life on a firm foundation.

That is the trusting part—believing He is working even when we **don't see it.**

There is a song called *Way Maker*. The chorus and bridge say:

Way maker, miracle worker, promise keeper,
Light in the darkness.
That is who You are.
Even when I don't see it You're working,
Even when I don't feel it You're working.
You never stop. You never stop working.

Even if you aren't there yet, friend, believe that God is working on your behalf!

December 25

"And Mary said, 'My soul glorifies the Lord and my spirit rejoices in God my Savior.'" Luke 1:46 (NIV)

While Joseph was wrapping his mind around God's new plan for His life, Mary was working it out and trusting God in her own way. She had surrendered her heart as the Lord's faithful servant, and now she was going for a visit with her relative, Elizabeth, for words of wisdom, confirmation, and blessing. When Elizabeth's child leapt in her womb, Elizabeth called Mary the mother of my Lord. At these words, Mary broke out in words of praise as recorded in Luke 1:46-58.

The King James Version translates the first line of this praise song, "My soul doth magnify the Lord." When something is magnified, it becomes bigger than everything else around it. By magnifying or glorifying the Lord, Mary was leaving the minute details of her life in the hands of her Mighty God. She was rejoicing, in spite of the certain turmoil and trouble that lay ahead back in Nazareth.

God could have sent an angel to Mary's hometown so that everyone would believe her and Joseph's story. Instead, He reserved His heavenly host to visit the shepherds who were out in the fields the night of Jesus' birth. God's glory and might shone around them as the sky was lit with messengers declaring that the Christ child had been born.

As Mary pondered the visitors that brought praise and honor to God's Son that first night, she must have been drawn back to the many events that had brought them to this moment. Once again, God was being magnified as He took care of their little family.

God can be magnified and glorified in your life. As He reigns as the Mighty God, the Everlasting Father, the Prince of Peace, in your heart, your problems will become smaller as He is magnified.

December 26

"Let him lead me to the banquet hall, and let his banner over me be love." Song of Solomon 2:4 (NIV)

We used to sing a song in Sunday School about God's banner over me being love, complete with hand motions. I can still sing it today. But when we peel it back, remove the "Christianese" and think about this verse in adult-think, it packs a punch.

First, God has a great banquet hall where I am invited. He leads me in and seats me as His guest. That in itself is a beautiful picture. After hosting Christmas at our house, I know the prep that goes into making the mealtime special and fulfilling. I can come to His table and relish in the aromas, flavors, and care that He has put into it for me.

To top it off, He places His banner of love over me. When we think of a banner, it usually conjures up an image of a long strip of cloth bearing a slogan or design of some kind. Whether we are close or far away, God's bold slogan over us is "I love you." His love compensates for my sin. His love is forever. Under His banner we find freedom, hope, healing, joy, and friendship. There is no condemnation if we are in Christ Jesus! (Romans 8:1).

As we end yet another Christmas season, I pray that you will sense God's love in your life. Give Him all your stress and anxiety. Picture His banner over you, and receive His healing and freedom. Worship Him with a new allegiance.

December 27

"Blessed is the one...whose delight is in the law of the Lord, and who meditates on his law day and night." Psalm 1a, 2 (NIV)

Do you want imitation happiness or eternal happiness?

Of course, that is a rhetorical question. But how do we determine one from the other?

There are a lot of imitations out there. Satan loves to make sin attractive and fun. It may satisfy for a brief moment, but we soon learn that it is not what we thought it was. The enemy's ways only lead to destruction.

A blessed life is tied to our God—He is the source of our pleasure and "happiness." When we delight in God's truth and reflect on it day and night, we are getting to know God, Himself. We tend to become the embodiment of the company we keep. If we are in step with the wicked and sit in the company of mockers, we will become like them and suffer for it (Psalm 1:1).

Our true joy and happiness come from walking with God. Delight yourself today in the Lord. He is the Real Deal!

December 28

"Do not let this Book of the Law depart from your mouth; meditate on it day and night, so that you may be careful to do everything written in it. They you will be prosperous and successful."
Joshua 1:8 (NIV)

If you want to live wisely, you need to make the most of every opportunity (Ephesians 5:15-16). If you want to be prosperous and successful, you need to be intentional and careful about structuring your day. I'm not talking about micro-managing your affairs. Really, I mean just the opposite.

The most important "structure" of your day is to begin and end with prayer and meditation of God's Word. When we bookend our days like this, the other things will fall into place. It will help us leave time and space to be available for God.

What a SIMPLE thing to implement, but simple does not always translate to EASY. We sleep too long in the morning or we are too tired at night. It takes discipline and discernment to recognize those interruptions and obstacles as a means to get us back on track. Worship music in the car on the way to work, audio scripture at night, or any other creative way to put our day in God's hands, should be our primary goal.

Be creative with the ways you keep God central when your schedule gets upended, or you just don't "feel" like opening the Bible. Vary your routine enough to give your quiet time some spark. Listen to the Bible on line or read it outdoors. God is just waiting for you to make the most of your time with Him.

December 29

> "No longer will there be any curse. The throne of God and of the Lamb will be in the city, and his servants will serve him."
> Revelation 22:3 (NIV)

Are you ready for the party?

No...I'm not talking about your New Year's Eve party.

I'm talking about the heavenly party where there will be no more curse on anything (Rev. 22:3). Everyone will be celebrating before the throne of God, worshiping, singing, dancing, serving, and bowing before Him. I'm not sure how it will look, but I can imagine there will be a combination of raucous joy and reverent gratitude, even though those things seem like opposites.

May I encourage you to put your life into the hands of the Party Planner—the One who gave His life so that you might experience His joy and peace for eternity. The Savior of the World, who gave up His heavenly throne to become one of us is preparing a magnificent celebration!

You don't want to miss it! Get ready for the party!

December 30

"In the beginning was the Word, and the Word was with God, and the Word was God. He was with God in the beginning. Through him all things were made; without him nothing was made that has been made."
John 1:1-3 (NIV)

Happy New Year's Eve-Eve! Are you staying up until midnight tomorrow night? We probably will go to bed after the ball drops in New York City (9:00 pm our time).

Whether the night owl or the early retiree, I'm sure you have been contemplating goals for the upcoming new year. Here's a comforting thought: God doesn't expect you to "get it together." In fact, Colossians 1:16-17 reminds us that all things were created and are held together through Christ. John 1:1-3 tells us that all things were made through Him.

Goals are good, but remember that God will meet you where you are and help you with your action steps. New Year's resolutions will come and go. Some may be kept, others may be broken. But that's not the point. Let the Creator of the universe teach and guide you. He holds all things together, and that includes you! Without Him nothing was made, and nothing will give you purpose without the Word being in the middle of it.

December 31

"Remember the Sabbath day by keeping it holy." Exodus 20:8 (NIV)

One of the reasons I go to bed early on New Year's Eve is because I love to watch the Rose Parade live the next morning. Did you know that the Rose Parade has never happened on a Sunday? Tournament of Roses officials decreed in 1893 that the Rose Parade would never be held on a Sunday so that it would not interfere with the churches that lined Colorado Boulevard. When New Year's Day falls on a Sunday, they postpone the parade to the following Monday.

I love the fact that the organizers are keeping the Sabbath holy. That might not be the intent, but I will take it. We would do well to keep other things off our plates on Sundays, reserving it for the Lord.

Anyway, I hope you enjoy the Rose Parade tomorrow. It is my all-time favorite holiday parade to watch on TV, so you'll find me in my PJ's with my coffee, sitting in front of the screen, oohing and aahing at the beautiful floral floats and bands from all over the world.

Have a very Happy New Year tomorrow (no matter what day it falls on)!

Made in the USA
Columbia, SC
19 December 2024

5f332d6c-6235-4dc4-8290-ad4c1bb21b3aR01